Hiking the Yukon Quest

1000 miles and one of the greatest trails on Earth

By Dr Mark Hines

Copyright © 2025 by Mark Hines

A Healthy Body Publishing Book

0-9553800

Published in 2025 as a Health Body Publishing paperback, ebook and audiobook, Oxfordshire, United Kingdom

ISBN: 978-0-9553800-9-9

For information regarding permission to reproduce any material from this book, contact Healthy Body Publishing, United Kingdom

The moral rights of the author have been asserted.

All rights reserved

This book is sold subject to the condition that it shall not, by way of trade or otherwise, be lent, re-sold, hired out, reproduced, stored in a retrieval system, or otherwise circulated without the publisher's prior consent or in any form of binding or cover other than that in which it is published and without a similar condition including this condition being imposed on the subsequent purchaser.

Printed and bound by CPI Group (UK) Ltd, Croydon, CR0 4YY

In Extremis: Book Four

Hiking the Yukon Quest

1000 miles and one of the greatest trails on Earth

By Dr Mark Hines

A Healthy Body Publishing Book

Oxfordshire, UK

The Author

Dr Mark Hines works as senior lecturer in exercise physiology at Oxford Brookes University, England. He has undergraduate and Master's degrees in exercise physiology, and a doctorate in biomechanics and neuromuscular physiology. He is a Senior Fellow of the Higher Education Academy. Mark's academic and research interests include biomechanics, diet and nutrition, injury prevention and rehabilitation, and extreme environments physiology. His ultra-endurance running journey began in 2005, and his first race was documented in his book on *The Marathon des Sables*. Mark writes books on diet and exercise, and details his various adventures. He also delivers training courses for athletes looking to participate in ultra-endurance races in extreme environments.

Acknowledgements

Acknowledgements are traditionally positive. However, there were interactions during this expedition that were so acutely painful to me, that recollecting them for the sake of this report made me wince. I suffered this way for your benefit. You are welcome. On a not entirely unrelated note, I would have finished this book years earlier, but was side-lined by the cost of living crisis and the covid lockdowns. The lockdowns should have afforded me more time to write, but I was desperately preoccupied with trying to make cash to not get kicked-off a Scottish campsite, whilst simultaneously searching for edible fungi or living off weevils.

On a more traditional front, I would like to thank the people who truly supported me to help this book reach publication. I would like to thank those who gave me financial support during extremely tough times, which helped me generate the first draft from rough notes. Had this not occurred when it did, I would have lost too much accuracy. I would also like to thank the team of reviewers who gave me feedback to raise this work to *even* greater heights. Any complaints should therefore be directed to their doors. Finally, I would like to thank the people who have read my previous books, and who were so keen for this publication. Knowing you were waiting helped to motivate me to write and edit, when I might otherwise have resorted to experimenting with recreational drugs and committing crime. I would especially like to thank Jacqui, who bugged me more than anyone else to get this finished. Thank you all – I truly hope the long wait was worth it.

Dedicated to the Memories

of

Larry 'Cowboy' Smith

&

Lance Mackey

Legends of the Yukon Quest

Preface

As a British adult, my most acute memories are mostly reserved for the sorts of things that have caused me painful embarrassment, persisting as a sort of personal torture. It is therefore an extremely pleasant relief that one of my clearest memories is really a rather lovely one, from time spent in the Yukon. I still remember it quite vividly: That first time I stood in Shipyard's Park in Whitehorse, on what for me was a cold February day in the sub-Arctic; my breath crystallising in the frigid air. The sky was a rich blue, and everything beneath it laden with a blanket of white snow, sparkling in the sunlight; glistening as though it were filled with diamonds.

I was amongst a small crowd, lining the start of the 2009 Yukon Quest, and next to me stood John, as majestically as ever; a good friend and occasional racing companion. We had known each other since we were carefree boys of twenty-seven, running gaily in short trousers over sand, and skipping together through the woods.

More specifically – for the intelligent reader so often craves the finer details – we both competed in events in the Moroccan Sahara and the Amazon rainforest, and now here we both were, somewhere cold and forbidding. We were in *The Territory* to compete in the human-powered race that followed the Quest, and had been recommended to watch the dogs leave across the start line, lashed to their sleds, before it was our turn the next day.

I was so glad to be there for it. There is something quite incredible about witnessing that pure, raw, clean energy of a team of dogs, as they flex the elastic in their harnesses and lines, pushing and heaving and pounding their bodies against the weight of the sled, the musher, the foot brake, the ice anchor, and the handlers, all straining to hold them back. That excitement was a sight to behold. I cannot recall any occasion when I have seen any athlete so excited, committed, and eager to commence a feat of endurance. They barked and whined and howled and tried to force the start.

When the moment arrived – when the handlers stood clear and each musher set the dogs to running – as a team, the dogs accelerated, the musher still standing on the foot brake in an effort to control their pace, and they all blew past us at an impressive speed. Fifteen individual journeys of a thousand miles all began in this precise moment, and it was magnificent.

Who knew what trials lay ahead? Each musher would finish with a new collection of stories and reflections. The mushers and the dog teams would grow as individuals – and as teams – over the days that followed. This spectacular Yukon land was spread out before them; waiting to welcome them; to test them. The next day it would be my turn to join the fray.

Time on these frozen trails is a gift. It is one of the purest, most satisfying and rewarding gifts I have ever come to know. It is a time to learn from nature, from oneself, and from those we happen to meet along the way. It is a time to dwell on your life and, in so doing, you can fix all your problems. This has been my experience, at least. For example, at the time of writing, I am single and own an old Land Rover. Bliss.

Time on the open trails is time to contemplate anything, everything or nothing. It is time for peace. It is time to enrich your soul with experiences of one of the wildest and most beautiful landscapes on Earth, in one of her harshest environments. It is time to think about those who came before, seeking their dreams and finding them, or meeting their end, or, for the vast majority, arriving at something in between. And it is a time to reflect upon all the poignant, stirring, brilliant words, written long ago by those magnificent and wonderful literary giants of the Yukon: Robert Service, Pierre Burton, Jack London, and Mark Hines.

But the time ran out: three times running. I set out from Whitehorse in 2009, 2011 and 2013, and I ran and jogged and hiked and bled and froze and sled-hauled for more than four hundred miles to Dawson City. And that is where it ended three times, because that was as far as the human-powered race went. But how much was I missing? How much more did the sled dogs and mushers get to see and experience that I did not? I had been tested and I had met the challenges I faced each time; I had searched and found the ways to overcome the trials and tribulations, and I finished. But I was left wondering, pondering, deliberating, and dreaming about all the rest of those trail miles, between Dawson City and Fairbanks.

For me, the Yukon is the only place on Earth that truly feels like home. I am not alone in this. There is a breed of us that feels this draw to the Yukon. It is a timeless yearning; existing long before us, and something that will endure within those who follow in our own footsteps. There is something about that land that makes it stand out; standing alone.

I am not a religious man. I am not a spiritual man. I do not really believe in anything at all, although I often find myself hoping for much more from the world around me. I do not believe that I have a soul or a spirit. But, if I did have a spirit, it is right here in the Yukon where that spirit would soar. It is a place like nowhere else, and it is such because of the landscape, the environment, the wilderness, and the people. All of these together make this land what it has become to me, and I am drawn back here again and again. It is the land where I feel that I belong.

In the days and hours leading-up to my first race in the Yukon, I reminded myself that this was a place in which tens of thousands of people have made themselves a home. They live here and they work here. Children walk to school, and play outside, in temperatures not encountered in my homeland of England since the last Ice Age. It is not some alien landscape, or an uninhabited desert: it is a populated land, albeit populated by more wild animals than wild people. However, it arguably boasts more wild folk than most places I have visited.

Yukoners go about their daily lives in much the same way as people might anywhere else, with a few modifications here and there; less queuing and probably less to complain about in general. Their ethos is different, too; I know nowhere else that people do so well to have their work-life balance so full of living. In my experience, when Yukoners talk to me about what I do, they mean for life: for fun and for leisure. Work is seen more as a well-managed side-line to the real business of living, and living in the most splendid place in the world at that.

I am not drawn to the Yukon because I equate suffering in the cold with ambition, or with pride or fuel for the ego. My reasons are entirely the opposite: I typically manage myself to preserve all the comfort I need to enjoy this incredible land. Nor does the Yukon appeal because 'I like the cold', but for all sorts of reasons – including the environment, which just happens to be cold at the exact same moment that it is also so exquisitely beautiful, and so calm and peaceful and silent. I dreamed of a new journey here, and my return to attempt to experience the full Yukon Quest route evolved into everything I dreamed it might be, albeit with a few added challenges I might have quite happily done without.

****

I have come to realise that those unfamiliar with sled-hauling might feel unequal to fully appreciating how physically exhausting this enterprise can be. I suppose the best I can offer as a corollary is that, sometimes, it is like trying to move very fast whilst actually progressing very slowly, as if through treacle, or the next victim in a horror film. Where a rucksack might be, instead there is a harness, attaching you to an absurdly heavy sled. The result of all this is that forward progress is hampered by the feeling something weighty is dragging you backwards, whilst your feet sometimes sink or slide about as if in wet mud or sand. The feeling and intensity can be harder than marathon running, but for much, much longer, typically further, and oh so much slower. Sometimes it is worse. When conditions align, it all works so well one practically flows majestically along the trail.

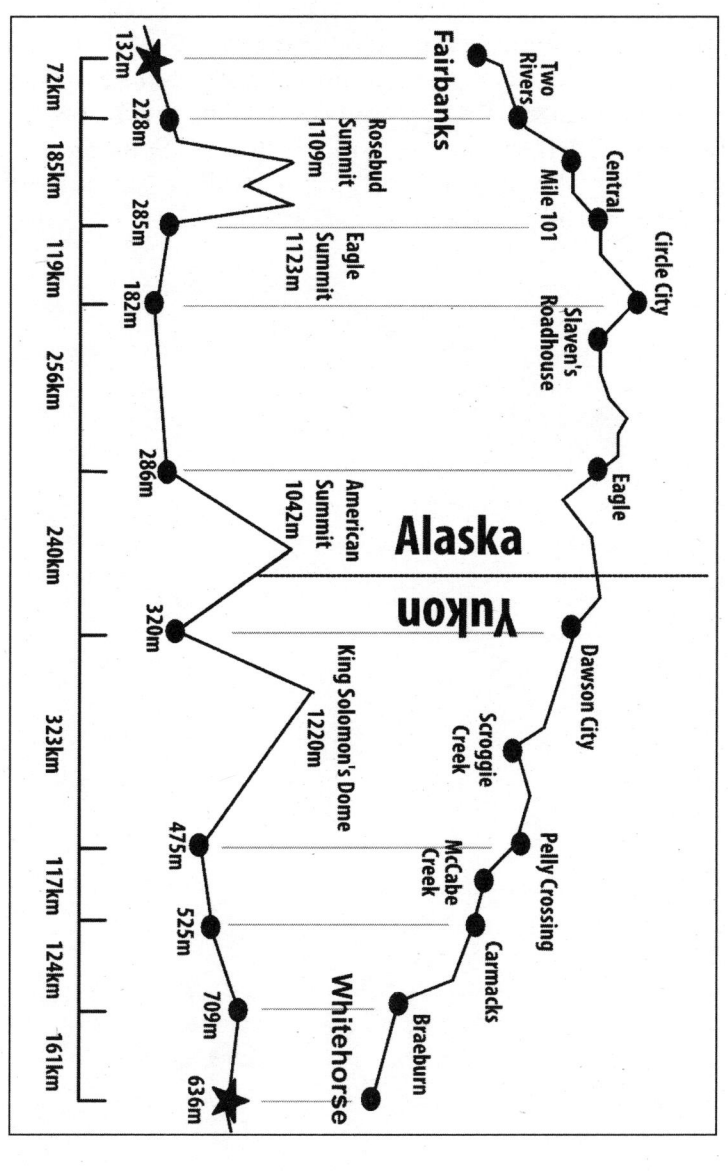

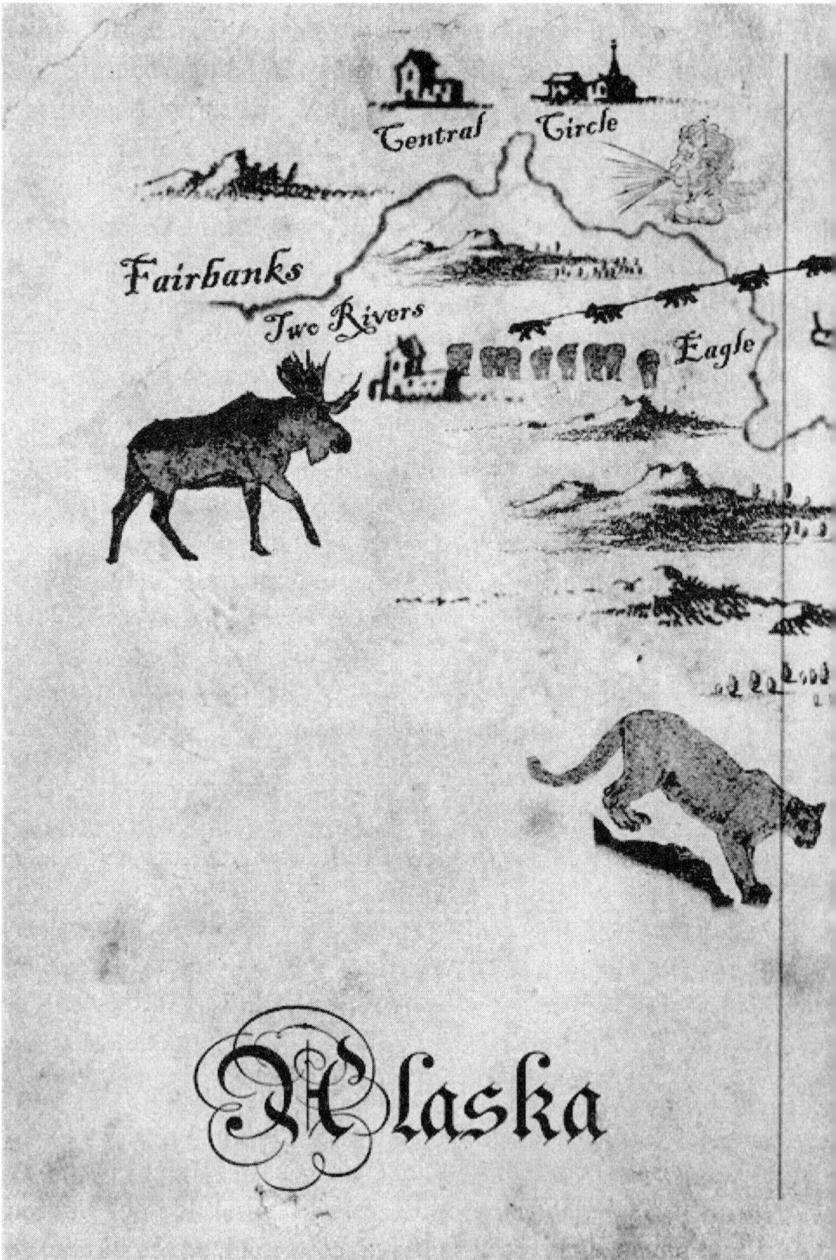
Central
Circle
Fairbanks
Two Rivers
Eagle
Alaska

Chapter 1.
Leaving Fairbanks

The day was young; no longer in its infancy, but brightening into its spotty adolescence; its attitude cold, its will aloof and mysterious, and its air greasy. The brave hero of the hour left his mouldy hotel, striding-out magnificently – a spectacle almost too marvellous to behold (or, indeed, even imagine) – a tall, thin, brave, bearded man, clad all in black, making his way resolutely, boldly, heroically and bravely, across the hotel's car park, with his trusty orange plastic sled, which he had only recently purchased from the REI in town, bravely sliding and scraping over the ice behind him.

A route down to the river, located just adjacent to the Yukon Quest's Fairbanks cabin, had not yet been put in, but soon enough our brave hero bravely stepped down onto the frozen river, and a new adventure was heroically underway.

I believe I can confide in you, now that we are getting to know one another, what a challenge it can be to write an autobiographical account. Originally, this opening was much longer, but I worked tirelessly in your favour, distilling the crux of the matter down to just its barest bones; the absolute concise perfection of the story that the world needed to hear, and no more. I am therefore at liberty to report that, if you want to know anything at all about Fairbanks, you will simply have to Google it. If you want to know about my shenanigans in town up to this point, and, indeed, my life so far, perhaps including education, work experience and past romances, you are now left with no alternative but to imagine it. This is for the best and you are most welcome.

****

Some people might consider that, at the start of a 1000-mile journey, a chap might look quite splendid. Certainly, when on a race start line, surrounded by other racers, it is easy to feel a sense of camaraderie, belonging, and, if standing-out at all, then it is as something to be respected and admired, simply for being there.
In truth – for I hold no secrets from you - by myself, all alone, only moments ago packing equipment in a hotel car park, at the start of a solo journey where I knew little of what lay ahead, and even less about my chances, I actually felt like something of an arse. What if it all fell apart on the first day and it was all for nothing, and the end came about through something any local would laugh at, whilst shaking their head in disbelief?

As a Britisher, I maintain that the only thing to be feared more than death itself is any slight episode of mild embarrassment. At the news of any silly calamity, the rest of the world would surely shrug its shoulders and move on, but the person afflicted would cringe whilst reliving the moment for the rest of their existence. It did not bear thinking about. I am not alone in this.

Many of my bravest and most heroic friends feel exactly the same way. Dying in some unpreventable tragedy, such as falling through thin river ice and getting sucked under by strong currents, or freezing to death in some devastating blizzard which tore trees from their moorings in record low temperatures, or being savaged by a cougar incensed by our presence, are all deaths we could live with.

Position us on the verge of some embarrassing end, and, before we take that High Road, we will be seeking out cougars to irritate and antagonise into action. And, in such a way, perhaps the records will report a noble death at wild hands, glossing over the fact we had also somehow set fire to our tent, clothes and sleeping bag, had no other survival equipment, and thereby died out in the cold; nude but for some ill-thought-out underwear, not spectacularly far from a hotel car park.

The actual bar for what qualifies as an embarrassing end is set to a standard many would not imagine at all embarrassing. All any adventurer can really ask themselves, is, if informed about the specifics of the event, would Ray Mears nod his head in respect, perhaps shedding the occasional tear for a good person cut short in their youth, or, would he shake it in disappointment and contempt? It is a tough standard, but a fair one. It is the fear of Ray Mears tutting at me which helps to keep me on the straight and narrow, striving to make only good decisions.

Indeed, one reason I was keen to get going, was simply to start accumulating respectable distances. The more progress I made, before disaster walloped me between the eyes, the less foolish I might feel about the whole thing. Plus, the sooner I got out of town, the sooner I would be by myself; immersed in my own little world. Each step offered a trifle more protection from embarrassment, in all its myriad forms.

Having made my way down to the river I reached the trail: A trail of about 1000 miles (1600 km). More than half of this trail was new to me. My limited insights had come from reading race reports, written by the Yukon Quest dog mushers and trail support, and from studying maps. I had learned that this year a route deviation featured around Fortymile, not far along from the border between Alaska and Canada. Here the route would lead me across a mountain range, along the Top of the World Highway. If you have no idea what is at Fortymile, and have never been on the Top of the World Highway, then we have something in common.

Learning about changes to a route, when you know neither the original route, nor the deviation, is quite abstract. Would I even make it that far? Would the trail still be 'in' when I got there, or since snowed-over and imperceptible to me? I hoped my GPS would be sufficient, but this was an unknown that would come towards the end of lots of other unknowns. It was also happening close enough to Dawson City that, as long as I could improvise my way somewhere along that trail, Dawson City could hopefully draw me in the rest of the way, whether through my GPS mapping, natural pathfinding, the increased trail activity, light pollution, or something else.

It was now the end of January. I was starting-out a week before the sled dogs, and the official start of the Yukon Quest, commencing on February 6th. There were already local trails, and the trail teams for the Quest had now begun setting-up the race trail. I anticipated it being enough to get me through the first week or so. If winds or snowfall covered the trail in the meantime, the trail team would break it again at some point, after which the dog teams would come through.

In my mind this gave me a total of about ten days of trail, which would be good enough to navigate and progress along. After that, I would just have to muddle through towards Dawson as well as I could, whatever was thrown at me. From there I was in familiar territory, and reckoned I knew my way well enough. I had sled-hauled between Whitehorse and Dawson along that trail three times, plus sections of it on snowmobile to support other events, and to help clear away trail markers. It was not quite 'back of my hand' familiar, but it was more than this alien ground I worked my way along now.

In truth – whilst we are being so open and honest with one another like this – my focus was all about reaching Dawson City. It was this section between Fairbanks and Dawson, which was so unknown to me, that I was quite anxious about. As long as I could reach Dawson City, I reassured myself, I would then have experienced the entire Quest trail, and that would be enough. The thought of proceeding from Dawson to Whitehorse was more of a dream than a dependable and realistic objective. There were simply too many miles to go; too many unknowns of course and conditions, both bodily and environmental.

Thinking about such an endeavour in any serious sense of micro-planning, timetabled progress, and macro-achievements is unreasonable, in my experience. Trying to imagine it in real terms of the minutiae of getting from the start to the finish is like staring into an imperceptible, dark and icy abyss. One discovers oneself staring into the black, icy eyes of a vast monster, and, as one stares searchingly for hope and promise, so the monster stares back, searchingly, I know not what for. This land can be enticing, encouraging and welcoming in one view, and dangerous, forbidding and terrifying in the next. But it is never vindictive or malicious; with experience we come to know the possibilities of what might lie ahead, and, as with so much in this life, most of the limitations are only within ourselves, after all.

All a person can do is commit to the adventure; to make a start, and, while the conditions are favourable, to work hard and make solid progress. And, when conditions turn against you, so you dig in; working harder than you ever imagined possible. Celebrate every milestone; every break, every camp, every bend in the river, every town and every mountain. My greatest strength is the miles already behind me when I begin this venture. I have endured before and this offers me confidence I might endure again. I have faced problems on the trails and I have worked through them; finding ways to use what I have available to continue to make progress.

And so it will be here; reaching the finish is just a matter of maintaining progress; working through the problems as they arise. As apprehensive and as anxious as I am, deep down there is an element of confidence that I might just be able to pull this whole thing off. The only monsters are the demons in my own mind, accompanying me along the frozen trail, tempting me with doubts. I know them well enough. They grow quieter with every mile passed.

It was a cold, fresh morning, and the sun sat low in the sky as I pulled against my harness, making those first few miles along the Chena River and out of Fairbanks. The cloudless sky was a brilliant blue. The snow glistened along the river and riverbank. There was the slightest, lightest of breezes caressing the river. The ambient temperature was a civilised -4 degrees Fahrenheit (-20 Celsius), which is a perfect temperature for optimal sled-hauling conditions, leaving the trail crisp and firm underfoot. Buoyed by the environment, and with some scarcely qualified hope and enthusiasm, I began my great adventure.

Chapter 2.
Progress

This was a low-snowfall year. The advantage of this was that there was a limit to the amount of snow to sink through if the temperatures warmed-up. The disadvantage was that if the trail became blown-over by fresh snowfall, or just high winds, it was too thin to feel and distinguish from the snow around the trail. Thus, progress can be faster, but navigation less certain.

This initial section of trail, headed out of town, passed a good number of homes early-on. A road nearby was busy with traffic. From down on the river I gazed up at the houses. All this would be behind me soon, and I would be alone. Anyone gazing about might have wondered what was passing along the river in front of them. As for me, I am always happy to be out in nature, creating distance between myself and civilisation: it applies here as much as anywhere else on the planet.

The sled felt heavy as I dragged it along. This was the heaviest pulk I had ever hauled. The second heaviest was the first time I raced from Whitehorse to Dawson City. Then it was heavy because I did not have a clue what I was doing, and had adopted a kitchen-sink approach to kit choices. This time I was hauling enough food to get me to Whitehorse, and plenty of fuel for my Kovea Booster+1 dual-fuel stove. Now, as I felt the harness strain across my hips and shoulders, I wondered what I might afford to lose from the pulk.

I utilise a 'straw-that-breaks-the-camel's-back' approach to endurance travel. I concern myself with considerations of the added load, resistance, and the impact of these on workload, energy requirements, overuse injury risk, and a variety of other inefficiencies, risks and challenges.

Each day the sled will grow lighter, as I work through my food rations. The sled was heavy but it was moving, and that was what mattered, for now. The thought of shifting it up and over mountains, or even riverbanks, was not an appealing one, but I would work out how to cope with such obstacles as and when they arose.

When racing over trail in these conditions, the sled glides easily over the ice and compacted snow. My racing sled is so light that, on the whole, I barely notice it, unless there is a dump of snow or I am going uphill. Over those gloriously hard-packed Yukon trails, on cold days, when the trail is like an iced pavement, my sprightly sled is like an enthusiastic puppy, so keen to get going it almost pushes me along. Out here, where the trail has not had so much use, it is an older, lazier and sluggish sort of retiree mutt that languishes behind me, flailing in the snow. It sits, it lies down, and it must be dragged along unwillingly on its belly. Such was the start to my Yukon Quest: a steady pace under heavy load, rather than a surge and a flourish.

* * * * * * *

In case you happen to be wondering what the well-dressed man is wearing, as he minces along frozen rivers in suburban Alaska, just outside Fairbanks, I shall talk you through the repertoire. My baby-soft skin is protected about the legs by a baselayer of Sub-Zero F1 leggings, and an outer layer of Rab Vapour-Rise Guide trousers. These trousers work so well in this environment that Rab stopped making them years ago, just to spite me, thus ensuring I am not too careless with the current set.

My torso is wrapped in an Alpkit long-sleeved baselayer top, although I sometimes use Rab baselayer tops instead. This area of my body does not tend to get cold enough to worry about. It is only when the temperatures plummet that I rely exclusively upon a Sub Zero F1 top. Worn seductively over the baselayer top is draped a Rab Vapour-Rise Guide jacket, offering warmth, insulation, wind-protection, and pockets.

About my feet are some spectacular trail running shoes: specifically Salomon's XA Pro 3Ds – the Gore-Tex version, which I find useful for shedding snow. I wear Injinji socks, which fit over each toe individually, helping to prevent blisters, and a thicker pair of socks over those. Gaiters complete the footwear division, adding warmth and preventing snow getting in amongst my socks and feet. Snowshoes are worn when the trail softens up.

I make use of a thin pair of liner gloves, and pull on a pair of cosy, expedition mitts, whenever it is cold enough to necessitate such drama. Around my neck is a fleece neck gaiter, which helps prevent cold winds blowing down my back, or my chin from rubbing against my jacket zips. Upon my majestic head is a Buff, although, if it gets cold enough, I use a rolled-up balaclava as a hat. I carry a very warm Rab Batura down jacket, complete with fur ruff, but, because one detests showing-off, I only wear this when the temperature drops below about -31 Fahrenheit (-35 Celsius). During daylight hours I wear a pair of stylish, category four, Bloc Eyewear sunglasses, which protect my eyes from glare and snow-blindness. When called for, I replace these with a pair of Bloc goggles, adapted from a set intended for mountain bikers, which have no tint and are excellent for use in blizzards.

Out of all this, it is the footwear that seems to concern people the most. Folk unfamiliar with hiking – or running – in this environment, tend to imagine we must need to wear something like a pair of hot air balloons on each foot. This is not the case. The only way we generate heat is by moving, and, as the golden rule, the more we move, the more muscle is involved, and the greater the warmth that is generated. Big, insulating boots are quite restrictive, impacting potential to generate heat, whilst simultaneously increasing risk of overuse injuries from being horrible, heavy and clumpy. Boots are fine if your feet are already warm and you need to either stem the loss of heat during limited activity, or you happen to have an external source of heat, such as hot air flow to the lower reaches on a snowmachine. One does not attempt to walk or run ultra-marathons in big, clumpy boots.

Reflecting on my racing background, it is rarely the foot athletes who suffer with the cold, and more commonly the skiers who get it in the toes. Ski boots are typically very restrictive, and the act of skiing involves a limited and controlled movement, reducing scope for generating heat. Similar is true with bikers, so they tend to wear boots that are better at insulating (to capture the limited heat produced), and they 'top up' by walking and pushing their bikes, whenever their feet noticeably cool. One adapts to both the environment and the mode of travel, and compromises accordingly for the goal of safely and efficiently reaching the finish line.

* * * * * * *

I did not weigh my sled before the start, but various individual items – such as the sled itself, food, sleeping bag, shelter, fuel and emergency clothing – could be calculated. Overall, I was hauling between 88-100 lbs (40-45 kg), as opposed to the 22-33 lbs (10-15 kg) I would drag when racing. Still, part of the plan was to experience what it was like to be self-sufficient for the expedition, carrying all that I needed to succeed to Whitehorse. This weight was still very little compared with many 'traditional' approaches to sled hauling, which contrasted with my own attempts at 'fast and light' travel. A luxury of this trip was that I would encounter hospitality along the way, in the form of cabins, villages, towns and friends, but nevertheless, I took with me everything I needed.

The compacted snow of the trail crunched beneath my feet. It was perhaps a curious thought, but even with 1000 miles ahead of me, I felt some confidence now I had taken my first steps along the path. The full distance, according to some reports, is considered to be around 1015 miles (1633 km), so at some point on this first day I expected to go from a four-figure distance to three-figure one. Granted, I would then have three-figures to deal with for 900 miles, but simply having less than 1000 miles remaining was a comforting thought. Getting through it, and all that.

There was a small question about whether the 'considered' distance was measured accurately using GPS, or estimated by mushers, based upon their known speeds with dog teams, but we need not get too caught up in the details. The trail of the Yukon Quest provides an ambitious distance, with the total varying from year to year, according to differences in river sections, any re-routes, and any changes to the location of the finish line. For example, some years the ice on the Takhini or Yukon rivers 'opens up' early, forcing the race to finish a marathon distance or so before Whitehorse.

I would be navigating using a route plotted onto my Delorme PN-60w handheld GPS, and my Suunto Traverse watch. I also had a route description, and a single trail map that consolidated the whole route onto an A3 sheet. Obviously that would be insufficient for micro-navigation, but it was an easy way to see the Yukon Quest checkpoints, towns, general heading, rough lay of the land, and to track progress. The best map I had was on my handheld GPS, which had come with full mapping for the US and Canada. I could zoom-in to get a sufficient level of detail to see what was around me. It lacked names of every road, river and lake, but it was good enough for covering this sort of distance.

I would be passing cabins that were accessible to folk such as myself, and cabins owned and lived in by chaps who want to live off-grid in the wilds, or else to stop in when out hunting and trapping. I would never have to go more than about 230 miles (370 km) between villages or towns, and I would have some of those cabins available to me at far shorter intervals than that.

Whilst it would be an injustice to suppose I was intending this to be an elaborate glamping holiday, it would be equally unfair to assume this was approaching the remoteness and hardships of a real Arctic expedition. But then, nowadays, there are arguably too many expeditions lacking the realism we romanticise, thanks to flights to convenient starting points a stone's throw from the finish, or groomed highways to move along. So perhaps I should not downplay the nature of this expedition too much either; it was not going to be too remote, and nor was it going to be too easy. It was a Goldilocks expedition: just right.

As I strolled further along the river, so I took in more sights along the riverbank. The Steese Highway disappeared behind me as I passed Fort Wainwright to my right, and with it the bulk of the heavy, city traffic. I could still hear roads nearby, and houses over to my left belonged to the various residential streets and estates, in this area of Fairbanks.

As I progressed along the river, so I left the central residential area and moved into suburbia, followed soon after by the rural outskirts. There were still roads off in the distance, occasionally coming into view as they paralleled or crossed the river. During the first 7 miles (11 km) I skirted around the military base, and a couple of signs on the riverbank warned against boats landing, or anyone entering the land. It was momentarily confusing to consider that this was a river that flowed for most of the year; travelled along by water craft rather than on foot, skis, fat bike or snowmachine.

There was plenty of military activity about, mostly in the form of helicopters, droning and buzzing into earshot, and briefly popping into view. I looked forward to the point when I would be far enough away from the military bases to have some quiet and calm – the luxuries I enjoy so much in this frozen world.

I passed beneath a bridge and paused for a few moments. I had been working hard with the sled-hauling, and this bridge was the first road bridge I had seen since leaving Fairbanks and the Steese Highway. As I stood there, contemplating my position in the universe, I heard a sound I wish I had not. It was a deep, booming sound, that seemed to reverberate across the river, and it was almost alarming.

Once the initial panic subsided, to be replaced by the middle and later stages of panic, I was able to allocate some attention to considering what it might have been. It was probably not gunfire, which ruled-out the military base in the first instance. Nor was there a marauding pack of usually-armed rednecks to be concerned about; at least not yet and not here. Rather, the booms seemed to have been generated by the river itself. I do not recall having heard such a sound before, but I could best place it as the sound of forces beneath and within the ice acting upon it. There were no visual clues to support this, but nothing else seemed to fit the sounds and how close it was. Indeed, it seemed to have come from directly beneath my feet.

I was aware I was at no real risk, at least not until spring, and, whilst the ice might crack here and there, it was far too solid and tightly packed to actually move or open until then. Nevertheless, these 1000 miles were not going to complete themselves, and there was no need to linger idly by. I chalked the icy boom up as a new experience, regretted its occurrence, and continued on my way. The land opened-up more now, as I left the vicinity of the military complex behind. I was progressing further and further from the city, and entering a more rural Alaska.

In some places, the houses existed bunched together in small riverside settlements, in others they stood alone. At one collection of houses I spotted a young lad and his father, staring out at me through French windows. There seemed no attempt to be friendly; to wave or to otherwise reach-out to me. It became the boy, his mother, father and dog, all imprinting their noses against the glass, staring at the freak hauling a sled along on the far side of the river. I continued on. There are of course walkers, skiers, and dog strollers who make use of this river trail, but perhaps not so far out of town, and almost certainly not dragging such a mighty sled behind them.

After three hours, I sat down upon my sled, to have my first proper break of the day. With the temperatures not being too extreme, discipline could be lax. I had not been wearing my down jacket or my expedition mittens so far today. The mitts remained with my trekking poles, there for if I needed them later on.

The breaks were a chance to take the weight off my feet, and to have some food. I had no real meal structure, beyond regular breaks and a bag of food for each day. I would begin with some South African droewors, perhaps some biltong, a small handful of dried fruit, and a golf-ball-sized, high-energy, homemade chocolate truffle. All-in-all the food of champions.

I realised at once that I should have ordered more than just the 100 grams of dried tropical fruit for each day. The stuff was delicious, and a great source of nutrients, including much-needed fibre, which was otherwise absent from the expedition diet. I also should have made use of some flavourings with the truffles. Granted, they tasted absolutely fine, but the last time I made them I had infused half the batch with strong black coffee, and the other half with a good single malt whisky. I was unimpressed with this inexcusable oversight. One has experiences.

What was important to me about my food selection was that it was all ready to go. It did not matter if the temperatures dropped below -58F (-50C); the food could be taken from the bag and eaten as it was. I also did not need to sit around getting cold whilst I heated-up water to add to freeze-dried food. I do not claim for a moment that mine is the only way, the right way, or the best way. My approach is quick and easy, and the food full of quality nutrition and energy, with the added benefit of it having real texture, which many freeze-dried meals so despairingly lack. Mine was an unusual approach, but one I had always used and been happy with.

For water, I have a 5.25 pint (3 litre) water bladder, in a small pack on my back, between my baselayer and midlayer clothing. The rationale is that it is lighter than Thermos flasks and more convenient – there is a hose from the bladder that reaches under my arm and connects to the front of the pack. I shortened the hose to ensure the mouthpiece never stuck out from within my layers, where it might freeze in the open air. Whenever I want water it is there and ready. The bladder, hose and mouthpiece are all insulated from the outside by my clothing, and bathed in my body heat. It is impossible for the water to freeze unless I am some hours dead, in which case, upon reflection, dehydration is the least of my troubles.

If I need more water, I can use my stove to melt snow or ice. If the stove fails, or if I run out of fuel, I can build a fire instead. If I cannot build a fire, I have a separate 1.75 pint (1 litre) flexible water bottle, which I can use to melt snow in, using just my body heat, tucked away within my layers of clothing. Others happily make use of Thermos flasks, just going to show that this sort of activity can be played out successfully in more ways than one.

As I continued along the left side of the river, a snowy owl took flight from a tree close by, gliding low across the river and up above the far bank, scoping me out for a moment or two before sweeping back, flying directly overhead and seeking-out a new perch over to my left. It was such a beautiful bird with such perfectly white feathers. It was a pleasant welcoming into a land that was becoming more remote with each step.

Shortly after this, I came across a sight no less majestic, but far more familiar; a Yukon Quest trail marker. These markers were used on the Canadian side too, and, as I had not seen any before this point today, I had wrongly assumed the trail crews had not yet put them in for the race. The markers are tall and slender wooden stakes, with a few inches of red paint at the top, and a few inches of black paint beneath that, with a reflective, rectangular strip orientated in portrait, stapled in the middle of the paint.

A little further along, I encountered more markers. This time they guided me onto a trail raised up on a high section of ice, with double-markers on either side of the trail, crossed to create an 'x'; warning me of danger on or close to the trail. This was some cracked ice that may have presented a danger to snowmachines and dog teams, but was not an issue for steadily lumbering me to move across.

The markers also indicated that I needed to remain on the raised trail, and not take a lower trail across bad ice. The brilliant trail teams, who masterfully 'put in' the route each year, have experience in finding the strongest, safest ice, and avoiding weak ice and other hazards. Knowing there were markers in place to highlight such areas, and to guide me, was wonderfully anxiety-relieving, offering some considerable relief. I expected the markers would be removed after the Quest passed through, but they were here for now, and that was a settling, navigational bonus.

Chapter 3.
Fairbanks to Two Rivers

Seventeen miles (27km) from Fairbanks I passed beneath the Nordale Road bridge, a useful landmark on this early part of the journey. It was late afternoon now, and the sun was already on its way down. Only another steady 5.5 miles (9km) and the trail would lead me from the frozen river, off into frozen woodland, and later on to frozen fields beyond.

I took a break a couple of miles after the bridge, enjoying the view of an elegantly built, large log home. Smoke rose from its chimney, drifting out across the river, hanging in the air as a thin and flat cloud, moving so slowly it appeared as frozen as all the snow-covered land beneath it. In the evening light the smoke was lit by pale blues and pinks against the darkening sky. The scene was stunning, captivating, wondrous and unexpected. I relaxed for some moments, in my element, drinking it all in.

My trail was nothing more than snowmachine tracks, so whenever such tracks led from the main river trail elsewhere, I would scan beyond them to see where they headed, ensuring they were not actually the trail I should be following. I saw such a path enter the woodland to my left, on a clear passage through the trees, but without trail markers I supposed this was not the Quest route.

I persevered, albeit with slightly less confidence than before, and with a nagging thought that I might be going adrift. Although I had a GPX route from the 2010 Quest on my handheld GPS device and watch, I was sure there was an error in this section, as it seemed the musher whose route I was following, had taken a trail that did not fit with the description in *The Guide*.

Darkness grew steadily around me, as the early evening began wrapping up and night closed in, and I mentally braced myself for my first night out on the trail. A swarm of homes hove into view along the right bank of the river as I continued south. The trail wound along the river, with another deviation to the left and into the trees, which I decided to head towards and explore.

It is important to share with you that my progress along the trail is not what one might consider 'stealthy'. The plastic sled makes a scratching, scraping, bashing sound as it bumps along the hard, icy trail. Plastic conduit, which I employ to cover the ropes between sled and harness, are crossed to give stability on descents, but bang into each other and generate more noise. It might be surprising to imagine the total ensemble can seem so loud, but when there is nothing else but purest silence, what we must consider is that I contribute nothing short of an assault to the ears of every animal in range, and it is a generous range at that.

Where there once reigned peace, stillness and silence, now there is a blundering Englishman, generating an unholy ruckus. My presence brings with it a sort of plague or curse to the peace-loving fauna. The disturbance is on a par with what we might expect to hear, if I were to have my trusty old Land Rover – Doris the Defender – dropped from a great height, onto the percussion section of the Royal Philharmonic orchestra, whilst they performed Verdi's *Requiem* inside quite a large fireworks factory, as the brass section fled for its life. It is a good battle cry as I move deeper into the wilderness, whilst the denizens therein scramble themselves into action, departing the vicinity long before I can see any of them. Even the dead ones.

As sparsely populated by homes as this area has become, there are still some rather pretty dwellings to be admired. One consequence of all the noise I am creating is that attention is drawn to me, as I make my way towards the sharp climb up from the river. A young woman stands at a large window in her cabin; gazing out at my chaotic form scrambling to get up the riverbank.

The climb up was only about the length of the average male walrus (around 3 metres or so), but it was tough. The steepness of the slope meant I had to kick-in with the front of my feet to gain purchase, and with the heavy sled I could not just charge up, but had to ensure each step held firm before taking the next. My poles were pressed down into the slope, as rigid supports protecting me against falling back. One slip of foot or pole could be managed, but a combination totalling at least two would see me plummet in a graceless collapse. I reached the top, grateful my efforts brought me to where I needed to be, and more than a little appreciative my observer had not had to witness me make a total shambles of it. I lacked grace, but I got the result.

At the top was a trail intersection, giving me options to the left and right, and no trail marker within view. I fired-up the GPS to take a look – I kept it off when not in use to preserve battery life – and, as I waited for it to power up and find some satellites, I detected movement over to my left, a little off the trail. It appeared that someone had just left the trail into the woodland, maintaining distance from me but heading around to my front. A second set of legs followed the first into the dark woods.

Might these be locals whom I could ask for confirmation that this was the Quest trail? As I looked, I struggled to get my head into gear. I had already been away from civilisation too long. The second pair of legs had been distinctly grey, long, thin, and atop surprisingly petite feet. Had the first pair of legs been the same? My mind asked the question, but my short-term memory just shrugged a response and looked another way.

As I pondered these matters, it slowly dawned on me that it may very well have been a moose. If this were the case, two things were definite. Firstly, caution was required, to ensure I did not inspire the beast to charge or otherwise stomp me into smithereens. Secondly, I had probably been unreasonably optimistic with my expectation of gleaning useful navigational assistance.

For those unaware, moose are the most dangerous animals to be found in The North at this time of year. Granted there are bears, wolves and mountain lions, too, but the bears are now sleeping peacefully, snoring gently and with only mild flatulence. The wolves are no real threat to people, and one is extremely lucky to even see a cougar. Moose are big, lumbering, bad-tempered, ill-humoured, defensive pricks. If they see a person ambling along a trail, they tend to form a dim view almost immediately, to which they conclude the best form of defence is attack.

We do not regard moose as docile or intelligent ungulates. Ideally we regard them from a very safe distance, whilst sitting upon a snowbank, making no sounds at all. In my experience, expanded to include vicarious experience – which I confess is still limited – if a moose is spooked at close range it might run away in the confusion. If a moose is spooked at very close range it might attack. If it sees you approaching from a distance, it could be minded to charge.

I checked the trail in both directions again, hoping for a shining beacon of light to hail me the right way, but was left wanting. My GPS was ready for consultation, with the track showing I should continue along the river, although I remained doubtful this was actually the case, or an error from the 2010 GPX track.

It was around this time during my deliberations that the moose chose to break the ice of social intercourse, and sauntered over to initiate a meeting of our two minds. I had no idea what it could be that the moose wanted to confide in me, but, as I am generally inclined against moose society – for one has prejudices – I quickly put away the GPS and, well, heroically I ran away.

I emerged by the top of the riverbank further along, and saw the trail descending onto the river, with an intersection to head back along the river in either direction. I headed down to give the trail here a chance for a short distance (approximately 495 corgis' lengths, measured from booper to pooper, or 300 metres, for readers more accustomed to the metric system). This did match the GPS but seemed contrary to *The Guide*. It made no sense that the trail would exit the river and then re-enter it a hundred or so beavers' lengths further on. More likely, these were simply two access points to the same trail, and the route actually went back in the other direction. Without trail markers, or anything else to give me confidence the river route was correct, I performed an about-turn, and headed back along the path towards the woods.

Knowing there was a marauding moose up ahead, potentially still reeling with the harsh and cutting emotion of my devastating rejection, I decided to move briskly here. I was hoping that the noise generated would prevent the moose concluding it was being snuck-up upon, and would therefore be unsurprised by my closing proximity. Up ahead, at about the location I had originally ascended from the river, I detected movement. As I approached, still at lively pace, the moose was alerted to my coming, and seized the moment to hoof-it elsewhere. About 60 washing machine widths later a trail marker emerged from the darkness, and confidence grew I was indeed headed in the right direction.

* * * * * * *

After a day progressing along the iced-up water course, it was a pleasant change to be nestled onto a woodland trail. I hold no complaints about the river, but I do feel even more at home in the woods. There is more security here. The temperature was dropping now, and it was a little less cold than along the river. Amongst the trees I can set myself a good camp for the night. If the occasion warrants it, I can even get a fire going. If I felt too cold I could potentially build myself an insulating spruce mattress. I can whittle away at sticks to make tools. I could even build a raised sleeping platform with a fire the length of it close by, complete with wind-break-cum-heat-reflector. All these possibilities, and more, are present in the woodland.

In short, I felt secure in the woods, because it was an environment I could use to my advantage, and it supplied all the natural materials I needed; not only to survive, but to survive *well*. Tell me I would need to stay alone out here for six months, and I would build myself a fully operational bar within a fortnight, complete with a microbrewery and traditional pub lunches (food served daily, from noon until four o'clock, with roasts on Sundays. Muddy paws welcome).

The trail weaved through the woods before bringing me out in a small, open section, devoid of foliage. Perhaps it was a pond or creek, but there was no way for me to know at the time. I had only seen that single trail marker, and there were no more here, but as there had been no other trails it seemed reasonable this was the correct way. The trail led me away from the river, and soon I was passing fields I anticipated from *The Guide* and maps. The night sky was clear and the stars bright. In the Far North the stars appear so much brighter and larger than at lower latitudes, and it is typically a joy to travel on such clear nights.

* * * * * * *

I persevered, maintaining my habit of taking breaks every few hours, and chose to sleep at around 10 pm. When racing I would push late into the night, but for a solo expedition I had no need to rush, and health and self-preservation were the focus. There were sections here where the trail widened, and short deviations off the trail where snowmachine riders had passed, or had pulled alongside each other for a natter. These were the Holy Grail of camping spots, because the sections were off the main trail and packed down. Without these, it is often necessary to don snowshoes and stamp down an area to create firm, flat ground. I found an appropriate area adjacent to the woodland and set up my camp.

My night's accommodation was a compact, weatherproof, chic, single-skin, Rab Latok tent. It took two internal poles crossed-over to erect it, and nothing else. I did not need any loops to feed the poles through. As the tent was only up when I was inside it, there was no need to peg it out (a fairly labour-intensive practise in the snow), and I had already cut-off the peg loops and guy lines before leaving the UK, all to save weight. Erecting my bijou accommodation was, with me, the work of a moment.

Inside my little den there was about enough room for my sleeping mat, sleeping bag and me, and I brought in my jacket and spare clothes bag to use as a pillow. I also brought in my food bag, not that I was hungry now, but eating is an important way to generate heat. The standard response to feeling cold is to ensure sufficient insulating clothing, sufficient food intake, adequate hydration, and to increase movement. The food might be a useful companion in a crisis.

I removed my mid-layer vest and jacket, negotiated myself inside the sleeping bag, and pulled down my trousers, so as to give the clean sleeping bag a treat, and to allow the heat from my body to more effectively warm the bag. I kept on my baselayer, mostly for convenience, and kept my trousers around my ankles, to save time when preparing to exit the bag in the morning. Into the sleeping bag I brought my trail shoes and water bladder, both within a drybag, which I kept the tent packed away inside during the day. Within the sleeping bag I used a vapour-barrier liner, to protect the sleeping bag's down from moisture, although for comfort it only came up to my lower chest.

It took me a while to drop-off to sleep. My heart was still pounding from my day's efforts, attempting to facilitate some recovery of my laboured muscles. Some unsettling palpitations startled me on more than a few occasions. The startlement led to further palpitations, and in no time my heart was beating a complicated but broken rhythm all of its own. Doubtless any passing cardiologist, with an empty wallet and extensive gambling debts, might have thought this was to be his lucky night.

Palpitations are, with me, usually rare, but unusually high rates of exercise, stress or alcohol seem to be factors, coupled with an unfortunate genetic issue where I lack efficiency in absorbing magnesium. The result of all this was that it took longer than anticipated for my heart to slow and calm. My efforts with the heavy sled had taxed me more than I was used to, and, I am ashamed to admit, beyond what I had trained for in the lead-up to this expedition. My mind was busy with thoughts of the day; what I had accomplished, and just how much I still had left ahead of me. Excitement also played its part in keeping sleep at bay.

What lay ahead remained a daunting prospect, but I had managed my first day, and that was an important confidence-booster. I had made progress along the trail, navigated myself successfully (with only the one problematic navigational moment, just off the river), avoided getting tangled-up with an inquisitive moose, and taken regular breaks to ensure I was well-fed; my water intake had been sufficient, and I had not had the water bladder or hose freeze-up. Now I was set for my first night. All I had to do, for the remaining miles to my finish point, was repeat. I had done everything necessary within this day, and all that was required to guarantee success was more of the same.

I stirred a few times during the night, roused from my sleep by the cold. This concerned me, and I could not think from where the heat was escaping. It occurred to me that I had noticed the down at the back of the sleeping bag shift as I initially laid back in it, and, by sleeping on my side, I only suffered a cold arm and not a cold back. It was not a particularly cold night, and the temperature could not have been much below about -13F (-25C).

Was the problem with me? Was there a way that my internal thermostat had gone askew, or was it really a problem with the sleeping bag? I had definitely eaten enough, and I was sufficiently hydrated. I drank some water just to be sure, and tried for more sleep.

An hour or so passed and I awoke shivering. As I lay there, on my side, I started to rapidly pull my knees up to my stomach and straighten-out again, doing the best I could to exercise and generate some heat. It worked for a little while and I fell asleep again, only to wake once more, a little before five, this time shivering intensely.

What the reason was could no longer be dwelt upon. I was shivering and had been feeling cold for hours. Eventually I would exhaust my body's fuel for shivering, and then I would no longer have the capacity to warm myself. How desperate my situation was, I had no idea, but with frustration, annoyance, peevishness, and various other such negative (but not strictly tautologous) emotions, I rallied into action.

Within a few minutes I was dressed, my equipment packed away, and I was moving as fast as I could along the trail. I was warm again in moments, but tired and annoyed with myself. If the issue was with the sleeping bag, how could I possibly entertain the idea of getting through a month out here, or however long it might take me to reach Whitehorse? Was it a problem with the distribution of down insulation in the bag – something I could easily fix – or was it something else?

I have only been cold once before when sleeping-out in this environment, and that had been in a different bag and in predictable circumstances, due to a cold breeze wafting through the doors of a large, wall tent. My recent situation made no sense to me. Another night would tell – I would try to improve lofting and could place my down jacket beneath the sleeping bag for added insulation. For now, it was time to accept that a new day had begun, and, by the end of it, I would have accomplished many more miles away from Fairbanks, bringing me closer to Dawson City.

As I arrived at one corner of a field, I saw a dog team heading along from the far corner, perpendicular to my own direction, as we headed towards the same corner. The musher's headtorch lit up the dogs' backs as they ran along. They were all well gone by the time I reached that corner and took a right turn. Still, I hoped they might be doing an 'out and back', and would pass me by. There were fields, there were roads far off, and there were distant buildings. All remained dark.

I passed a few driveways and saw some houses. I heard the local dogs first. My lack of stealth was clearly irritating them from some distance. Another road junction and I found myself along a residential road, with homes on both sides boasting plenty of land.

After a few minutes I passed a petrol station with a shop, and, tempted though I was, I could not think of anything I needed to buy. The food I was already dragging was heavy enough. I passed a store to the left of the road, and then a launderette to my right. The latter advertised showers and Wi-Fi. It appeared open and empty, and I decided I might as well treat myself to some inside space and warmth, to take my first break.

Inside I stripped the extra layers, did some minor kit faffing, and made use of the toilet. I had pulled-up in an empty parking area, abandoning the sled within a parking space. A driver pulled in and greeted me inside as if it was all the most natural thing in the world. He made use of the toilet and then went on his way. He made it seem so normal it was weird. As I sat there, dishevelled and scruffy, filling my face with dried meat and chocolate truffles, the packed sled sitting outside waiting for me, I wondered what it could be the locals were used to seeing, if they could imagine I was a picture of normality.

A check of the map on my GPS confirmed my location as Pleasant Valley, just after Two Rivers. This featured on my little map of the route as a key point on the trail, ahead of the main checkpoint on Chena Hotsprings Road. I had completed the first noteworthy chunk of the journey, and that felt satisfying.

Chapter 4.
Two Rivers to Angel Creek Lodge

I left 'Soapy Suds laundromat' in philosophical mood, as launderette users often do the world over. Stepping back out into the frosty morning air was a pleasing experience. The temperature was a few degrees warmer than yesterday, but remained sufficiently frigid for optimal trail conditions. I had had a good rest in a warm place that I had not expected, and now my mind was all for the trail.

I pulled on the harness, backed the sled out of her parking space, and set-off at brisk pace along the road for a few miles, before crossing to pick up the Quest trail through woodland. A frozen pond lay still and silent off to my right. The trail weaved and the land opened up. As I created distance from the road, I found myself immersed in a sublime, sub-Arctic winter wonderland.

The trail was hard-packed and wide, and progress was as good as it gets. The sky was clear and a deep blue; the air appreciably still, calm and fresh. The land tended towards flat, and, in places, teased me towards very gently undulating. Far off in the distance stood grand wintry hills and mountains. The sled was hard work on the ascents, short, gentle and forgiving though they otherwise were. Although, upon reflection, the weight of the sled made it fairly hard work even on the flats. Still, overall, I was in my heaven, and all was right with my immediate world.

The trail paralleled the course of both highway and Chena River for many miles. The road itself lay only around eight football pitches away (about 600 metres), but there was little traffic, and I rarely heard or saw any indication of its presence. Indeed, if I had not seen the map on my GPS, I would not have realised the road was so close. I would have this trail for a total of 35 miles (56 km), between where I joined it after Pleasant Valley, and the Quest checkpoint at Mile 52 of the Chena Hotsprings Road.

* * * * * * *

In the early afternoon a familiar sound steadily rose in the air, as two snowmachines approached from ahead. We all stopped and I chatted with the front rider for a few minutes. They were part of the Quest trail team, and had been out checking the trail. I was asked if I would be staying at Angel Creek Lodge that evening, which came across as a recommendation as much as a question, and I nodded in both agreement and approval of the idea. The Lodge was 2 miles before the checkpoint, with the CP itself not being open this year. These were the first people I had seen on the trail, aside from the dark figure of the musher in the morning twilight.

I smiled and assured the trail guys my mission was to give this Quest trail my best shot, and I would see how much progress I could make. Nice and simple; no stress. I was here to enjoy it and to experience new lands. I thanked them both for their work, as I appreciated what they did for the Quest, and for me as another trail user. I let them know I had supported the Quest the year before at the Scroggie Creek checkpoint in the Yukon. We were all one inter-connected, Far North-loving family. We wished each other well as we continued on our respective journeys.

Not long after this I saw a moose cow and her calf cross the trail, about eight blue whales' lengths ahead of me (175 metres), and a bull moose some seconds later. I got my camera ready to take the family portrait, but, by the time I reached their crossing point, they had all been consumed by the wilderness, and were now nowhere to be seen. The woodland was not at all dense, but they had somehow managed to melt away into the landscape. Onwards I marched.

There were plenty of animal signs within sight as I progressed along. The animals that had approached close to the trail, or crossed it, left the story of their journey for all to see in their prints. There were tracks of squirrels and rabbits and moose, most noticeably. I gazed at them as I moved along the trail, detecting their direction and who was where first, and how long ago that might have been.

There is a lot to be discerned just from the appearance of animal prints. Newer tracks overlaid the older ones. Fresh tracks were defined at their edges, whereas older ones had softened, and the prints more or less filled-in with snow. The recent histories spanned back over the past few days, since winds or snowfall filled-in all the tracks and histories that were there before. All those stories of all those lives; so many critters eking-out an existence across the snow, over frozen earth.

During the middle of the day the temperature must have warmed to close to 5F (-15C); what I would consider warm for the time of year. It was lovely, really. The trail was firm, the sun shone through a clear blue sky, the views were astounding and glorious, I had spoken with friendly folk, and I was absolutely in my element. Reflecting on all these moments, my cup of happiness runneth over.

* * * * * * *

As evening approached, I began to notice feelings of exhaustion creeping up on me. My muscles were working harder than ever, although none were individually, overtly knackered. Hauling a sled is not, contrary to popular imagination, a feat of strength, but one of endurance. When muscles are engaged in strength work, they fire for seconds only, before fatigue forces cessation. When muscles are doing endurance work, they are contracting again and again and again, and can do so for hours or days. The heavier the sled, the more endurance fibres must be recruited to the cause. During the course of a day, they would all be called upon to come to the aid of the party, and contribute to my little scheme of accomplishing a respectable distance.

My progress was consistent, but the strain of sled-hauling was a bit of a shock to the system. I am sure it is not uncommon for endurance athletes to reflect that they could have trained for longer, or a bit more specifically, for their event. For most of us, the realities of daily life encroach on the time we would rather set aside for training. I would integrate as much physical activity as possible, around my days in the biomechanics lab, or when trying to earn sufficient cash to avoid starving to death as a poor doctoral researcher. It was always a struggle, especially with my research demands, and the fact that the wolf was stuck to the door like it had been secured there with a nail gun.

Still, despite all this, I had trained and prepared myself as well as I could. The weight of the sled was beyond what I had dragged previously, and that took its toll. Muscle fibres that liked to sit back and put their feet up during a race, only logging in a few solid minutes of work here and there to keep things ticking over, were now being recruited constantly, and at a level of intensity sufficient to give cause for concern to my nervous system's HR department. I knew how I could have optimised my training, had other commitments not been such a factor, but now here I was, feeling like an unqualified chancer. My body was calling on me to rest, recover, reassess, repack, and do better. A lot better.

I was quickly coming to terms with the fact that progress was nowhere near as solid as what I would expect when racing. The heavy sled slowed my pace, and, although my breaks were still 10-to-15 minutes every few hours, I would also stop fairly often to take photographs using my DSLR camera. I was not much of a photographer, but I was committed to learning my way around a camera, and this added another element, and another cause of delay to my progress. Still, I could always hide the camera away if it slowed me too much.

As the evening drew on, so the unwelcome, and frankly distressing, feeling of bodily fatigue increased. I was annoyed I was not finding this easier. Fitness had never been an issue during previous exploits in the cold. It was all about the heavy sled, and I was wondering whether I could jettison some of the contents to lighten it up a bit.

It was night when I came into view of a bridge where the Chena Hotsprings Road passed over a river. This was 24 miles (38 km) from Pleasant Valley. Another bridge would be 4 miles (6.4 km) later, and 3 miles (4.8 km) after that would be Angel Creek. However, at my current pace this meant two more hours of work, and that was feeling like it would be a push. The bodily fatigue was being compounded by the limited sleep I had obtained during the previous, rough night.

I was more than 70 miles (112 km) from Fairbanks, which, considering I had had a relatively short first day, was not bad progress for non-racing. Still, non-racing distances, coupled with fatigue that more than equalled levels experienced when racing, rankled with me. I was still early enough into this adventure to feel a heightened fear of failure. I needed some recovery and a chance to think intelligently about what lay ahead.

Time-off during an expedition can be tough in itself. Sitting down for extended periods requires work to keep warm, such as preparing and tending a fire. Angel Creek lodge was up ahead, and I was now forming a plan to camp before getting there, completing the remaining couple of hours in the morning after a really good sleep. I would then take the rest of the day off at the lodge, to review kit, and to start fostering a better frame of mind for the 'long game' of reaching the finish line. A thousand miles called for a measured approach, and I was racing nothing but the coming spring.

The trail took me onto a small knoll, from where it descended to pass beneath a bridge, less than the length of one felled Giant Sequoia tree (90 metres) away. I stamped down the ground adjacent to the trail here, and set up my camp. I got comfy in my sleeping bag, lay awake for a while with my mind excited, after which it relaxed and calmed, and I drifted easily off to sleep.

A few cars drove past on the nearby road, but I was mostly undisturbed. It felt like a cold night, but not so much as the previous, and I achieved a welcome, restful, long night's sleep. I remained in my sleeping bag the next morning, until the sunlight was pouring into my little man cave, and I made a point of a more relaxed than usual start to my daily exertions. I did not have far to travel today, and I needed to prioritise recovery and adaptation. Whitehorse was still an awfully long way off.

I tidied away my kit and moved on, heading beneath the first bridge and into woodland on the far side. The trail undulated here and the road was soon out of view. A little further on and the trail brought me back to the road and the next bridge. A sign advised me to duck, although presumably it was intended more for the mushers, standing up on the backs of their sleds. The trail weaved for another couple of miles through woodland, out of view of the road. A sign directed me off the main trail to Angel Creek Lodge, so I took it, shortly after to be ejected into a small, sparsely populated residential area.

The first property declared no trespassing. A road shot off to my right, which I avoided to continue perambulating along the narrow trail. More homes and cabins, but they were all either uninhabited through the winter – easily seen by the lack of broken trails to the doors – or else signed as private property and no trespassing.

I reached Chena Hotsprings Road, and saw no signs or other clues to the whereabouts of the lodge, just a sign to my left that a bridge spanned Angel Creek. I headed back to the start of the short road I had just come along, removed my harness, and went for a more thorough exploration along the trails, unimpeded. The second time I reached the highway I took a right turn and found the lodge a little way along it. An enthusiastic, barking dog was first to greet me, and I took a moment to savour the sight of someone who really took pride in their work. A human emerged shortly after. He greeted me warmly and was efficient in issuing me with a cabin for the bargain price of $65 a night. I went off to retrieve my sled, making use of an unsigned trail as a shortcut back through the woods.

Chopped wood was stacked-up outside the cabin, for the stove within. The door was front and centre, from which I entered the cabin to have my first look around. A wood burner stood in anticipation to my right, in the corner, and there was a dressing table and litter bin to the left. In front was a double bed, with just enough space to walk around it on three sides. There were a couple of small windows and paintings on the wall. The floor was carpeted, and the low ceiling was a foot or so above my head height. All in all, it was a cosy little cabin, which had everything I needed. And a dressing table.

My first priority was to get the wood stove going. There was plenty of wood, and getting the fire started was, with me, the work of a moment. Getting heat out of the stove took a while longer. The flume and front vent were fully opened – as far as I could tell – but it was thick metal, and, with small wood burning to catch bigger wood, it took its time before it was roaring away, and the stove was doing its job of radiating heat into the room.

The result of sitting still in a frozen cabin, after a couple of hours of generating heat from sled-hauling along the trail, really was quite remarkable. I quickly grew cold, and now discovered myself sat on a chair, with legs akimbo around the wood burner, with my torso huddled over it, extracting the steadily generated heat from the stove by apparently humping life out of it. It was some time before I dared to sit up and remove my outer layers. The wood stove did get up to its proper heat, and within no time I had the flume and vent almost entirely closed down, and the cabin soon at a perfectly luxurious temperature.

I brought in my sled and took the sleeping bag out to warm it up, ensuring it was entirely dry and checking it thoroughly, looking for weaknesses or cold spots by spreading it out over the large double bed. The lofting at the front appeared fine, but there seemed to be a lack of down in the back of the bag. I would promote the lofting as best as I could, to see if that made any improvements, and continue to use my down jacket to add insulation, and to compensate for any deficiencies in the back of the bag. In all other regards the bag was fine.

From my sled I took out my food, my spare clothes, my stove fuel, stove equipment and everything else. I would examine everything and be ruthless about whether or not there was anything I could leave behind.

I headed over to the main building, seeking a change of scenery, but on finding it closed I returned to the cabin, to continue faffing with kit, and attempting to beat my shambles of a life into some sort of order.

I took out my Sena action camera and microphone, and made a video diary of my first 70 miles on the trail. The fact that I was two miles from the first official Quest checkpoint was largely irrelevant, as this year it would not be open, but it felt good to be close to another important Quest waypoint, nonetheless.

My usual tactic in the races was to have only cold food, such as dried meat, dried fruit, and the chocolate truffles. As I would only be melting snow for water, I had a stove and fuel that I would not otherwise require. I was carrying dehydrated soup for each day, so as to treat myself, but the treat of dragging the weight of 30 sachets, plus sufficient fuel, had now worn-off, particularly as I had not yet needed to get the stove going. I put my titanium pot on the wood stove and made myself a soup now. It was a pleasure to eat, but not sufficiently so, for me to want to carry about a couple of pounds' worth on the sled. I decided I would leave most of them when I moved on, and take perhaps half a dozen with me as an occasional bit of variety.

In the evening the main building was open, and I went in for some dinner. The place was dark and cluttered. There was a vast wood stove in the middle of the room, and various pictures, paintings and antlers, all hung in general disarray all around. There was a television behind the bar. I treated myself to a refreshing beer and a hearty burger, all of which was a delight.

That taste of a beer and a hot dinner transported me back to the familiar; to thoughts of many days of hiking, when I have retired to a cosy inn for the night, together with the comfort of traditional fare and local ale. It would be very rare for me to consume alcohol during a weekend of running, but when hiking the familiar restorative was very much the norm. After finishing my one beer, and the best burger I could remember ever eating, I filled my water bladder from the kitchen tap and returned to the cabin.

That night the luxury of a big, cosy bed, with a soft mattress and warm sheets and blankets, was not lost on me. I had filled up the stove and then closed down the flume and vent, to help keep it going through the night, and had stacked-up some wood next to the stove for when it had burnt through what was in there. I drifted easily off to sleep, grateful for the recovery time, and expectation of a lighter sled tomorrow, and, therefore, looking forward to my next day on the trail. My thoughts were of what lay between this cabin and the Milepost 101 checkpoint, namely the climb up Boulder Summit and along Rosebud Ridge. I considered that I was taking proper care of myself – making good decisions – and that this was the key to making it all the way. *There was a chance.*

Chapter 5.
Angel Creek to Rosebud Ridge

I awoke from my cosy slumber feeling refreshed and well-rested. Whilst it may have been a stretch to state that I was a new man, I was, at the very least, a factory reconditioned man. I dressed and headed to the main building for breakfast. Some overly fussy and hard to love individuals might have turned their noses up at a microwave-warmed, thin and soggy cinnamon bun with a coffee. To the inexperienced, this might sound like a bit of a raw deal, but to the chap out in the wilds, who expects nothing but cold snow (preferably white), the food he carries with him, and outright abuse from the environment and every single thing living in it, that coffee and soggy cinnamon bun would keep him going for miles, with cause to reminisce frequently on that delicious, bountiful breakfast. I would be dreaming about that cinnamon bun, and with considerable affection, for days to come.

Without the luxury of a shower, I was left to treat myself to a standard expedition 'pits and bits' wash in the bathroom, before heading back to the cabin, to tidy everything away on the sled. I left the majority of cup-a-soups on the dressing table, together with my 4-kg tin of Coleman fuel, which I now optimistically decided I could do without, considering I already had a full fuel bottle and would be able to resupply later, if required. Not having taken the 'kitchen sink' approach to expedition packing, there was not anything more I could really leave behind. My spare clothing was limited to a couple of items in case I fell into water, and everything else had its place in helping me to make progress along the trail.

I expected to use wood stoves in cabins dotted along the trail, plus whatever I could find at any checkpoints, or other places of pseudo-civilisation. The result of this cull was a sled with a fighting weight about 11 lbs (5 kg) lighter than when it left Fairbanks, ignoring the food already consumed.

I floated out of Angel Creek just before 10 o'clock, buoyed with the rosiest of feelings. I planned to promote recovery and keep my days relatively short during this first week. It was not the bold start I had expected, but I was adapting my approach to play the long game. I was grateful I had so effectively dealt with the pulk's weight problem, as slightly warmer temperatures were already softening-up the trail.

The soft trail allowed the sled to sink lower into it, with the effect that I had to really pull the sled through. I was very much aware of how much harder this meant I was working, compared with what I was used to on this trip, and generally. Granted, I have worked hard in the past, sled-hauling through poor trail conditions here and there, but never for full days. This was shaping-up to be hard work, and I would have to raise my game to manage it. Blundering on regardless was an unlikely strategy to win me through, to the happy ending we could all marvel at. Still, this awareness had only a marginal impact on my spirits, as I was coming to terms with the nature of adapting to – and overcoming – the challenges presented.

Angel Creek to Rosebud Ridge

I passed cabins, signs for cabins, Chena Hotsprings (closed), sites with machinery and vehicles, and the occasional minor road. Through the woods I came to a section where the trail team had been busy wielding chainsaws – their focused effort to clear what had become a congested area of trail was staggering. They had worked hard to support the Quest, and I was certainly grateful to make use of their efforts now.

When outside of the woodland, the scenery was magnificent, not that I held any passionate objections to hiking through the woods. On the contrary, but the views of the surrounding low-lying hills and mountains were breath-taking. From *The Guide* I expected a fairly long and easy slog for the first 17 miles (27 km) from Chena Hotsprings, then a steep ascent at the start of the climb up Boulder Summit. I accomplished many climbs along the way towards Boulder, and dismissed each as clearly not steep enough to be noteworthy for *The Guide*.

As I headed along through another patch of woodland, I detected that my peace was about to be violated from the rear. It was a sound I sometimes miss due to the noise of the sled, but I caught it now, and just about in time. It was, with me, the work of a moment to fling myself majestically from the trail, as a dog team came running up alongside me, and the musher brought the team to a halt. A second team came to rest just behind the first.

I was not entirely surprised, of course. It was late winter in Alaska. The Quest trail was being put in. I had spoken with at least three other people during the preceding days. News of my forging a path across Alaska would have reached the tantalised local townsfolk. Big, strapping, brave men such as these were always bound to have been first to take to their dog teams, to begin searching me out. One has one's public.

Had I been making an adventure in the summertime, the schoolchildren would have doubtlessly been bussed-out to nearby roads and trailheads, armed with binoculars and posters with my name poorly spelled across them, to see me pass close by. Attractive single women would join excursions sponsored by the local dating app for lumbersexuals: 'Timber'.

Here, in the midst of winter, I shall miss their company, their warmth, and whatever treats they might have had in store. Still, this is Alaska, and the women are hardy. I fully expect to cross over the coming mountain, and there find a welcoming committee of slavering wild maidens awaiting my thrilling arrival, almost certainly led by Sarah Palin.

My two new human companions made a poor attempt at explaining their presence out here on the trail with me. They regaled me with a tall tale about how they were training along this section of Quest trail, before heading over to Anchorage for the Iditarod in March.

Today they planned to head up Boulder Summit and along Rosebud Ridge, descending down the other side before reversing their route. A likely story, of course. I fully expected they were only going over the mountain first to ensure the stage and seats were all set up ready for Sarah's arrival.

Having exhausted their thinly veiled excuses, muttering something incoherent about having to push on before their dogs got cold feet and seized-up, they moved ahead of me along the trail. This is because sled dogs are famously appalling athletes, of course. Certainly not being such finely-tuned sportsmen as myself, they could not match my ability to hold-up and shoot the breeze for half the day without any ill-effects whatsoever. Off they went – the chancers – and I followed on.

The dog teams were soon out of sight. Their endurance running pace was not much more than mine, perhaps only around 5-6 mph (8-10 kph) or so to my 3.5 (5.6) with this sled, but theirs was relentless. There was no break in their rhythm, nor pauses to take-in the scenery, to check navigation, or to take photographs to share with their loved ones back at the kennel. They did not turn to check their kit on the sled nor to look back along the trail. They ran as an optimised, finely-tuned unit, and cruised comfortably away. I followed-on, about as finely-tuned as a broken piano.

* * * * * * *

In the evening, a section of woodland trail brought me to a short, steep ascent. The climb was at least a couple of moose high (at the head – so at least 6 metres) and it was brutally steep: any steeper and it would have been an overhang. I was digging my feet in, and making good use of my poles to stop me from slipping backwards.

I had no idea how anyone would do this on a fat bike – my alternative mode of transport. It must have been a mission for the mushers with their sleds and ridiculous dogs. Presumably, the first two dogs had to be launched over like grappling hooks for the rest to follow.

There are a variety of skills the professional athlete has at their disposal in moments of impending doom, such as this. The most important approach to tackling a near-vertical climb of snow and ice, whilst hauling a heavy sled, requires a combination of starting momentum, grunt, fury, misplaced optimism, and a fair spread of denial. Equipped with all these in spades, I gathered pace and committed to the climb.

A casual glance from witnesses would have led them merely to report a flash of activity, concentrated around whirling arms and legs; all limbs flailing around in an almost cartoonish fashion, whilst movement of the main body and sled progress upwards at a slow but steady rate. A more careful onlooker would have been rightly baffled by the whole bizarre scene. The feet complete a combination of scrambling upwards, whilst simultaneously kicking-in steps for themselves, as the trekking poles offer both support against the downwards pull of the sled, and somehow stabilise the feet, whilst also producing upward momentum.

Succeeding up these steep climbs is so unusual and complicated a procedure that I mostly manage them without any real idea of how it happened. My brain's higher centres – preoccupied with both the physical task, and the essential need to prevent me from being terrified at the peril I am being propelled through – ensure that I am only left dazed and confused, with my mind swimming in a grateful fog during and after.

This was the very base of the mountain, and the climb levelled-out after those initial, perilous few steps, so I could gather my composure before the climb-proper continued. The longer, steep climb – as described in *The*

Guide – was now ahead of me. I could not discern the height or shape of the mountain, because I was now far too close to it for that, a bit like trying to take-in the scale of a large house when already standing in the porch. Further away my view had been obscured by woodland.

The main climb would be split into a couple of sections. From where I stood, what I now faced was less of a slope and more a wall of slippery snow and ice, extending far up above me. This was presumably only a little worse than the view the Wildlings had directly before their ascent of *The Wall*.

It was too high for momentum to carry me up this time. I could see the gradient eased a little about halfway, which was where I would recover myself before continuing on. I took a few moments for deep breaths, and to get philosophical about this vague mystery called Life, and then it was time to commit to the climb. The sled still felt heavy as I made my start, but I was grateful for the items I had sacrificed at Angel Creek.

The first couple of steps were the easiest. At that point I still had the sled sitting on the more level trail beneath. The steps that followed were tough, because that was when I had to shift my whole body forward, and take the strain of the heavy sled onto the slope, whilst ensuring my footing and poles gave sufficient purchase to prevent a disastrous backwards slip.

I kicked baby-step, after baby-step, into the slope, straining hard against the resistance, and making it halfway up before I could dare to pause for a moment and take rest. My eyes were focused on the trail, and I could see where the dogs had pawed their way up, slipping here and there.

Onwards and upwards. The strain was telling on me, but I knew I was good to make the end of this section, as long as I avoided a slip. Instead of the bold chaos of the first short climb, now everything had to be deliberate and controlled. I brought one foot up a little and kicked it into the slope as best I could. I repositioned both poles higher up, and took the strain of the sled as I then brought my second foot up. This was always the point when I felt most vulnerable; most likely to fall.

The trail was soft and slippery, and my eyes sought-out tell-tale elements that appeared more favourable: a dog print, a section of a few inches that were slightly less steep than the rest, snow a couple of centimetres deeper than the snow around it, some exposed saplings or a spot of mud. Anything that appeared a better option than the surrounding trail became my whole world, as I focused intensely on kicking my feet into the slope, and negotiating my way up.

As I neared the top of the first section, I was alert to a strong wind blowing over from above. Still with some minutes remaining on the climb to the top, I could feel the wind in my face, biting at my exposed skin. The cold, forbidding wind was something I could do without, and I wanted the climb completed before having this to contend with.

The air alone was not so cold, perhaps a civilised -5F (-20C), but it was a strong wind that took the effective temperature down to below -40F (-40C), and I could not risk frostbite to exposed skin. I braced myself in my precarious position on the steep climb, tucking my head down to protect it from the wind. I was wearing a fleece neck gaiter to limit cold air moving down to my baselayer (and to help prevent any zips rubbing against my face), and I had a Buff as a second neck gaiter inside the first. It was there for occasions such as this. I quickly took my hand to the Buff, pulling it up to cover my face just below the eyes. I pulled my midlayer hood over my head too, and continued working my way up the slope.

At the top of that section I paused to recover from my efforts, taking the time to soak in the view around me. I still had the final section of the climb to the top to complete. When the sun sets this far north, it drags its rays on the way down – the twilight lingers long here. I enjoyed gazing at that last gleam of light before the sun was gone. I could not remain drinking it all in for longer though, because the wind was already clawing into my clothes and trying to sap the warmth from me. I still had some way to go up, too; the remainder of this slope and onto the summit, then the ridge and the descent. I could not rest properly until these were all behind me.

At least the opportunity to rewarm was at hand. The trail now proceeded up an even longer, steeper slope to my lefthand side. How the trail team had managed to place a marker in it I had no idea – I would not have liked to try the slope in either direction on a snowmachine. With the dog teams, the mushers would have let the dogs haul the sled with the musher pushing it from behind. Going up on foot would be a real challenge with the sled. What made me feel a bit better was knowing that an American, Jeff Oatley, had done this with a loaded fat bike earlier today. I had seen his tracks on and off since I started this morning.

Getting up this slope was some of the toughest sled-hauling I have ever attempted. I was gripped with an entirely well-placed terror, that if I slipped it would be a disaster. The sled would pull me backwards down the slope, and I would become entangled in the hauling shaft, ending up at the base in a jumbled and broken mess; ropes around my neck, and my limbs distributed in the snow across a wide area. This climb certainly felt further than the last, and I had to take my time to prevent a fall. Occasionally a foot would slip, or a pole, and I always managed to shift weight onto the other three contact points and recover, but there were times when it got close.

It was the last moments of dusk as I reached the top of Boulder Summit. I had heard mushers talk about Boulder and Rosebud Ridge. Now here I was. Trail markers led the way along the ridgetop to my right, and further from view towards the descent.

The route ahead was undulating; it was high, and it was exposed. The wind was surprisingly not as strong up here, and the view of the jagged mountains around me was absolutely staggering. I briefly entertained the idea of camping there, just so I could enjoy the views in the morning. Reality dictated, however, that if I were to attempt such a thing, Fate would hurl a hurricane at me to whip me from the summit, ending me with my limbs distributed in the snow across a wide area.

****

Darkness fell as I continued my way along the high ridge. The trail conditions varied, but overall the conditions were fair, and my path easy to follow. The night-time mountains now reflected the starlight, giving their slopes the drama of a silvery, metallic sheen. As my gaze returned to seek further ahead, I became witness to one of the most incredible sights I have ever beheld.

High up on this mountain, under this frozen, starlit night, the first returning dog team appeared over the crest of a round, distant summit, descending briefly to head to the centre of the ridge, and towards me. The second team moved into view close behind, presumably close to the first here for safety, and for easier communication between teams.

The dogs appeared as black as the night itself. A silvery sheen blazed across their backs, where their musher's powerful headtorch lit them and the ground directly ahead of them. As they caught the light from my own headtorch, 14 pairs of eyes burned towards mine like dazzling stars, or demons. Moving fast towards me as a unified, silent, and ghostly team, they conveyed a majestic elegance, but most of all it was something raw and otherworldly; it was primal, and *it was wild.*

Two teams of 14 dogs, their sleds and their mushers, travelling in a way that has worked here for over a hundred years; this relationship, this bond between the dogs and musher. Witnessing it here on top of the ridge made for a special moment. I watched them in awe and with a deep respect as we advanced towards each other.

I raised a hand to greet the mushers as they passed by, and they did the same. The conditions were too harsh up here for anyone to stop for pleasantries. We all had to be somewhere else, and that somewhere was off the dark, windy, frozen mountain. I turned to momentarily watch the dog teams disappear from view. I dreaded to think what the descent would be like for them. 'Rapid', I expect.

I turned my attentions back to the trail. The summit I now crossed was at 3640 feet (1100 metres) above sea level. The night sky was clear and beautiful, and I became absorbed in looking upwards and all around at the stars. The necessity to protect the sled kept me frequently checking on the trail in front of me. In areas the minimal snowfall and brutal winds had left a stony ground exposed. My lightweight plastic sled would not fare well being dragged over sharp stones.

After a couple of miles the trail began leading me down; off the mountain. The descent with the sled was troublesome, as it tried to overtake me, clearly even more interested in getting off the mountain than I was. I gave up at one point and decided to sit on the sled, but this only ended in predictable carnage, and considerable embarrassment for both of us.

I could only steer at slower speeds, and at slower speeds I was better off walking. At faster speeds the best I could hope for was a deep trail, where the edges could guide the sled around. Here I did not have that, and when the trail went one way I continued straight; ploughing into powder, capsizing, and having my face indelicately thrust into the snow.

I picked myself up, brushed off the snow, and pulled the sled for a while until I could sit on it again. I was not downhearted. After all, one total disaster was just the beginning! I resolved that it was simply going to be one of those nights, and I made my peace with that. I managed about three such rides in total, before finally accepting defeat, appreciating as I did that I was not making sufficient progress, before the inevitable tumbles, for it to be worthwhile.

The problem was that I had to remove the harness to sit on the sled, and I could go neither fast nor far enough to justify the time to remove the harness and pull it back on after. I resumed a more efficient, more traditional, and less exciting format. The land off the mountain was open at first, with the trees small and sparse, and areas of woodland visible further along. All around were foothills.

Up above and to my front, I was treated to the northern lights, drifting and waving me along the trail; the ethereal green curtain that sways, weaves and dances in the thermosphere up to 372 miles (600 km) towards space; a gift from the sun in the middle of a dark night. Someone must have been whistling to them from somewhere. It was a welcome sight, and I became absorbed in the scene as I moved along. No matter how many times I see them, a good northern lights show remains the most spectacular, beautiful, and captivating sight to behold.

The trail undulated but there was nothing overly aggressive left for me that night. I passed where the dog teams had turned around, after which I found myself on a poorly broken trail; I was the only journeyman here since winds had blown-in the track. I had not been the only traveller, though. Another set of solo tracks belonged to a wolf; perhaps the biggest wolf tracks I have ever seen. It had been moving along the trail headed in the same direction, and, although on the same day, the tracks were more than a few hours old.

I continued along the now wooded trail for a while. At a spot where the trail was wider, care of snowmachine activity, I set up my camp for the night. It felt good to know I had started-out well-rested today, and now felt more positive about the journey ahead, helped by the lighter sled. I had managed the first of the big climbs. Eagle Summit and American Summit were ahead, plus the detour over the Top of the World highway. After those I would have King Solomon's Dome and the Black Hills on the Canadian side, and I had crossed those three times before.

As far as I was concerned, there were four previously unknown mountain ranges to cross for this year's Yukon Quest, and I had just accomplished the first of them. I had enjoyed fairly good conditions today, and succeeded up some incredibly tough climbs. On the descent I had had a little fun riding on the sled, and enjoyed the scene of the starlit sky and northern lights. It had been a good day, and I now felt that things were going my way. I pitched my little mountain tent inside one of the wolf prints and slept well.

Chapter 6.
Milepost 101

The heroic climb onto Rosebud Ridge had begun around 19 miles (30.5 km) after leaving Angel Creek. It had been a heady night of dark skies, high winds, dog teams and silvery mountainsides, for no more than 4 miles (6.5 km) before the descent began. The descent totals about 5 miles (8 km) to Birch Creek drainage, and I had camped-out somewhere in between. From the drainage, it would be fairly flat going to the checkpoint at Milepost 101, and a total of 43 miles (69 km) after Angel Creek. I had accomplished most of the descent before erecting my night's lodgings.

Thinking about all this, no matter how hard, was not going to get me any closer to that checkpoint, which is one of life's curses. It was with me the work of a moment to half dress, clamber out of my sleeping bag, fully dress, pull on my trail shoes, pack away all the sleeping kit into drybags, hurl it all towards my sled, and then climb out of the wolf print after it. I pulled on the harness and began making progress, wondering whether I might be too early to see anyone at the CP, setting up for the Quest.

Those gigantic wolf prints were still clear as I progressed along the trail that morning. The scenery was beautiful; staggering even. There were hills all around and woodland closer by. There was another azure sky above: a pleasant, crisp, but not cold morning. All was well with my world.

I triumphantly negotiated some tricky areas of overflow as I crossed a moderately wide river, without getting wet, which I always considered a victory. I manage these sections of abject peril whilst channelling my inner water boatman; striving to exhibit an outward appearance of majesty, poise and purpose, more closely approximating that of a world-class ice skater. The reality bears little such resemblance, I regret to report. Reality presents the world with something closer to the progress of a washed-out drunkard of an aged and arthritic ice skater, recently shot in the leg.

My onward path brought me close to the Steese Highway, before diverting me back a little way along unbroken trail. A few paces along the soft trail gave me pause to halt and reassess. I pulled on my snowshoes to give them their first airing of the expedition, and to maintain something approximating my desired pace.

The trail brought me back close to the road, and up ahead I could see a cabin on each side. I moved along, hoping the checkpoint would be one of them, not that I was expecting much there, or even an accessible cabin, but it was another important landmark on the Quest route.

I passed the two cabins, fairly dejected that the checkpoint was not either of them. A small cluster of cabins lay a little further ahead, mostly hidden from view beyond a small rise. I made it up to those to be confronted by a hive of human activity. There were cars, snowmachines and actual people milling about.

The spectacle of all this was almost alarming, after my recent days of minimal interactions. I brought myself to a halt close to a cabin, and a woman kindly informed me there was food, drink and a place to spend the night. I struggle to imagine what more wondrous and heavenly words have ever been uttered in the history of humankind.

I responded by asserting I would be happy to work to earn my keep, although this was obviously a blatant lie. However, and because some folk are equipped with only a rudimentary grasp of sarcasm, and apparently even less ability to read the scene in front of them, I was actually put to hard labour. My first job involved helping to shift a sofa out of a cabin, with a secondary task for the out-of-puff sled-hauler being to inflate a pink flamingo (checkpoint mascot or practical joke on me, one cannot be sure).

One of the volunteers came to look at my sled set-up, and to engage me in enlightening intercourse. He reckoned he managed about 1000 miles of snowshoeing each winter, hauling from 100 to 200 lbs (45 – 90 kg) of kit on a sled. He had a formidable background as a hunter, trapper and outdoorsman, and, for his knowledge and experience of bushcraft in this environment, I could have hung on his every word for days on end. Whereas, during a race, I enjoy shooting through checkpoints like beaver fever, on a solo expedition my priorities are quite different. I was not interested in setting a fastest known time, but to soak-up some experience and understanding, both of the environment and its people.

The richness and appreciation that comes from insights of the locals cannot be conveyed by a single person writing a book: you need to be confronted by each person, to look into their eyes, and to hear the interest and passion in each voice. Each individual conveys their own stories in their own way, with their own emphases and excitement, and this creates a rich tapestry of the people, who are as beautiful and wild as the land itself. The listener benefits from the ebb and flow of ideas and passions that align them, and those that distinguish them as individuals.

I was recommended that, considering how gnarly conditions and the trail had been over Eagle Summit just before now, it would be advisable to crack-on and get it done. I was scarcely tempted though. Good conditions are important, even vital, to a successful mountain crossing, but I had too much to lose already. I had managed myself well from Angel Creek to here. I was feeling fit and well-rested. I reflected upon an air of impatience and excitement, just to get over the mountain, but decided that, sometimes, restraint and a more measured approach can be best. I was not racing, after all.

To push on might leave me exhausted, reducing the quality of my experience, or advancing me into a descending spiral of needing more and more recovery, from pushing too fast too soon. Plus, this was my first chat with an interested local, and it was likely the CP would be buzzing with other fascinating folk later on. One does not wish to alienate those nearest and dearest to me with this stark switch from my normal, introverted and anti-social ways, but I actually *wanted* to spend time with these people. Of course, the sad fact might be that all my friends and acquaintances back home are *the worst*.

I also wanted to be feeling fresh, fit and ready for that climb. Besides, I had a strong suspicion there would be trail-breakers coming through imminently, ahead of the first dog teams, and they would therefore be breaking trail for me, too. I was not only thinking about the mountain at my feet; I was thinking about the several hundreds of miles that lay beyond it, and all the conditions, trials and struggles waiting for me out there.

I was now with folk who welcomed me as a fellow Quest volunteer, and, as my goals included seeking-out the most positive experiences overall, here I would spend the night. Eagle Summit would still be waiting for me in the morning. At this point, I would happily exchange perfect conditions now for a little less-perfect in the morning, if it were the difference between feeling healthy and strong tomorrow, or overworked and knackered tonight. Rosebud was likely the toughest climb of the Quest from this direction, but Eagle Summit would take a fair second place, depending on the conditions.

According to *The Guide*, I was now 127 miles (204 km) from Fairbanks, so had less than 890 miles (1430 km) remaining, and with a little over 400 miles (643 km) to Dawson. I was feeling in good health, with fair weather conditions past and expected. I was feeling better with my kit, and, 127 miles in, I now had a better idea of how much food I needed.

I was making slower progress than anticipated, but I was only getting through about half my daily food rations. Granted, I knew my appetite would increase, and food intake with it, but for now I had a surplus of food, and that surplus was a dead weight on the sled, requiring more calories to drag than if I were without it. I would dwell on this issue and make the necessary changes in the morning.

What followed, that afternoon and evening, was an entirely unexpected delight. I had not anticipated the checkpoint to be staffed by the time of my arrival, although I knew there was a chance. To be welcomed in as a fellow volunteer, given a few tasks, and, in exchange, to enjoy food, drink and wonderful company, was far more than I had hoped for.

There were trail team members congregated here, with many expecting to head out over Eagle Summit (just a few miles from the checkpoint) in the morning. Others had arrived from the direction I had come in from. Mention was made by the team of the massive wolf tracks, and questions raised about my security when sleeping outside, and whether or not I had gotten wet when negotiating the stretch of overflow earlier that day. This commonality of observations and experiences on the trail was a passing bond between us. Discussing a shared experience such as this is not entirely unlike folk discussing a sports game, film or TV programme they have recently watched, but the living experience in nature is so much deeper.

Topics of conversation therefore centred around nature, wildlife, racing and the great outdoors. All anyone talked about were subjects close to my own heart – my own passions – and it helped me to feel truly at home, inspired and motivated. The food was superb and the beers flowed, followed by spirit-based jellies. I maintained some restraint with the alcohol, but the merriment was contagious. A team from the highways management arrived with some cooked ribs to share, and there was much rejoicing.

By this time, I was sharing a table with a couple of volunteers and the checkpoint manager. One of the volunteers, Nate, was a good young man with an interesting background working with people in distress and with mental health issues, but was here in a technical role, to manage the communications side of things. I could have listened to him all night long.

Nate was much vexed when he posted a photo on Facebook and someone recognised me almost immediately. "Yeah, right," Nate ejaculated, "like someone is going to recognise the random walker guy who just showed up here." Well, to borrow from Ron Burgundy: *People know me*. I checked the name and confirmed this was the case.

The northern lights were present that night, and blissfully welcome. They were not as spectacular as the night before, but I was just grateful to be able to see even green mist-like cloud moving in the sky above. It remains a novelty to me, no matter how weak or strong the aurora happens to be. It is always a special sort of pleasure to look up into the sky and see the lights there, full of green, waving down to me.

Following that night of bacchanalian revelry, I headed to a cabin, where I attempted to sleep on a bunkbed. The cabin was shared with Mike and a hunter; a man who slept with his rifle and pistol close by, and who snored like the worst I have ever known. This was funny at first, but I soon found myself toying with the idea of sleeping outside, and acknowledging the point that one of the luxuries of sleeping out is the all-pervading peace and tranquillity. How I found any peace – and slept at all that night – remains one of the universe's great mysteries.

Chapter 7.
Milepost 101 to Central

Despite the earth-shaking, cabin-trembling, deafening snoring that I contended with last night, somehow sleep overcame me. I was aware of this fact because I woke up in the morning, albeit groggily – so groggily, in fact, that I was too groggy to be absolutely furious. I would have slept far better if – at the first signs of the snores refusing to abate – I had clambered down from my bunk, left the cabin in the dead of night, at -22F (-30C), in my underwear, and sought-out a noise-cancelling snowbank to bury my face into. Granted the frostbite would have become agonising, but at least I would have found rest.

Over coffee and a cooked breakfast, Mike kindly scribbled out a list of cabin names and locations on the back of my A3 route map. At least that is what he told me he was doing. Before evolution selected archaic eye cells to form together, adjusting themselves into a fairly efficient concave shape, eyes were quite flat and ineffective. A leech has eyes like this – many light-sensing cells that make up an eyespot – sufficient only for detecting light and dark. Due to my extreme tiredness, my vision was probably now only just beginning to approximate that of the humble leech.

As the coffee steadily did its job of transforming me into a functioning hominid, I slowly felt that I might be about equal to the task of legging-it up and over Eagle Summit, and tumbling down the other side and into Central; the next town and Quest checkpoint. At a distance of around 28 miles (45 km), it was scarcely over a marathon, and, aside from this not unsubstantial bump between here and there, I thought this looked to be a good stint for the day. And who knew what waited for me in Central? Food? Supplies? A quieter place to sleep? All good things, I was sure.

I was in no rush to leave the delightful company of my new friends at Milepost 101. This was not so much because I enjoyed their company – although I certainly did – but because a group of them were due to head-out on snowmachines over Eagle Summit, so would be breaking trail for me. I planned to bide my time a little, to allow the trail to set before I followed on.

It was mid-morning that I harnessed-up, expecting to set-off after them in tepid pursuit. One mountain, a cheeky marathon or so, and then Central. I discovered then that the trail team had not, in fact, yet left, and were still organising outside. However, if I waited longer I would not reach Central until late, and I was growing impatient to get going.

They would pass me soon enough, and doubtless before I was onto the climb itself. The sky was overcast, but that seemed to have the benefit of it not seeming so cold; not that I mind the cold when I am heading up a mountain. Sled-hauling uphill is hard work, so cold is not a problem.

Eagle Summit is known to be a tough climb; and potentially a dangerous one for the dog teams. The mountain stands 3652 feet (1113 metres) above sea level, and it has a reputation. In 1916, Hudson Stuck successfully navigated over the mountain. He later wrote: "The Eagle Summit is one of the most difficult summits in Alaska. The wind blows so fiercely that sometimes for days together its passage is almost impossible".

It is now a hundred years later and time has done little to tame the climb for winter travellers and dog teams. Some Quest mushers have been reported to state it is the toughest section of the whole race, and even the toughest section of any sled dog race anywhere in the world. Fierce winds, drifting snow, and steep slopes make it a grim ordeal, and those conditions are encouraged by the surrounding landscape, channelling the winds into the mountain.

In 2006, Quest mushers faced the worst storm in the race's history, with hurricane-force winds trapping several mushers and their dogs around the summit, while a handful endured hell to reach safety. Lance Mackey arrived in Central and told the onlookers that he had never been that scared in his life. It took snowmachine teams from Mile 101 and Central, plus National Guard and Alaskan State Troopers – all hampered by continuing blizzard conditions throughout the next day – to rescue six mushers and 89 dogs from Eagle Summit. None were left behind.

* * * * * * *

My first few miles took me past an old mining area, complete with dilapidated cabins. They must have looked inviting once, and I pondered on when that might have been, and what the area might have looked like in its heyday. They probably still looked like cabins, but new. And that was probably when mining was starting-up in the area, late in the 19th century. That more or less exhausted the subject, so I looked to the trail to inspire me.

The track undulated, and there were saplings and brush to negotiate self and sled past. The trail team passed me as I worked my way through this section, about halfway to the start of the main climb. I was in snowshoes by now, care of a soft trail, and, although the snowmachines helped break the trail for me, it was churned-up and still easier to manage with snowshoes.

A couple of hours after leaving the checkpoint, the trail began heading gently upwards, and across the base of a hill. Two of the trail team returned from the summit and reported on conditions. Visibility was not great on the mountain, and the trail was soft, but at least there was now a path for me. They would head back to Milepost 101 now, and remain there, just heading out in either direction to help pack the trail ahead of the dog teams. Three other snowmachines were now continuing beyond Eagle Summit to Central.

The trail led me up through a short valley, where I could see huge tripods up on the hillside to my left, and which appeared to stand about as tall as I did. They would be there year after year, to help guide travellers in adverse conditions, including during white-outs. I had seen similar during the Iditarod the previous year, in the Alaska range. The Quest trail markers missed the first of these, as the trail continued up the valley, then taking a 90-degree left turn to head directly up the slope.

The climb was a long slog, and, although steep, it did not compare to my experience on Rosebud. I was even able to take a couple of selfies on this one, which helps to illustrate the lack of peril. The clouds were low and I had no views from the top. The white clouds met with white mountainside, messing with my mind, as I had no visible horizon. I imagined that hours in such a place could become quite disorientating. Still, the tripods and markers showed me the way.

The toughest part of Eagle Summit was not the climb to the top, but rather the contouring journey from close to the top to the start of the descent. The trail led down from the top, meandering across to the right, towards a ridge, necessitating a marginal climb. I felt like I was heading along the upper section of a vast satellite dish; the sled ever-ready to take some unfortunate initiative, and fire itself down the slope, instead of following me along. Because it was in a peculiar mood, rather than always trying to slide downhill, sometimes it cartwheeled downhill instead, ejecting its contents into the snow in its wake: It was a bastard like that sometimes.

My ideal sled set-up comprises one large sled bag, into which all my kit goes, and that bag is secured tightly onto the sled with straps. With such a set-up, when the sled turns over, it is not too difficult to get it righted again. My current set-up involved a fairly large kit bag, with sleeping mat secured on top, which took up the back half of the sled. A 20-gallon (90-litre) drybag, containing my sleeping bag, sat in the front half, with the day's food bag and camera bag behind it, clipped onto the front of the kit bag. When I was not wearing my snowshoes, they lived under the drybag at the front. This whole set-up was absolutely fine until it was not, such as now.

Although all the kit was connected to the sled in some way, the various bags all somehow manage to ensure that, whenever ejected, they found themselves dispersed over a wide area, despite still being connected to each other and the sled. It was baffling and impressive in equal measure. I did not have sufficient cash for a proper sled bag this year, so was improvising, which was not going spectacularly well, as now evidenced.

Moving back to right the sled whilst I was wearing snowshoes was also inconvenient, as they were better suited to forward progress than about-turns and finer manoeuvrability. These constant pirouettes were particularly trying and lacking elegance. I had now tied everything down as well as I could, preventing the whole unit from rolling off to seek adventures without me. It was still a time- and energy-sapping embuggerance though, and my frustrations grew. I dreaded to think what it would be like to do this with a bigger sled, and 14 dogs all harnessed-up to it. I imagined dogs and kit would be everywhere, the musher flailing along in the snow behind, trying to bring order and sense out of all the chaos. In my own way, I was grateful for the simplicity of my approach.

The main descent, in which self and slope were heading in the same direction, was unfathomably worse. Now the sled attempted to overtake me, which was not helpful. I admired its eagerness and energy, but I had been labouring under the belief we were partners. The sled was pulled along via fairly elastic paracord. I had PVC conduit over the ropes, and these were crossed before being secured to the harness. This gave me the benefit of a more stable set-up, and prevented the sled from repeatedly crashing into the back of my legs, which is always an agonising experience. Instead, the increased speed in the sled would cause it to attempt overtaking manoeuvres, to whichever side of me I least expected.

If the sled succeeded in moving ahead of me, the tension from the poles, through the harness and onto my waist, would make forward movement difficult, awkward or even impossible. On those occasions, I had to perform a movement more familiar to performers of Sufi whirling, to bring myself out ahead of the sled, and with the poles back in their correct position.

Sometimes I could outrun the sled, and tuck it back into position behind me. Most often, the sled would just careen off to one side, traditionally with the added bonus of then tipping itself over. Although it was not a long descent, there was sufficient scope for each of these moves to feature multiple times. There was no option to sit on the sled and end up in a snowbank, as the trail was too shallow and the slope too varied. I might have ended up in a tree and with the sled in an adjacent valley.

Once off Eagle Summit I could begin rehabilitation from all the trauma proper. I emerged from the snowy and mountainous chaos in philosophical mood. In life one has experiences. The trail now undulated for many miles through woodland, and across a creek. My route took a sharp right turn and led me through another mining area. Thirteen miles (21 km) from where I began that day I crossed the Steese Highway. On the other side I met with two of the trail team, who were making their way back to Mile 101.

I was warned of a long creek section with about 4 miles (6.5 km) of overflow. I was given the good news that at least they had broken through a lot of the ice with their heavy snowmachines, so now it was good and open and I could get my feet nice and cold and wet. I thanked them earnestly, hoping their next bowel movements might feature flaming pineapples.

It was late afternoon when I reached the overflow. Initially it was good and well-frozen, but I soon found sections where my feet started to fall through. It was clear to me where the snowmachines had fractured the ice. My misplaced optimism made me incorrectly believe I could somehow float across, without punching through the unbroken ice around the periphery, as if I were an Arctic Jesus. I was not, and the obvious resulted. I suppose it was partly because I knew I would be in Central that evening, and able to dry-out my shoes and socks, that I jettisoned caution to the wind. In any case, my feet did not sink in too far, so I mostly got away with it.

The trail brought me off the river and onto firmer ground. It was night now, and the stars were once more my companion. There was woodland and open fields. I soon alerted local dogs to my presence, and, in the distance, I could see the light from a cabin. I crossed a road before rejoining the trail on the far side. I was entering Central now, only a couple of miles from the checkpoint, and it was shaping-up to be another good day.

I was so pleased, in fact, that I began singing a little, although, as I loathe the sound of my own voice, I have no idea why I did this. It has been said that if Pandora were to be beaten by curiosity and open up her box for a quick squiz, the first thing to come flying out of it would be the sound of me singing. And the world would hold its breath and shudder amidst the ensuing cataclysm, and humanity would know its doom. Still better than Coldplay, obviously.

I took a moment to pause my perambulations and stare up at the Milky Way, soaking it all in. Spending so much of my life in light-polluted towns, I embrace these opportunities to savour clear skies, and none are better – in my experience – than the Arctic skies. Whether it is brilliant stars, an easily perceived Milky Way, or dancing Aurora, I never tire of gazing up.

I was now back out on the road, passing a few homes and businesses, including an inviting bar. I kept going though, not content to rest until I finally arrived at the Steese Roadhouse; the race checkpoint here in Central. I soon reached that key Quest milestone. Volunteers from the race had expected my arrival, thanks to word from the trail team. A couple of regulars took note as I deharnessed and headed within.

It is a strange and unusual position to be in, both for adventurer and spectator alike. For me, I had journeyed 160 miles (257 km) of a 1000-mile (1600-km) expedition, arriving with a beard frozen from exposure to recent temperatures below -4F (-20C), and having successfully hauled a sled over Rosebud and Eagle Summit, along the toughest sled dog race route in the world. I had pulled up outside with my sled, and walked inside a nice warm bar and restaurant, closing the door behind me, and turning to be confronted by a sea of faces staring at me.

Well, I exaggerate the scale of the operation. Central itself has a population that probably only breaks into triple digits when the Quest blows through. I was confronted by a moderately-sized puddle of faces staring at me.

For them, they were enjoying a restful drink on a pleasant winter's eve, not too many miles south of the Arctic Circle, and their peace and tranquillity was disturbed by the presence of an odd-looking chap with a frozen face, who had just sauntered in from the cold, black night, as if his was the most ordinary occupation in the world. I could see that I needed to put everyone at their ease. I ventured a cheery "Hullo!", and, seeing that I was on a precipice, followed it up with a "Nice night for it". With my evening's lecture concluded, people responded a kindly greeting, and returned to seek reassurance and quiet counsel in their drinks.

I then sallied forth to the bar, offering a nod to the Quest volunteers all huddled around a table, bid a good evening to a young lady who had just emerged from the kitchen, and pulled myself up a chair at the bar. I confided in the barkeep that I would like a bottle of Alaskan Amber, and he confided that a chap sat a little further along the bar would like to buy it for me.

During my whole life I have had many people buy me drinks, and, perhaps, some of these individuals may be thought of as friends of friends, or friends of family. Never, during any of it, have I had a drink bought for me by someone strange to me. If this is the sort of thing that comes with professional adventuring, I told myself, then it is clearly the career for me.

I raised the bottle to salute my new chum, thanked him kindly, and took a sip of the fine nectar. Because I am not an alcoholic and I had had my moment, I followed the beer with a can of V8 vegetable juice, knowing that now everyone was very much left bewildered; baffled at what my next move could possibly be.

The barkeep informed me they had only recently bought the roadhouse, and had worked frantically to get everything set-up to open ahead of this year's Quest. I assured him his work was well worth it, and I and all were hugely grateful he had managed it.

John – my new BFF and beer purchasing chum – invited me back to his house, which was apparently situated next door. I joined him and his friend there, and a party ensued. I enjoyed one more beer, sat in the comfiest, softest armchair in the world, and watched on. People came and went, drinking beer and enjoying a recreational smoke. John and I had a pleasant chat about the drives and desires for feats of endurance in wild lands. His wife had recently headed-off to begin a journey of her own, under her own steam, a little further south.

The conversation flowed amongst the partiers, although it was quite different to that of my kindred spirits back at Milepost 101. It was a very different living and attitude here in a town, and I felt like something of a misfit, although we were perhaps all misfits in our own ways. That is how we end up here. It was different at Mile 101, because people had travelled far and wide to be involved in the Quest, which was our common ground and interest. The heterogeneity here, or, at least, the stark difference between myself and those for whom the Quest was not the be all of their existence, made it difficult for me to engage. This was my shortcoming and not theirs, of course, but I was too tired to try harder to fit in. I excused myself to an early night, and slept well in someone else's bed.

Chapter 8.
Central to Birch Creek

I rolled out of bed in the dark at around seven o'clock. I tidied away my kit in the dark, and legged it back to the roadhouse, also in the dark, for bacon, which was also suspiciously dark, but what they seem to rave for around these parts. There were already a few familiar members of the trail team installed, and it was great to see them and to briefly catch up.

One of the team was in his early seventies, and described a ruined shack down the trail where they had tried and failed to get any warmth into the place, so abandoned it and made progress to here. The breakfast at the roadhouse was very well-received, even forgiving the crimes against bacon, and I enjoyed it all whilst chatting with another Mark, an engineer from Canada, who had been asked to join the trail team at short notice.

The trail team set about organising themselves, and I, inspired by their initiative, thought it would be a good idea to do the same. After a quick check with the Quest checkpoint volunteers, I established that none of them was entirely sure which way the trail led, which is why it is often better to enquire of the trail team for such advice. The GPS is good, but it helps to at least start off in the right direction, in case the GPS route is not quite right, or is baffled about present location. When a GPS track has come from a single musher in a single year, there is always scope for a little error.

The early morning light was just winning-through its victory over the night's darkness as I launched away.

The trail left the roadhouse to the south, paralleling a road as far as Circle hot springs, about 8 miles (13 km) from town. From here, the trail headed east to an airstrip, where I arrived a couple of hours after my breakfast and treated myself to my first break of the day.

Airstrips on the snow are fairly straightforward to spot, in that nothing else looks quite like them; flat, rectangular, white, and free from brush and trees, somewhat like a fluffy albino cricket pitch, scaled-up. The first of the dog teams overtook me here. I was already well into enjoying my break, and sat tight, off the side of the trail, as they ran past.

Seeing a dog team racing along is a wonderfully humbling experience. Each dog will work longer and harder each day than I do, consuming miles like they were born for it. It is a scene I never tire of.

I harnessed myself, keen to make more progress. I reached level with the end of the airstrip, where the route proceeded through a section of woodland and brush, before dropping me onto Medicine Lake. It was noticeably cooler here than in town, and on the lake a mist had descended beneath a grey sky, making the white trees on the periphery stand-out amongst an otherwise bleak landscape, with the low morning sun burning through the clouds.

The trail leaving the lake was fairly deep, soft, and punchy. I fastened my snowshoes on now, to help promote efficient onward progress. I met Mark and an accomplice coming back, and we all stopped for a very brief natter. I was reliably informed that I had about 12.5 miles (20 km) to go before the trail would lead me onto Birch Creek.

Central to Birch Creek

On Birch Creek I could expect temperatures considerably colder than in Central. I would have a total of 47 miles (75.5 km) along the creek. Mark advised me of a potential campsite, but not knowing exactly where the 'canoe landing' was, I could only hope it was obvious. A large, flashing neon sign with 'Canoe Landing', and a dozen or so canoes leaning against it, with fireworks going-off upon my arrival, was what I really needed in order not to miss it. Without that elevated spot, I might be in for a cold night on the creek. The guys were reluctant to hang on longer to chat. The trail here was narrow through the brush, and they had concerns about coming head-to-head with a dog team in this area.

One of Mark's roles was to widen the trail as much as possible, but there really was not much that could be done through this particular section. A snowmachine can happily ride over saplings, but even if the trail is widened in such a way, the saplings will spring back up and present a barrier to the dogs. In any case, the general lie of the land and the spread of trees, saplings and brush, limited the scope for much ambition when it came to trail-widening.

The motivation for widening elsewhere, such as along the 47 miles of Birch Creek, was to make it easier for dog teams to pass each other. There was always such a need during the Quest, but this year there was a routing difference too. There are two races in the Quest; the 1000-mile race and a 300-mile race. The 1000-mile event finished in Whitehorse, and the 300 traditionally finished in Circle.

Ordinarily, teams in the 300 would do an out-and-back along the Yukon River from Circle City, but this year the ice conditions on the river were too rough to permit this, so teams would turn around in Circle and finish in Central instead. This meant teams in the 300 coming back along the trail, facing teams from both the 300 and 1000-mile races coming towards them. Hence the need for trail-widening.

The trail between the airstrip and the creek was some of the worst I have encountered. The way was certainly clear and well-broken, but also being soft and churned-up it was a tough slog with the sled. I was also frequently looking behind me for approaching dog teams.

* * * * * * *

It was late afternoon when I reached Birch Creek and descended onto it. My target for the day was to get as close to 40 miles accomplished as I could, before leaping onto an inviting campsite. The earlier, soft trail, had slowed me down, making it hard to judge distances and progress, but I would simply go as late as I dared. I harbour no great fear of *The Darkness*. Still, I consider a healthy fear of pushing fatigue to the point of sleep-monsters, and poor decision-making, to be fair enough.

Sleeping on the creek would mean a cold night, with dog teams passing me by throughout, disturbing my peace with their noise. What I ideally wanted was an area where the trail led up onto the riverbank, and was wide enough (and/or flat enough) for me to set up my camp on the good, raised ground, far enough from the trail to not interfere with the Quest teams, and that little bit warmer for being off the river. I was not overly optimistic, particularly as it would be dark as I looked for my camp. I suspected the wily mushers would have nabbed all the best spots.

This was a tough day, not only because of the trail below, but because of the sky above too. The trail was better on the river, where the limited snowfall had been packed down more than elsewhere. However, the grey, overcast sky hampered the enjoyment somewhat.

On a grey day, where the horizon is difficult to perceive, the sky and land are almost indistinguishable. The view lacks depth and contrasts, and there is no brightness to the day. It all appears dull, flat, lifeless and murky. The whole world is in greyscale. The days sleep like this, and, although I know the land is beautiful and wondrous and captivating, I cannot see it in these moments with my own eyes. I can only imagine, and wonder at what it must be like on a better day. Onwards I moved, hoping for clearer, brighter days ahead.

The creek was, for the most part, flat and fast, which helped to buoy my spirits. There were occasions where the trail led me up to the riverbank, but these were gentle, easy climbs, and any additional efforts from the ascents were compensated for when descending, shortly after. These were fast miles, easy miles, and, without the scenery to draw me in, my mind happily wandered into daydreams.

For the most part, the creek was lined with woodland, with hills sometimes further off, sometimes closer. Occasionally there would be a cabin. I was unable to determine where the canoe landing was. Any wooden structures on the riverbank had been engulfed by the snow. Mark had told me there would be tracks going in all directions when I got there, but now that I surveyed the trails on the creek, I could see tracks in all directions at various places, and I did not even know for sure if he had meant snowmachine tracks or just animal tracks. Wherever the landing was, I had passed it.

I sled-hauled long into that dark night. By nine o'clock I was content that I had accomplished enough and had earned my rest. Still, an hour or more after that brought me to no good campsites. I knew that my standards for what constituted a good campsite would deteriorate the further into the night I pushed. I reflected on so many perfect campsites I had already passed, and had knowingly passed, in the hope of gathering up just a few more miles before I slept.

A sense of desperation began creeping stealthily upon me. I was tired now from my efforts earlier in the day, and I did not want to push into the early hours of the morning, only to miss out on daylight if I overslept. The trail brought me within some yards of the riverbank on my left side, and a patch of riverbank would have to suffice. I had paused to examine similar spots before, and had dismissed each of them as being too much effort to reach. Now I was tired and my need to call the day a day reigned supreme.

I brought the sled off the side of the trail, and unpacked everything that might inhibit progress of the dog teams – they can get distracted with alluring smells, such as might occur if I left my food bag near the trail. I had taken my snowshoes off for the better river conditions, and put them on again now.

I snowshoed up to the top of the riverbank to get a good look at the area. It appeared flat, and there was a section without brush or saplings to damage the tent. There were moose tracks, but it was not a main animal trail, and the moose had passed through at least a day before. I stamped down an area for the tent, and headed back down to the sled for the kit I needed.

I did not fancy the chore of bringing the sled up my poorly compacted path, so double-checked it was well-off the trail before leaving it. I then proceeded to take each item I needed – my tent, sleeping bag, sleeping mat, clothes bag, food bag and down jacket – and enthusiastically launched each up to my camping spot.

I trudged back up, pitched my little camp, and crawled within. It had been a good day for progress, and tomorrow I would arrive at Circle City, population between 150 and 200, comprising mostly sled dogs passing through on important business, with the normal citizenry of about 70, plus various breeds of humans there for the Quest. The checkpoint would be open because the race was in full swing, indicating I might even manage to blag some food and somewhere warm to spend the night.

It was with warm thoughts that I settled my head down onto my clothes-bag pillow, and began drifting off to sleep. It seemed to be only seconds later that my heart was in my mouth, and I lurched up to what seemed like a freight train almost running over my tent. The rumble of movement felt deafening; the river ice trembling. I was alert and shaking from adrenaline, wondering what fresh hell was about to kill me now. It passed as momentarily as it had arrived.

It could not have been dogs. It simply could not have been. Sled dogs are petite, light, and this far into the race they are moving steadily rather than fast. It could not have been dogs. Had a musher swapped-out his dogs for a team of stampeding, furious bison, perhaps? It seemed unlikely, but, having exhausted all the probable options, this is what I was left with, and – however improbable – it had to be the answer. Satisfied with my Sherlock Holmes logic, I lay back down.

As I lay there, waiting for my heart to navigate its way back down into my chest, for the palpitations to ease off, and for the cold sweat to dry up, a second and then a third team passed. Nowhere near as formidable as the first, to my dazed and bewildered senses here in the tent, but each team was surprisingly fast and committed.

I would have loved to watch them moving past. I was still in awe of the spectacle of those two teams moving over Rosebud Ridge, in the depths of that inky black night. It was colder now; the trail firm and flat, and the teams were presumably in their element, perfectly comfortable, and moving well. Dog teams truly are extraordinary. I drifted back to sleep, occasionally reawakened by the sound of another passing dog team. It seemed that nature was getting its own back, for all the ruckus I make with my noisy sled bashing about behind me. Still, I appreciated the fleeting, passing company of the four-legged athletes, and it was with those warm thoughts that I eventually found sleep for the night.

Chapter 9.
Birch Creek to Circle City

Despite a few rude awakenings, I slept well. In the morning I packed everything away, enthusiastically hurled it back down to my sled, harnessed-up and moved off. Today I would see the remaining dog teams that had not passed me during the night, and, hopefully, I would see someone I knew at Circle (whether a musher or support crew).

In stark contradistinction to yesterday, I was now being treated to a cloudless blue sky. By midday it was even feeling fairly warm for the river; somewhere around -4F (-20C). I paused to greet a musher, who was resting his team off the trail, and preparing them food. He looked up at me with a beaming smile, taking in the view across the glistening white, frozen river to the soft white hills beyond, and the azure blue sky as he did so, and he called out 'It don't get any better than this!' I grinned back and agreed with him completely. We had a brief chat and I moved on, allowing him to continue his work, and happy with the spirit of our conversation. I did not even correct his grammar, which was unusual for me, because I like to be helpful.

Here we all were: a few dozen Quest 1000-mile and 300-mile mushers, and me, probably all absolutely loving the experience of being out on the river, under the blue sky, on a good day. It was far from cold, and we were all simply enjoying the wonderful world we were moving through. It all felt utterly beautiful, and that spectacular northern beauty flowed from the sky far above to the ground below, and to the depths of my being.

What made it even more wonderful, was the thought that we were all sharing this together, all at home in the outdoors, in a place so many others would see as some harsh, frozen hellscape, and full-on suffer-fest. For us, this approached our heaven. The experience can vary by the day and by the moment, or all at once the most peaceful, calm, inviting, forbidding, freezing, heart-warming, beautiful place on Earth, and I love it and know of nowhere better. For all these long days of focused and determined activity, it was our shared playground, out in the heavenly wilds of the world's Far North.

It was just after midday when I arrived at the Steese Highway Bridge. I moved the sled off the trail and sat down upon it, facing back in the direction I had come from, and proceeded to get myself outside of some food. I was just packing everything away when I saw a dog team approaching. I stood at the front of my sled, ready to move off, waiting for them to pass first.

I do not know precisely what the dogs were waiting for, but the lead dog did not seem keen on moving ahead of me. He just sort of looked up at me, and his eyes said: 'After you, good sir'.

'No really, I couldn't.', I tried to explain to him: 'You're so much better at this sort of thing than I am. Please you go first.'

'Couldn't possibly, my good man' returned his stout expression.

If you have never met a nonplussed sled dog, then I strongly recommend it. Even better is 14 of them, accompanied by a frustrated musher, getting more irritated with them by the second. There may have been 14 dogs, but their attitude was as one. And it was very much not the attitude of the musher. The lead dog simply looked up at me, enquiringly, expectantly. Thirteen others gazed on with vacant looks; with lost looks.

I apologised to the musher and she explained how her dogs were just confused and curious. Onwards she went, with me falling-in behind them. From the bridge it would be about 17 miles (27 km) to the exit from the river, and 8 miles (13 km) more to the checkpoint. I suspected that opportunities for me to inflict chaos into the lives of mushers was diminishing by the mile.

Darkness was already falling as I approached the exit from Birch Creek. The trail led me around open land, and the night sky became clear and spectacular. There were no northern lights at this time, but the stars looked impossibly close and bright. I moved along whilst craning my head back, or else twisting around, in an attempt to identify as many constellations as I could. It was another stunning, cool, crisp night. Following the relative heat of the day, and my own body heat bolstered from my exertions, I felt refreshed now, as I drew that cold air deeply into my lungs.

Far off in the distance, I saw what I took to be the headtorch of a musher, heading back from Circle and towards me. I looked ahead along the narrow trail, wondering when I should step off to wait for the team to pass. The team rounded a bend in the trail ahead, with only a few hundred yards separating us, and they were closing the gap fast. I ran on to find an open area to my right, a dozen or so yards ahead, and came off the trail. The team passed.

Sometime later another team approached, and this time I moved off to the left. The team had come to a stop, perhaps imagining I was a dog team moving at speed, and I called them on to pass. The musher was full of gratitude that I had made room, but this was their trail and I was merely taking advantage of it. The right of way was entirely theirs.

I did not see any more teams for a while, before a distant headtorch came into view, scouring the landscape from left to right. I searched for somewhere to step off the trail, but continued on, reckoning they were still a good way off, and there would be plenty of options for me further along. The bright and extremely powerful headtorch continued to search the landscape from left to right, and they were barely any closer – was the team lost, or simply unsure of which way to turn at a junction? Were they taking a rest?

A little further on and the beam continued to move across the land, and my memory went back to a scene from *Airplane*, where a commentator, monitoring a flight's position from a control tower computer, declared an unflattering observation about the pilot being all over the place. I was practically in Circle City before I had established the light was in fact a beacon, set-up to let everyone know where Circle City was. Sometimes, and probably more often than the local average, I can be such a muppet.

Along the trail I passed a couple of buildings, before reaching the turn-off for the fire station; the checkpoint for the Quest. Getting to the checkpoint itself was a leisurely process, as a multitude of volunteers were loitering outside, waiting for the last few teams to arrive. Because of this, folk were only too happy to chat with the random weirdo who had just arrived on foot with a sled. All good people, and it was an absolute pleasure to pass the time with them. But – for there must be a But – I was feeling angst that my day was not done until the harness was removed and I was inside the checkpoint. I agreed to chat with them inside, and headed off.

I abandoned the sled between a pick-up truck and some Portaloos. It seemed the place it was least likely to be in the way or to get run over, particularly as it was on a snowbank. I left everything on the sled and headed within the fire station.

The checkpoint was a moderately-sized warehouse building, with one fire engine parked along the righthand side, taking-up about two-thirds of the length of the building. Between me and the truck were rows of tables and stools, set-up in perpendicular fashion to the truck, each with space for eight people to sit and eat.

Along the other side of the station, more tables had been arranged together almost the length of the wall, with food and a hot water urn. Facilities for heating the food were against the wall. At the back of the room was a charging station for electrical devices. There were two doorways at the far end; one to an office, and one to a sleeping area. In the main room, behind and above the truck, was a huge air blower, doing its job of keeping the area within cosy and warm, despite the cold night and thin walls.

I was delighted to spot Mercedes, a vet I had spent time with when volunteering for the Quest at Scroggie

Creek. She had not yet been alerted to my presence, so I snuck up behind her, placed my hands on her shoulders, and declared that I did not care what anybody else thought, to me her purple hair was simply wonderful. She was in the process of thanking me for the kind words before the penny dropped and she linked the offensively British accent to its owner.

A warm hug followed and I was sent off in search of food. The German volunteer responsible for dishing-out food was a little reluctant, but as there was a full table of vets and officials rooting for me to get fed, and as all but two of the teams were now in, I was given a very much appreciated hot meal. Having volunteered with the Quest before, I did not feel too guilty; more of a kindly passer-by there to ensure none of the wonderful food went to waste. And I also made a solemn vow to donate to the Quest for the kindnesses given to me.

I sat with Mercedes and we had a chat. I met Mike, a fellow Englishman, and conversation turned to our roots. Mike mentioned that he had 15 sled dogs in England, which he ran in a forest. "Not Thetford Forest?" I enquired, in astonishment that he clearly must be that chap who runs dogs in Thetford Forest. He conceded that he was, and I informed him I had known of his business for years.

I confessed to Mike that I hailed from Sawbridgeworth, a small town he knew of, and he confided in me he was from Brandon, a small town I knew of. So, there we were in a remote, isolated and tiny little settlement in northern Alaska, barely 50 miles south of the Arctic Circle, and we meet a fellow Englishman from the same part of England, scarcely a stone's throw apart. How wonderful! Mike was there to help a couple of Norwegian mushers with their teams, and I met one of them now.

Mercedes informed me that Russ was there, too; a race veteran and Quest official who had been with us at Scroggie. He was apparently enjoying a delightful and well-earned sleep in his truck, so Mercedes excused herself as she went to disturb him with news of my arrival. In he came for an equally-warm hug, and there was much rejoicing.

They had both been at Milepost 101, and heard talk of a chap sled-hauling the Quest trail, but had not realised it was me. Whilst chatting and being positive, Russ gleefully expressed how good everything was so far this year: "It's not even cold!"

I do appreciate that, for the outsider, to consider that our lows so far of -31F (-35C) were not cold, might seem odd. Out here, cold does not even get a consideration until it has declared itself below -40F/C. At those temperatures, we are all more at risk of frostbite and lung injuries: people and sled dogs alike. Above -40 the trail is good, the air feels cool and crisp, and progress can be fast and easy.

Mercedes was concerned that I was already looking thin, now only 215 miles (346 km) from the start, with still around 800 miles (1287 km) to go. Russ was concerned that I was not carrying a gun, but that was only natural, because he suffers with being an American. The trail guy, Mike, had already assured me that everything was friendly at this time of year.

Wolves do not bother people, and bears are sleeping. Moose are the biggest risk, but far more to dog teams than a person. I can sit by the side of the trail and wait for a moose to move off, whereas dog teams move fast and can surprise a moose, the latter becoming entangled in their harnesses, then rapidly stamping down on them in a panic, and in such a way can kill an entire dog team within seconds. For this reason the mushers need firearms, but I, without such speed and a dog team, do not.

The next section would take me along the Yukon River to the town of Eagle. It was something over 160 miles (257 km). Russ advised that that distance along the river was, in his words, a mind-fuck, but that the river ice was not too bad this year, with about a dozen crossings in total, from one side to the other, which was about the same as usual.

Russ elected to take this moment to share an hilarious and heart-warming tale, about a time when he was mushing the Quest in the opposite direction outside of Eagle. He was on the Yukon river looking up at the top of the riverbank, only to see a pack of wolves standing there, looking down at him. His dogs, all as one, looked up and saw the wolves looking down at them, too. Also as one, his dogs then looked down to the trail where they – still as one - just kept powering along. As one. There was only a need to move away from the area, and looking up brought them no comforts.

Mercedes confided that she enjoyed the experience of Russ and me exchanging stories, and she considered that we had far more in common than what separated us, even though neither would want to be doing this the other's way.

Another official took this moment to inflict himself upon us. He, not knowing me, was ready to make all sorts of outlandish assumptions. His first comment was that Chris McCandless does not get much sympathy around here, which struck me as an already known piece of trivia, but of no relation to my own endeavours. He continued to press this point home, and demonstrated to me quite clearly that he had absolutely no idea what he was drivelling on about.

At this point I must ask my reader to forgive some minor recklessness. I am compelled by a solemn vow – a bond between self and reader – to convey with absolute honesty the tale of my journey. Not a stone may be left unturned, and every detail is shared openly and without prejudice. When each step is a moment of heaven, I have no doubt that my reader will feel that they are taking those steps with me. When I am tormented by foreign foes, so my reader stands with me against them.

It is for this latter reason that I am compelled to assign my tormentor a new title, for, I believe, should he be given his real name he might readily find himself at the mercy of an infuriated readership, incandescent with rage that this buffoon might have had the impudence to sit smugly before us, under the misguided optimism that his words counted for something. The man's name, I must therefore tell you, is absolutely not Jack. Nor was it Gertrude, but Jack is the name I have settled upon, to relate my interactions with this blight upon Alaska; this boil on the lardy and mottled arse of humanity.

As Steven Covey teaches us: "Seek first to understand, then to be understood." Jack assumed I was some hippy type who was chancing it out here. Presumably, he thought my sled was filled to the brim with dream-catchers, incense sticks and sandals, and that all my rice had my name on it.

By assuming I had no real experience here, Jack presented himself as a drivelling imbecile, and I viewed him as such from that moment on. To me, there were no risks or dangers applicable to me which were not also applicable to a musher (to greater or lesser extents), and I was sure he did not hold such views towards mushers, considering he was one.

When Mercedes confided with me that he was judging my trail shoes, I knew for sure the sort of gross ignoramus I was now dealing with – someone at least 20% worse than any other type of ignoramus (sorry). To judge a stranger doing something that stranger has fair experience and successes in, whilst the judge has no direct experience themselves, nor any vicarious experience from observing other foot racers in this environment, nor even any awareness – it seems – that foot races occur along the Quest route, with racers generally managing themselves alright along it, was to me like a congenitally blind man judging me for the colour of my socks.

Whilst I do not wish to labour the point further, as Wilde tells us, the best means to get rid of temptation is to yield to it, so I confide in you here my true thoughts and feelings on the matter. Jack was, in short, unqualified to hold opinion, but that he had not only formed an opinion, but proceeded to voice a sort of derogatory view based upon it, gave me cause to consider the man a very specific sort of disaster area.

Specifically, I was convinced he owed trees and oxygenating algae an apology for putting their good works to waste.

If your experience of footwear in the Far North is based upon standing on a sled pulled by dogs, or sitting upon a snowmachine, or walking from one heated container to another heated container (home to car to shops, for example), your counsel on the requirements of ultra-endurance runners is unqualified and worthless. Whilst the observation is true that I do not suffer fools gladly, my peaceful mind becomes easily distracted and agitated that such imbecility walks amongst us, so freely and unchecked, permitted to vote and to operate heavy machinery. Around here they even issue the living nightmares with guns.

Jack concluded his sterling presentation on the theme of proving himself the biggest arse in America, and left me to recover. As the menace dispatched himself away, through the exit, so I felt bathed in an exquisite sense of relief. He moved westwards, out of my life, and was swallowed by the night. I felt a pang of apprehension the Night might realise its error and regurgitate him back towards me, but such horrors were not realised.

I am, as you know, a chap who prides himself on his supreme tolerance, compassion and love for all worldly creatures, so it was only natural for me to wish him be promptly cut down and eaten by a pride of marauding badgers. Some might say this is unfair, but I reply 'At what cost to those poor, cold and hungry badgers?' It is the selfish and small-minded who think only of the one and not the many.

I was soon returned to peace, and, once more enjoying the revelry of sensible, intelligent companions, basking in the general delights of this wonderful hive of activity and focus. As a musher passed the table and headed for the door, he paused to wish me well on my journey, and I returned the wish to him. It was touching that there existed this connection amongst us, a stranger though I was, and it was appreciated.

I passed some time chatting with Russ and Mercedes, after which they both headed off to get some rest, and I permitted myself to retire to the sleeping area. There was only one other person in there. Some folk were sleeping on top of the fire engine, others wherever they could. There had been an option to pay for sleeping space at the local school, and to have a shower there, but I did not find out about that until too late. I made myself extremely comfortable on a camp bed and went to sleep.

Chapter 10.
The Race

A slow sunrise spread pinks and blues across the snow. Cool, crisp air bites the exposed skin. Wood stove smoke hangs in the air like it was painted there. Winter sensations. The last dog team is readying to leave.

Inside the warm fire station the race officials and vets and volunteers were getting ready to move ahead: Steve's Roadhouse, Eagle, Dawson City, Scroggie Creek, Stepping Stone, Pelly Crossing, Carmacks, Braeburn and the finish line at Whitehorse, and they will meet others moving ahead from the previous checkpoints, too.

Some staff join the team, others leave. 'Proper' jobs and annual leave, other races, family life: all the commitments that limit how much some can do. Others say 'To Hell' with the income and the jobs and the rest, and see the race through from start to finish, unwilling to allow a year to blow through where the Quest is not the biggest event in their lives.

During the last 24 hours every musher has come through Circle. Twenty-three mushers started the 1000-mile race out of Fairbanks, a week after I did. I sat having my dinner around half of them last night. Now they have almost all moved ahead. One dog team sits in the parking lot, resting, relishing in the pause, whilst their musher goes through his motions of sorting his kit and theirs, preparing their harnesses and lines, getting ready for the big push to Eagle City, then over American Summit to Clinton Creek and Dawson City. No Fortymile this year, so an added push over another mountain range awaits; waiting for all of us who can make it that far.

The Yukon Quest international sled dog race is underway across the Alaskan sub-Arctic. Beginning from Fairbanks, Alaska, 23 teams of mushers and their dogs have approximately 1600 kilometres of racing ahead of them, before they can finish in Whitehorse, in Canada's Yukon Territory.

There are racers representing Canada, France, Germany, Hungary, Italy, Japan, Sweden and the United States. The temperatures have not been overly cold, and this is definitely a low-snow year. Jumble ice on the Yukon River necessitated a reroute before Fortymile, downriver from Dawson City, over the Top of the World Highway.

Brent Sass is currently leading the race, but it's a long way to the finish and a lot can happen. Arctic weather can turn against mushers and the teams, and this year's mild temperatures so far might plummet, and wind or snowfall could obliterate the trail. Not all 23 mushers will reach the finish, but, whatever happens, they're sure to have some incredible experiences along the trail.

Race report by the author, MH

There is a purity and simplicity to the Yukon Quest. Good ole mushers and their teams, racing for 1000 miles across the Yukon and Alaskan wilderness. Changes that happen tend towards safety aspects, and safety of the dogs long before safety of the mushers. The trail-breakers cut the young willows that threaten to snag on dogs' paws and legs. A big expense for the mushers is all the dog booties the teams must wear to protect paws from ice crystals.

Vets and officials communicate as best they can, to relay details and concerns from one checkpoint to the next, with dogs getting retired and driven or flown home if that is in their best interests, but overall nobody cares for the dogs as much as their mushers do, many of whom have bred their teams and raised and trained each dog from the very beginning, and over generations.

Hughes Network Systems is sponsoring the U.S. portion of the Yukon Quest, a 1,000 mile international sled dog race, with its HughesNet broadband service. The company will provide high-speed Internet access and Voice Over IP (VoIP) service to enable communication for information such as weather updates, course warnings and other information to make the race safer. The service also enables officials to update results on the website and steadily feed information to fans and media around the world.

Hughes partner Will Johnson, owner of Alaska Satellite Internet, is installing the satellite terminals on the U.S. half of the Yukon Quest trail. Johnson flies the systems to the six U.S. checkpoints — landing on roads when no landing strip is available — sets them up, and will manage network operations throughout the race.

The Yukon Quest officials responsible for major operations during the race — Marshal Doug Grilliot, Manager Alex Olesen, and Head Veterinarian Nina Hansen — will rely on the satellite VoIP service to coordinate operations up and down the course. Telephone access between checkpoints enables them to speak directly to each other and their team

members to keep the dogs, mushers, support crews and Yukon Quest staff safe as they cross the Arctic terrain.
By Caleb Henry
www.satellitetoday.com/telecom/2016/02/04/hughes-sponsors-us-leg-of-2016-yukon-quest-race/

The first team into Dawson that goes on to finish the race wins themselves the Joe Feller Dawson City Award: 4 ounces of placer gold to commemorate the Great Klondike Gold Rush, and the first really substantial achievement of the race. All mushers and their teams get 36 hours of rest at Dawson: a protocol I intend to honour myself. Dawson is close to the halfway point, sitting just inside the Canadian border, so is the official crossing point.

Dawson is the biggest city on the Canadian side, other than Whitehorse, and it used to be the Yukon's capital. Dawson City: still so many hundreds of miles from here, including that long hike along the Yukon River, and over two mountain ranges. Who knows what hell awaits us all along that trail?

Not far from Dawson lie the two remote cabins at Scroggie Creek, where I was based last year as race support, helping to ensure the mushers had a warm place to sort their gear and access to the best fresh river water the Yukon had to offer. I remember meeting Lance Mackey there – a legend of the Great North American sled dog races – who sat in a camping chair in front of our 'hippy killer' wood stove, where we chatted for a while before he caught himself a solid forty-winks before pushing on. Other mushers came and went; all of them focused on the task at hand, and all of them good, honest, salt-of-the-Earth types you would feel honoured to drink a beer with.

Lance's trip to the Iditarod would be delayed as he was diagnosed with throat cancer in 2001. After extensive treatment he entered the 2002 Iditarod but had to drop out as his frail health was no match for the gruelling race. Taking some time off to recuperate and train, Mackey entered the Yukon Quest, another 1,000 mile sled dog race, in 2005 and won. He went on to win the next three years in a row making him the only musher to do so. He returned to the Iditarod in 2007 and again became the only musher to win that race four times in a row, a record that stands as of 2016. He is also the first musher to win both the Yukon Quest and the Iditarod in the same year, twice. He is most proud of the Humanitarian awards he has won during his career which validates the extreme care and respect he has for his sled dog team which he considers the true heroes of the sport.

By Smithsonian
Division of Culture and the Arts, National Museum of American History, Smithsonian Institution
https://americanhistory.si.edu/collections/object/nmah_1446116

Lance was not racing this year, but many others I had met and/or supported were. All but one had moved up along the trail now; on towards defeat or glory in the Klondike. Sass, Neff, Moore, Hall, Hopkins, Kohnert, Johansen, Barnes, Honda, Ellis, Dalton, Tweddell, Neese, Drobny, Strathe, Pace, Albrigsten, Cooke, Pierrard, DeBruin, Dos Santos Borges, Levy and Angelo.

The brave and the bold men and women of the 2016 Yukon Quest. All good things are wild and free.

Here we all were, stretched-out along the Quest trail – the mushers and their dogs, the vets and the officials, and now me holding on at the back – all out in the Alaskan wilderness, being wild, being free, trying our damned hardest to give of our best, escaping the follies of normal society to return ourselves to nature; to our true nature, to the place our hearts belong.

Our journeys flit from peace to punishment; from calm to calamity. We strive to be true to ourselves and we will become what we must when the conditions tax us the most. We will stare into the abyss and see it staring back. We did not come to this land to be tamed by it, but to grow in the face of the challenges. We will be whatever it takes to win through. Most of all, *we will endure*.

Brent Sass struggled with his team from the start, reporting that his dogs suffered with diarrhoea, and keeping them fed and hydrated was a real challenge. Brent's experience and his focus on the team brought him into Dawson City leading the race, with the dogs steadily recovering as they progressed along.

Allen Moore was second into Dawson, with Hugh Neff coming in shortly after. All three are well-known race veterans of this incredible event. The mushers are required to take a 36-hour rest in Dawson, where the dogs are thoroughly checked for health and fitness to continue, by the exceptional and dedicated veterinary team that accompanies the race.

Race report by the author, MH

Chapter 11.
Circle City to Brian's Cabin

I stirred, I woke and I rallied. I dressed, I acquired coffee, I checked my emails, I made use of an inviting Portaloo, I photographed the last dog team preparing to leave, and I sought breakfast. By this time, with only one musher still present in Circle, there was a flurry of activity on the catering tables, as volunteers – confusing themselves with heavy artillery – began dispatching breakfast burritos at my face.

Not that I needed the food. Getting through the food on my sled is a satisfying experience, knowing that with each mouthful my sled grows a little lighter. And the weight reduction becomes fully complete with the next morning's first dump of the day.

Hot, fresh food, which also happens to be different to the mundanity of eating the same frozen food, day in and day out from off the sled, is a welcome treat, nonetheless. Attitudes had changed by the morning, and staff were only too keen and eager to hurl food at me, rather than see it go to waste. Nobody wants to have to pack-out food destined for the bin. I ate one burrito and secreted two more about my person, where my body heat could keep them from freezing until appetite struck again.

I thanked all for their help, and prepared for the off. This had been a fantastic checkpoint. Now the Quest was moving ahead of me; their next checkpoint some 165 miles or so upriver, and I expected to be back on my own from now on. Still, these moments shared with the

Yukon Quest had been a blast, and added layers of wonderful experiences to my journey, as I always knew they would.

Stepping out into the crisp, cold morning, I set about preparing my sled. There was a beauty to this early morning, which held me captivated for a while, in spite of the frigid air and the need to get moving. I stood gawping, nonetheless, soaking it all in. The sky was a pale blue above me, and a light pink towards the horizon. The trees were blanketed in the purest white snow. The air was fresh, feeling as though it cleaned my airways, bringing my steadily waking body to life, invigorating me to my core. Light grey smoke drifted gently across the scene from the fire station's chimney. It was a serene and pretty sight, and a sublime experience. These are the moments that really help to make the journey something special; layers of the sublime added to the layers of other trail experiences.

I left Circle just ahead of the final musher. I had heard how one of his dogs had fallen ill, and he had driven the rest of his team some 45 miles (72 km) out of his way to carry him to a vet, before returning to the trail and continuing to the checkpoint. I descended down onto the Yukon River, and headed up and over a small island. I paused to turn around and take in one last look at Circle from the river. A few buildings lined the top of the riverbank, and a handful of people were standing around, gazing out over the river.

During my previous races along the Quest route, I passed hours travelling along the Yukon River. On those occasions, sweetly romanticised in my memories, it was this Yukon river that led me downriver out of

Whitehorse, and further on it was this same river that brought me safely into Dawson City. The river was fairly narrow in those earlier sections, closer to its source at Llewellyn Glacier by Atlin Lake, at the top of British Columbia, near the Yukon border. Here it looked like it stretched miles from one side to the other, although this was largely a result of so many islands nestled across it. I would have around 165 miles (265 km) along it on this section alone, the biggest single distance of river trail I have experienced.

I was prepared for the realisation of Russ's assertion that this would be a section of mental rough shag, but I felt quietly optimistic. Granted, most of the mushers would arrive into Eagle within two days, and I would take perhaps four or five, but it was all new to me, which helps to keep the interest going.

Although the island I stood upon was small, it offered a sound view of the river all the way across to the far bank, and a couple of miles in each direction. The jumble ice that constituted the surface was not as bad as that which I have seen elsewhere, on other journeys. The trail team had doubtless found the smoothest ways across. As I descended and set sail upriver, so my passage ventured from close to the riverbank to an island, along the island, and then back towards the riverbank. On rare occasions my way was fully across to the far side.

Crossing the river meant negotiating the jumble ice. The going was by no means arduous, although a trifle more effort was required than along flat trail. Jumbled ice blocks had been cut-through, and snow compacted on either side, creating ramps averaging around knee height, and maybe washing machine height at the absolute most. The sled would be a minor struggle on the way up, and would bang and bounce and thump down its short and sharp descent. What took time was not the undulating nature of the trail over this ice, but the meandering route it took. This was one of the ways the trail could differ by several miles from one year to the next, entirely dependent upon the ice conditions on rivers.

Following a descent onto the river from another small, frozen island, I turned behind me to see the last musher coming along. I accelerated to move into a section where a snowmachine had driven adjacent to the main trail, and gave the musher plenty of room to pass. Reigning his team to a stop as he came up next to me, we chatted away for a few minutes, of our ambitions and experiences on this trip.

As he continued off, so he held out his hand to give me the customary high-five, and, as was customary with me, I exhibited all my sporting prowess by missing his hand completely, like an arse. This was a repeat of something that had occurred along Birch Creek during the previous two days. I blame the fact I was secured to my sled, which limited my ability to turn and reach out far enough. I could not step closer and risk getting tangled-up with the dogs. These are my excuses, and I am sticking to them like a limpet.

The trail was flat where we had spoken, and now his team headed through a section of jumble ice ahead, with the winter sun low in the southern sky beyond. Watching his team move through this land was a magnificent spectacle; something impressive, pure, and familiar to me now. Still, the clear sky and low sun, casting long shadows out towards me from the team, made the moment that bit more beautiful and special to me.

* * * * * * *

Reflecting back on my day's swag of breakfast burritos, one of the challenges of these events is the amount of time spent with a very limited diet. The roadhouses and race checkpoints had really helped to insert some variety, and this made a huge difference. Still, when one is working hard, hauling the heavy sled for respectable distances on a daily basis, using up energy at a rapid rate, one is often hungry.

The meals I have with me are enough to keep me going, but they do not compensate for all the energy I am using. To replace calories in a balanced manner would require a sled too heavily laden with food to permit real progress. Instead, one slowly starves; such is the severity of the imbalance between energy intake and output. The effect of this, ignoring all the disastrous physiology, is that one dreams of food; real food. The fantasies make one's hungry, variety-yearning mouth water.

Whilst moving along, deeper into this stunningly beautiful day; with the blue sky above and the glistening snowy trail all around, so I dreamed. I yearned for proper food. Those breakfast burritos had literally given me food for thought. I wondered what it might be like to sit down to a big, hearty meal. My mind wandered and became distracted by thoughts of a well-laden plateful of a scrumptious dinner, followed in good order by some delicious, decadent dessert.

My mind swam with visions of all the substantial and satisfying meals within my cookbooks at home. I could picture the photos within, which were made real by my mind, and my mouth could almost taste the food. A James Martin hotpot had steam rising from it as I could see the rich gravy glistening, and the peas and carrots and roasted, fluffy potatoes, all calling out to be eaten.

I thought of all the recipes and salivated away. Those starchy, flavoursome vegetables nestled amongst big chunks of tender, perfectly cooked meat. Moments from the preparation scrolled across my daydreaming eyes, and I thought approvingly of James in his kitchen, preparing it all for me.

I could imagine him now – our gallant hero of the piece – as he worked his magic. I only tried to stop this line of thought because I was sure there were more pressing matters to meditate upon, but it was no good. I had scarcely wiped my sleeve across my face when all of a sudden the beautiful heroine of the tale, Nigella Lawson, had sashayed onto the scene, eyeing-up the ingredients for a sticky toffee pudding, and it was fast becoming too much to bear.

* * * * * * *

Later in the afternoon, I came across a trail marker carrying a sign written onto a paper plate, informing me it was a mile to Brian Asplund's cabin. A mile later and the trail led onwards, paralleling the riverbank, with a second trail leading up the riverbank. It was a short but steep climb over maybe the length of ten monitor lizards (10 metres), taking me up and off the river. The trail continued past willows and brush until I arrived at the abandoned homestead itself.

The first building, presumably a modest workshop in its day, was in a bad way; unsealed, broken and open to the elements. I then saw two other cabins and a raised food hide. There was no sign of an outhouse. There were also no signs of mushers having come through here; only the trail team on snowmachines. There was an abundance of firewood stacked outside the first cabin.

That cabin was aged and decrepit, with a roof that carried holes on the flat faces, and which was as good as entirely open at either end. The other cabin was, surprisingly, worse. For a start it had rolled over onto its side, presumably following a fit of despair.

Without taking anything from the sled, I held my breath and stepped within the first cabin, hoping for the best. It was dank and a little musty inside, thanks to dust and dirt on the once-carpeted floor. The ceiling was mostly intact, as were the remaining walls, save for holes here and there, and a poor fit of some of the slats. There was a large wood stove, which appeared in serviceable condition. There was one raised platform that would take a double bed, and a second in an adjacent room. There was a window, a bar stool, and a thin sideboard. What I had taken to be the remains of a workshop was once attached as an annex, or third room adjoining the main cabin, but had since been separated by the action of time on the wooden structure, and the hole it left filled-in.

I set to work getting a fire going in the wood stove, and brought in my sleeping kit, spare clothes and food. There was loft insulation lying around amongst the general decay that constituted the floor, and I began filling in some of the gaps in the walls with it. With the stove open it did not take long for the fire to take, but it was a while before the heat got into the cabin.

I brought in wood from outside, to save me doing so in the night, in the inky, frozen darkness. Everything now was about ease and comfort – I leave my suffering for the trail, and then exclusively for when more civilised options are not available. I heated-up some food and made some diary notes. You are reading them presently. Any good or utter tosh? One hopes for the best.

It was a relaxing evening at the cabin after a fairly short day. I reflected upon achievements to-date and what was ahead of me. I now had 145 miles (233 km) to go to Eagle, so perhaps four days if conditions remained good. Whilst it would not be accurate to declare that 'anything could still happen' – for I was unlikely to be stopped by earthquakes, volcanic eruptions, highly-organised packs of marauding velociraptors, abducted by aliens, taken-in by a tender and loving family of sasquatches, or suffer general calamity – of all the things with a *reasonable potential* of happening, I was allowing myself to feel a suggestion of confidence I could actually make it through, and pull this whole ridiculous wheeze off.

I considered that I had enough miles behind me, and felt fit and strong enough physically – whilst being injury-free – that I ought to be able to meet with all fair challenges, and to see my way through. There was sufficient chance to permit a welcome and relaxing feeling of confidence, at least.

Now I was in a cosy – if fairly dilapidated – cabin, set-up in bed, and looking forward to a peaceful and quiet night's sleep. I loaded up the stove, shut it down as much as I could (it was not in its best condition, and there were holes in both stove and chimney), and had a very warm, very pleasant night. Glamping simply cannot be any better than this.

Chapter 12.
Brian's to Kandik

It was fairly early when I roused the old carcass and launched myself off along the river. Whereas the route from Fairbanks to Circle had averaged east-northeast, from Circle the remainder would be mostly east-southeast, with an occasional emphasis on *South*. During the first week to Circle, I had enjoyed walking into the rising sun each morning, but from now I would find life easier watching the sunsets. Regrettably, my new direction will make gawping at the Aurora less practical. One considers such compromises during the morning sojourn upriver. One's meditations are not all Lancashire hot pots and sticky toffee pudding.

Between Central and Circle I had averaged 37.5 miles (60 km) a day for two days. Yesterday had been a quick and easy 21-miler (34 km). Today's goal was a respectable 40 miles (64 km). It would be a big day, relatively speaking, but the going along the flat river ought to be easy enough. Time would be lost in the meandering trail. There would be a cabin 22 miles (35.5 km) further along, but yesterday's 20-miler was to promote recovery from the longish stint into Circle. I would not need another short day for a while.

As much as I was not in any real rush, I did want to complete my journey within what I considered a respectable amount of time. There is a pleasure and satisfaction that comes with a good, strong day of progress; and the knowledge of a night's sleep well-earned. Shorter days are manageable, because I accept them as useful in promoting health and recovery for such a long journey, but my preference overall is to the more ambitious days.

The caveat to all this is, of course, my inclination to promote the overall experience, such as by maximising time spent with fascinating others, and utilising any welcoming cabins along the way. Even my longest days are not on par with my racing distances, but then the weight of the sled has something to say about all that sort of thing, too.

Tonight I was aiming for Slaven's Roadhouse, approximately 60 miles (101 km) upriver from Circle, and 105 miles (169 km) downriver of Eagle. I did not know what to expect at Slaven's. I was advised at Circle that, considering the Quest will have gone through ahead of me, it was quite likely for there not to be anyone around. If people had left Slaven's, I hoped for access to the cabin. If I had no access, at least there would be a way up to the cabin, and somewhere there to set-up camp close by.

There is a very real difference between sleeping on river or lake ice, and being just a little bit higher up. There is also likely to be shelter from the wind. Even a light breeze along open expanses of river can make it feel particularly cold. Opportunities to be off the river are valuable. During these expeditions one frequently flirts with discomfort, but only a masochist would seek it out for sport.

I reminded myself that 105 miles would be three days' work and not two, for such were my expectations from racing. I was grateful the trail markers were still in place. The thought that these would disappear at any moment was a source of some anxiety.

With such meagre snowfall this winter, the trail above the river ice was only an inch or so deep, and the untouched snow off the trail was a few inches at best. One good snowfall – or strong breeze – would be enough to cause the trail to disappear from view, and, being so thin and soft, it would be impossible to feel underfoot, with no real hope of distinguishing the trail from what was not trail.

I have navigated miles of the Pelly River with several inches of fresh snow above the trail, but with deep powder everywhere else, and to more than a couple of feet in depth, it was easy to work by feel. As a foot descended through snow then off the packed trail, so I could discern the bends in the route and adjust. I had actually managed to make progress at a strong pace then, and had been quite proud of myself for doing so. Here, I would have no such navigational giveaways.

I could follow the precise route only until it snowed, or until the trail became blown-in. After that I would be working marker-to-marker, knowing I was close to the trail if not actually on it. If the markers were taken-up, and the trail lost to the snow or wind, I would be guessing, with the predictable effect I would be struggling over jumble ice, weak ice, potentially snow-covered open water, and generally exposed to infinitely more peril than now.

For the time being, I kept a good pace in the fine conditions. The Alaskan scenery was wonderful. There were a few fluffy clouds in the sky, but mostly it was blue and the sun shone. The panorama varied off the river, from woodland to hills. The hills looked over the river with a timeless beauty, and a majesty that could be fully appreciated from here. The hills in winter hold snow-covered trees upon their lower flanks, above which a metallic sheen is presented by the rocky faces, stretching up to the tops, and around and between and over these lay blankets of clean, white, sparkling snow. I spotted a small herd of caribou a hundred yards or so ahead, breakfasting enthusiastically down from the riverbank, away from the trail, paying little attention to me.

I thought back to Russ's comments about the mind-numbing passage here, but I could detect none of it. For me it all remained a rich tapestry of sights and stories. I sled-hauled along the river, imagining it during a summer some hundred and twenty years ago, with the river in full flow, and paddle-steamers crowded with prospectors heading, like me, to Dawson City. They had the wealth to travel the Yukon River through Alaska; a far better option than the White Pass route into the Yukon.

Those travellers would have gazed around at these same hills, the same trees, and made progress under the same northern sky. They would have been excited, anxious, and full of hope for what they would find in Dawson. I, by contrast, knew that Diamond Tooth Gerties was there, and my anxieties were focused merely upon whether or not the old gambling-cum-entertainment wonder-hall would be open during my visit.

For those early prospectors, theirs was a journey full of dreams; of the hope of finding riches and glory in the

Far North – such a foreign land to almost all of them. I respected that; I romanticised it, and I recalled passages from Pierre Burton's book, *Klondike*, and the poetry of Robert Service. *This is the law of the Yukon, that only the strong shall thrive; that surely the weak shall perish, and only the fit survive.* That sentiment might not necessarily hold true nowadays, but 'only the strong shall thrive' resonated. I wanted to thrive here, not merely to struggle through in a suffer-fest.

I enjoyed taking my breaks amongst this captivating landscape. One human being, travelling alone, vulnerable to some extent but oh so free, feeling healthy, strong for the journey, but still apprehensive and unwilling to court confidence too much. All that mattered was this day. Tomorrow was too far off to be anything but a concept; an idea, a dream. Yesterday was already a distant memory, retired to history. All I needed was to take care of myself today, and the remaining days would take care of themselves; all the way from Fairbanks into Whitehorse. Such was my mantra.

And I did feel strong for what I had already achieved. I was not tired; my joints and muscles were not tender or beaten. I still worked hard to prevent injury and to deal with any recurring niggles, and they came and went. By dealing with each of them as they arose, so I had not succumbed to injury, or suffered with prolonged pain or discomfort. Everything was working, and I was confident for this day. That was all that really mattered.

As I sat on my sled, enjoying a break, immersed within and surrounded by this heavenly land, so I recalled my musher friend's statement, now another mantra for myself. *It just doesn't get any better than this.* And it was true. Alone, under deep blue skies and breathing the cleanest, freshest air, feeling cosy and warm on a cool day, making progress as an insignificant mammal, moving on his own individual and meaningless quest, I existed and felt a hippy-esque oneness with all of it.

Out here, alone, out of contact, I felt at my absolute best. My mind danced with the sense of freedom I have sought and earned for myself, and I felt grateful for that. *This is the life*, I told myself; however long or short it may be, and this day is everything. I was in my heaven; my own precious dream of reality and existence, and I was truly, deeply, satisfyingly happy.

* * * * * * *

Progress was slowed not by any fatigue, or any imperfections in the trail, but by my own desires to pause and soak-in the thrilling, astonishing, magnificent views. Occasionally I would take a photograph, and this took time, as fingers had to be exposed to the searching, biting cold, as camera settings were adjusted and tested. The views were breath-taking though, and I savoured every moment. A benefit of such a journey on foot was that I truly had the time to absorb and enjoy these scenes.

A beautiful hill or mountain would materialise around a bend in the river, and grow ever larger as I brought myself closer to it. I was drawn to the details of trees perched precariously on its cliffs, of cave openings, of the differences in shades caused by the shapes, to cuts into the rock, and the moving sun across its faces. Indeed, the passage of the low sun across the sky brought the landscape to life, as shadows shortened then lengthened, drifting steadily over time. The morning and evening sun brought even tones of red to the lower sky, and midday a dark blue lightened to pale, as light caressed the hilltops.

Not only was the length of time to absorb such views a benefit of this type of journey, but there is something important about expending physical effort, which makes a scene special, too. It is in this way that one feels a part of it; a part of the wilderness, of nature and of the scene itself.

To use motorised transport along this trail would not give the same sense of attachment, and, without the physical energy expenditure, the sense of fulfilment could never achieve the heights of gratification that I experienced now. It is wondrous in its simplicity, astonishing in its beauty, and sublime in the entirety of the experience. It is an indulgence like no other.

Out here, pulling a heavy sled along a soft trail, the miles may be long, with my body growing ever more tired, yet I cannot convince myself the miles are truly hard. Such is the awakening joy of travelling on foot in such a magnificent, stunning, wild land. Despite any apparent hardships and challenges, these are some of the easiest miles I have ever travelled, because the land just pulls me through.

On the east bank of the river, in the afternoon, I arrived at Richard Smith's cabin, 43 miles (69 km) from Circle City, and 17 miles (27 km) from Slaven's. It was a beautiful log cabin, and I momentarily wondered whether I should concede to a short day for the sake of staying there. I wrestled with the idea of settling for a second short day in a row, and, upon further reflection, felt I could not justify it. Instead, I satisfied myself with the sight of the cabin from the river, and continued on my way. It was such an attractive, *safe* cabin. Later on, in the dark, I might regret passing it by so dismissively.

* * * * * * *

As the trail took me from the east bank of the Yukon River across to the west, so I marvelled at the sight of exposed river ice; the snow having been windswept away, leaving the ice in clear view, in its varying hues of blue through to white, in some places flat and in others raised as small mounds, all with chaotic white cracks abounding through. The scratches of snowmachine treads showed me the way across to the far bank, as the trail proceeded south and around a westward bend in the river.

The riverbank was tall and steep as night approached. The far bank fell out of view in the darkness on this wide, vast river. Along my path, I noticed the tracks of dogs on either side of the track; their prints suggesting large huskies compared with the smaller dogs so common nowadays in the Quest.

As I moved on, so I began to question myself as to the nature of those tracks. If these were dog prints, the sled they dragged should have left clearer tracks overlaying them. A set of paw prints to the right moved off the trail and rejoined a few paces further on. That is quite a neat trick for a dog harnessed to a baker's dozen other dogs.

A couple of other sets of tracks deviated from the trail and re-joined soon after, too. Another moved off on the right, far too far for it to have been accomplished with even the most generous of connecting lines. It had rankled with me that the prints had been so unusually large for dogs, but at least now it all made sense, although this realisation was far from comforting. Russ might have had a different perspective to mine about the mundanity of this section, but his tale of a large wolf pack was certainly ringing true.

One-by-one, each set of wolf prints led away from the main trail, striking-out across the river, towards its centre. I counted about fifteen in all; a large pack that was following the Quest team ahead of me. A mile further on and the tracks came back onto the trail, although not so many. The pack had spread out along the river.

The dog team would have been moving consistently fast, and I suspected it was a tall order for the wolf pack to maintain interest when there was probably easier prey around. Fifteen wolves could bring down moose or bison, or anything else they put their minds to.

The snow was compacted where the wolves had circled or convened around areas of interest – perhaps some dog food or excrement, or a dog bootie. They had ceased to follow the trail so closely from here, and instead paralleled it, or left it completely to re-join later. How far ahead were they, and were they sticking to the river, or venturing up the bank, into the woodland? Might they turn around to find me, or already be stopped up ahead, for me to unwittingly move in amongst them?

It became harder to see the Quest trail, as the light from my headtorch began to fade. I paused to replace the batteries in the dark – I had been tempted to persevere until the light went out completely (as it might have lasted to Slaven's), but I could not risk trying to find batteries in complete darkness. There was still a little fading light on the southwest horizon, and I made use of it as I got the headtorch working again.

It would be a lie to state that I was entirely unconcerned about a large wolf pack sharing this area of the river with me. I was not scared *per se*, but I was alert and a little anxious. Statistically, people are simply not attacked by wolves. A wolf will not attack what it does not know. Wolves are curious though, and have been known to come up to people to sniff them, and even start biting at their clothes. I fought any dramatic distractions down as best I could, but I could sense them in the back of my mind, willing me to entertain a perilous predicament. *Melodrama* accompanied me along the river that night.

It was also the case that should I happen to be the unluckiest person on the planet, and to actually be attacked by wolves, I had nothing to protect myself with. Still, against fifteen or more wolves I would have needed a machine gun. I recalled Mike's comment that everything out here was friendly, and that would have to be true enough.

I certainly would have loved to see a wolf in the daylight, because I think they are striking, fascinating animals. However, I could not stretch to wanting to meet with a whole, hungry pack of them, socially, in the inky blackness. What really held me together was the consideration that, for hundreds of years, men have been shooting and clubbing the unfortunate and undeserving blighters to death. The wolves that survived either know to stay away, or tried their luck at being friendly, with the latter having now become sausage dogs, poodles and chihuahuas. Overall, I therefore expected to make it through unscathed.

****

I carried at least one spare set of batteries for each device, kept in a plastic bag in my mid-layer jacket. The rest were in the small rucksack that held my water bladder. They had to be kept close so they were not drained by the cold, although experience has taught me that some time in a warm pocket generally resurrects them. With a brighter beam I continued on towards Slaven's, wondering at the wolf tracks before me, and what the situation would be at the cabin (access, food, or a cheery but oddly hairy, big-nosed and long-toothed grandmother, sitting up in a bed).

The trail moved along the bank, becoming challenging in parts. Where the trail took me down slopes of angled ice onto the river, so the sled went sliding wherever the path of least resistance led it. I passed a marker with a plate, informing me it was a mile to Slaven's. No sooner had I seen that sign, that a new set of tracks appeared on the trail. These did not belong to a wolf, at least not unless it was wearing trail shoes.

Someone had walked out from the cabin and turned back. Half a mile or so later and there were a few more, and the tracks were fairly fresh – probably made this afternoon. Were they still lingering there? Did they know I was coming, and had they come out to look for me? And why did I always think that everything was all about *me*?

Another trail marker with another plate led me off the main trail, up a long slope to the cabin. Lights were on, smoke was rising from the chimney, and snowmachines were parked outside. I moved around to the far side of the cabin, deharnessed, and headed through a couple of doors into an ante-room, where there were pictures on the walls and boxes of snack foods on the floor. Another door led into the main room.

A characteristic, large wood stove, was responsible for the warmth that bathed me the moment I walked in. To the right a staircase led upstairs. A kitchen occupied the side of the wall to the left of the door where I now stood, and the kitchen continued along the left wall a little over halfway down. Between the kitchen and the stove, clothes were hung on lines and boots occupied floor space.

Two people greeted me in the kitchen area, as they prepared themselves some food. One was a race vet, the other an official. Although this was not a checkpoint as such, it functioned as a dog drop. The dogs that had been left were now sleeping outside, silent when I arrived, and were waiting to embark a flight to Knik, along with the 10 people sat at a long table, occupying the length of the right side of the cabin. They were mostly reading books, and the table was littered with bowls of snack foods. I was welcomed and made perfectly comfortable at the table, where I talked with those who were interested in talking.

The current denizens of Slaven's Roadhouse were employed by the Alaskan parks service, mostly young people, who made for some wonderful company that evening. I was shown how I could navigate myself to hot water, hot chocolate, cups and cutlery, and snack foods. I was made at home and felt instantly relaxed and at ease with my many new companions.

The volunteers would all be leaving later the next day, once the weather had improved around Knik, sufficiently for the bush plane to fly out to them. That night I opted to sleep on the floor behind the stove, where it was cooler than up above, on the next floor, which folk had already indicated to me as being something of a sauna. I had the luxury of less oppressive heat and some peace and quiet.

* * * * * * *

In the morning I was violently and relentlessly stuffed with sausage, and enjoyed some pancakes and coffee too. I did a little video interview for one of the chaps, who was interested in promoting outdoor pursuits in the Alaskan winter. All such good people, and I was sorry to have to leave. This was going to be a short day today to the next cabin, Kandik, only 23 miles (37 km) away, and I set-off as soon as I had my fill of coffee.

The alternative option was to camp between cabins, but with the trail only being on the river, rarely crossing islands, that would make for a relatively cold, uncomfortable night. I was too busy enjoying myself in these cabins for that sort of thing. Cabins had their own stories and histories, helping to initiate me into that aspect of the relatively recent, local cultures. Cabins were always a good experience, or at least an experience. I knew the feeling of being in the tent all too well, and the different cabins were far more stimulating, and therefore preferable.

The day was more overcast than previous ones, but there was no sign of new snowfall. The trail markers remained. A short climb up to the top of an island took me past a musher's flask. There was all sorts of detritus lying around; signs that someone had lived or worked here once.

I found a musher's iPod Nano in the middle of the trail, which I considered a good spot, considering it was grey, and so well camouflaged amongst the snow on an overcast morning. I checked the playlist and conceded this would be of little value in helping me along to Eagle. I would try my best to reunite it with its owner. I had the same model back home, and it was small, light and brilliant, with mine filled with far superior playlists to the abomination I had in my possession now.

The trail led over some islands and around others. With the skies clearing in the early afternoon, I was just crossing a section of jumble ice on the river when I saw two snowmachines approaching. I cleared myself from the jumble ice before they arrived, stepping off the trail to permit them to pass.

These two were also from the Alaska parks service, and their job was to look after the trail. They were travelling along now to clear away musher litter, and informed me the cabin at Kandik was well-stocked with wood, and the stove was still warm. They would be returning there later to clear away their kit and shift it all up to Slaven's, which was where they now headed with supplies.

I reached the cabin as the sun was setting over the hills. The scenery was so beautiful I took some time to photograph it all, before leaving the trail and crossing a creek to get up to the cabin. Once there I took more photographs, and had barely finished by the time the rangers came up the slope. They moved out as I moved in.

The cabin was wonderful. It was a standard log cabin, recently refurbished, with green moss on the insulation between logs. There were two raised beds in series along the left wall. In the middle of the right wall was a small wood stove. Nearer on the right side, against the wall where I entered, was a bench. On the far right side was a kitchen worktop area, with dried food stored beneath. There were a few wooden folding chairs. On the wall were pictures and kitchen utensils. There was a bookshelf above the furthest bed with some magazines and a few books on it. A window at the far end looked back out across the river, as did one along the left wall above the beds.

I stocked-up the stove and brought more wood in from outside. Before the rangers left they mentioned a woman wanting to do the route on bike, and I offered them my thoughts, mainly that the conditions were perfect for a fat bike, and now was the time. They let me know that what with so many people making use of the trail, they had no intentions of taking down trail markers anytime soon. This was fantastic news – I should be covered all the way to Dawson!

After the rangers left, I took one of two large ceramic pans from the cabin down to an adjacent creek. Below -4F (-20C) open water can ice-over and thicken-up rapidly, thus being capable of supporting weary travellers, even on surprisingly thin sections. I could see where the ice was very thin, so gingerly walked out to it, and attempted to gently and delicately break the ice open just a little, by giving it a thunderous stamp with my foot.

Despite the temperature being more than sufficient to freeze the water, this had hardly been realised on account of its fast flow. Thus, the ice was remarkably weaker than I had given it credit for, and my targeted stamp rewarded me with so much more than some fractured ice. Indeed, as I pulled my soaking wet foot out of the water, I considered that there may have been more subtle options available to me. Still, in life one has experiences.

Having disturbed the water with my enthusiasm, mud was brought up from the lower reaches, turning the recently crystal clear water dark and brackish. Nor did this water show signs of clearing-up again this season, so I even more gingerly retraced my steps, headed along the trail a few yards back towards the river, and, with extreme gingeriness – displaying levels of gingerytude never before exhibited by me – I began to work my way down a steep slope, towards a small section of open water, about a squirrel's length wide and a beaver's length long. The water was fast-flowing and looked good enough. I filled the pan as best I could and made my way back to the cabin, spilling only about most of it, as my foot squelched away in my wet shoe.

I heated the water up on the stove; a stove I had fully filled and opened up, and I sweltered in an atmosphere not far removed from that of a sauna. With conditions perfect, and the water now on the kitchen worktop ready, I stripped down and had my first proper wash of the expedition. I had some clean underwear and baselayer clothes to change into after, and it all made all the difference. I had been acutely aware of my growing filthiness, despite not actually *feeling* overly dirty. I was simply aware, as an objective fact, that I was unclean and extremely smelly.

Once clean, fresh and dry, I set about cooking myself a stew on the stove. I took my dried meat and dried fruit, boiling it in water for an hour or two, before adding one of about a hundred gravy sachets that had been left in the cabin. Despite it being broadly the food I was already eating all day and every day, taking it as a piping-hot stew made it taste utterly delicious. Nevertheless, I felt a little disappointed I had not helped myself to more snacks at Slaven's, or asked the rangers to bring some back with them. It had all been offered, and I had declined out of want to drag no more than absolutely required.

I had a peaceful, relaxing night. I browsed through some magazines and books, and savoured yet another perfect night out by the Yukon River. I was now 80 miles (129 km) upriver from Circle, with a little more than that distance remaining to Eagle. After Eagle, the next town would be the familiar Dawson City, and the comforts of a trail I have raced three times before. I assured myself I was doing well. This cabin was a perfect picture inside and out, and, nice and warm as I tucked myself into my sleeping bag for the night, I felt that, once again, I was in my heaven, and all right with my world.

Chapter 13.
Kandik Cabin to Eagle City

Morning arrived at Kandik cabin, washing over a meditative Hines, as he ruminated over his options for this new day's objective. Two fair possibilities presented themselves for consideration as my next *cabine de nuit*: Henry's place near the Nation River, or Mike Sager's place at Trout Creek. Henry's was 28 miles (45 km) from Kandik, and Mike Sager's was 36 miles (58 km).

It was instinctive to hold up Mike's place as the team favourite, as it brought me closer to Eagle, and to achieving a respectable day's distance. Still, the scheme to reach Henry's could be swung into action, if it was a beleaguered Hines that found himself nearing the doorstep, after some arduous feat, some calamity, or under threat of injury. One does not rush to eliminate a pleasingly acceptable Plan B from the menu.

It was another utterly wonderful, clear, fresh morning, as I loosed my moorings and set a meandering course southwards, continuing along the Yukon River. Progress was straightforward enough, mostly entailing bunging one foot ahead of the other, whilst leaning forward a bit to encourage the sled, and I got into my rhythm and headed upriver. As the hours of hauling carried me from morning into afternoon, the clear morning's sky was replaced by complete cloud cover.

Grey skies flattened the lands and stole its shadows and contrasts. Without the brilliance of blue skies and sparkling snow, I was left at the mercy of my philosophies to pull me through the day.

By the afternoon, my passage led me around a cluster of small islands by the Nation River. The number of turns, and the presence of the islands, made it impossible to see the far side of the river, and I became disorientated. Boot prints came into view along the trail. It seemed that two people had been out walking.

I knew that, by now, I must have been approaching close to Henry's place, but there were no signs directing me from the trail. I passed a section leading-off the main route, up the low bank into woodland, but it seemed to be closed-off against new visitors, and there were no signs of a cabin. I still wanted to reach Mike Sager's, but felt disappointed to be passing a likely route to Henry's, with no definite confirmation of it. I did not want to waste time running back and forth along mystery tracks, and between the trees, to confirm either way. Besides, I had no cause to take an early rest.

The trail continued to work its way on, and, after a mile or so, the footprints disappeared. For a few minutes I had the sensation I was moving around in large, sweeping arcs, almost heading back on myself. I was so perturbed that I confided my troubles in my GPS, seeking reassurance this was not the case. My GPS lent a sympathetic ear, before confirming all was well, navigationally at least.

I moved beyond the islands and could see the far bank again, with the trail leading around a bend in the river to my right, continuing a mile or so, and crossing the river to another island. It had begun to snow now, albeit it lightly and softly, but it did not bode well. Snow always slows the trail, potentially hides it from view, and generally makes progress worse. Onwards to Mike Sager's place, with meditations of concern, and in pensive mood.

As I approached the next island, I arrived at a marker with a plate on it. 'Stew for mushers, water for dogs, 3 miles' was the legend, and it gave me some hope. The trail led on, crossed to the far side of the river, meandering on for those few miles. How the trail crews worked-out these routes was beyond me, but I was grateful they had established the best way, so I did not have to make a shambles of attempting to do so unaided. It is a nonsense that anyone can ever claim such journeys are 'unsupported', when this experience without the trail would be infinitely harder, and vastly more dangerous.

I came to another small island, where the trail led me between that and the riverbank. To my right, snowmachine tracks disappeared into woodland, but again no signs that this was the way to the cabin. Considering the plate some miles before, I was expecting something here. Again, I confided in my GPS for help, and she showed me that a cabin was indeed along that unsigned trail. I took it, wondering how welcome I might be.

A short, close path led me from the river to Mike's. His place was of moderate size; two stories high, with a raised food store, as well as an open garage and wood store area, making up the compliment of wooden structures. The main cabin door was locked with a couple of makeshift bolts – designed to keep critters out rather than people. I opened and went within.

Kandik Cabin to Eagle City

Just beyond the door was a woodstove, and to the left was a staircase. At the far side stood a worktop area, with a kitchen to the right. Also to the right were shelves with jars of coffee, tea, cocoa, Tang and much, much more. A note on a table at the far side informed me this was not a public access cabin, but a private one, and visitors should leave it as found, or better. There were specific instructions regarding use of a propane cylinder and an upstairs window.

I headed upstairs to find a sleeping area, with the chimney coming up adjacent to the staircase. I returned to my sled, brought in and set up my sleeping gear, prepared myself a dinner on the wood stove, made my diary notes and went to sleep. A shame there was nobody around and no stew, but an extremely pleasant cabin, and appreciated facilities, nonetheless.

I had now covered about 120 miles (193 km) from Circle City, 335 miles (539 km) from Fairbanks, and with about 45 (72.5) remaining to Eagle. I was about a third of the way to Whitehorse, and only 200 miles (322 km) from Dawson City. I had no injuries and was moving well. I slept peacefully.

* * * * * * *

It turned out to be a hot night at Mike Sager's, care of a very efficient stove, and my having set myself up on the second floor, with all that hot air rising and washing over me as I slept. I passed an hour in the morning having breakfast, melting snow for drinking water, and doing a few exercises to release some muscle and joint stiffness, which had become steadily more nigglesome during the previous day. It would have been more efficient to melt the snow in the evening rather than the morning, but it had been dark when I arrived, and, having had so many mushers pass through ahead of me, I did not want to risk filling the pots with yellow snow.

With everything set, I locked-up and headed back towards the river. The snowfall had continued throughout the night, covering my footprints from the journey in. By the time I retraced my route to the main trail on the river, I saw that my nightmare was being realised. There were only a few inches of snow on the trail, but that was enough for the sled to sink down into it.

With every step I took, so the sled was pressing against the resistance of all the soft snow sitting in front of it. The sled was still heavier than I liked, and the snow too soft for the sled to have buoyancy upon its surface. I felt like I was ploughing the trail. I was grateful at this point that I had brought some fairly substantial MSR snowshoes, as opposed to the lower floatation, racing snowshoes, which I usually have with me on these adventures.

Dragging the sled had never been so difficult on this trip, and the trail was now lost. Passing snowmachines could break trail, but it would not be as good as it was before the snowfall – there would not be enough traffic to pack it down as well as it had been. This was not just a matter of the 45 miles (72.5 km) of trail between me and Eagle, but the trail as far as the snow was falling. The whole situation was outrageous. I should have joined a union.

What started-off as hard work began to feel impossible after a couple of miles. The snow continued to fall, and, in some areas, the trail had been fully blown-in, giving me more inches of powder to contend with. It was exhausting; far more so than climbing up Rosebud or Eagle Summit. My feet were sinking deeply into the snow, and the sled was hard work too. It was as disheartening as it was exhausting.

As my feet sank into the powder, they moved through a greater range of motion than on hard trail, and I had to work harder against the greater resistance of the sled ploughing along behind me. Because my feet were sinking, even with the snowshoes, it was harder to maintain any momentum, meaning my stride length decreased, and I was working so much harder for every short step and long mile. And the miles were so slow coming. Desperately slow. It was a case of more muscle fibres, working harder, for less progress.

I was moving perhaps a hundred steps at a time, sometimes pausing and standing to get my breath back, sometimes leaning forward over my poles, to rest my legs and back a little. On a few occasions I collapsed down onto my knees in the snow, burning hot and gasping for breath. My heart was thumping away in my chest, my lungs felt like they were burning, and my whole body felt too hot.

I was venting the heat as well as I could, but it was a mild day and an obscene workload, and all I could do was suffer it and endure. I reflected that if I was managing one mile an hour I would be happy with that. Onwards, slowly. It felt as though, whilst not actually beating me, it was trying really hard; threatening to become worryingly close.

Although I could still see one or two markers ahead, the trail was sometimes lost between them, and with such little snow on the trail before the snowfall, I likely would not have known if I was on the trail or off it. At times I would tell myself to reach the next marker before taking a rest, and giving myself a minute at each one. Then I would try for two markers.

All I could do was try to maintain some forward momentum. Nothing lasts forever: I would reach the end of the trail. Eventually. At some point conditions would likely improve, such as if other trail users broke the trail for me, or if the temperature dropped. I had enjoyed so many very good days before having to face this one, and good days would come again.

After a couple of hours of grim endurance, the trail led me across the river, and, on the other side – much to my surprise and deepest joy - conditions improved immeasurably. There must have been something in the way the wind moved along the river which had made the trail so bad on the previous side.

That is not to say that suddenly my passage was dreamy and delightful, such as if a hundred men or more had arrived with snowmachines, to pack down the trail, share coffee and snacks, and generally be a force for good in a troubling world. There was, nevertheless, a considerable difference between the amount of snow on the trail here, versus the hell I had just sled-hauled out of.

For one thing, I could at least detect signs of the trail now, and 40 or so miles (64 km) of this would merely be

Kandik Cabin to Eagle City

irritating, rather than wretched and improbable. I felt that a shorter day would be in order, even if that meant a meagre 10 miles (16 km) or so, because the risks of failure increased considerably with this additional workload. At my day's pace so far, 10 miles could take 8-10 hours, and my efforts and necessity for recovery were far greater than anything that had come before.

My pace improved, so I was now managing between one and one-and-a-half miles an hour, to give some indication of how dire my slow starting pace was. To think, I had been entertaining the possibility of reaching Eagle today. Now it was shaping-up to require at least three more days to get there, if my current pace became the new average.

I felt despondent as well as fatigued, beaten-up from my efforts in the snow, but I was not too pessimistic. There would be a cabin at around 15 miles (24 km), which perhaps I could aim for today, if conditions and pace permitted. It would be a record low for me, but such was the impact of so much fresh snow on the trail. It would at least be better than 10 miles, or five, or nothing at all.

It was not simply a matter of the trail being slow that made the going more difficult. With the white sky above a white river and white hills, everything was monochrome; flat, dull and lifeless. Everything was more difficult now. I got through by repeatedly reassuring myself that nothing lasts forever: not the snowfall and not even this trail. The weather would improve, the skies turn to blue, and at some point someone would be out on the trail with a snowmachine.

Some hours from Mike Sager's I could hear music on the wind. It was bizarre. It sounded like actual music; not just windchimes or similar, but proper music being played by people with instruments, or recorded music played on speakers. I stopped and listened.

I was expecting the cabin I was aiming for to be further along, on a fairly big island a little way ahead. Whatever music there was, or might have been, it stopped as quickly as it had begun. It had come and gone as I walked. There was always a chance I was going mad, a possibility that I could not rule out, and that many of my most upstanding supporters would more likely rule in; with a yard-long wooden ruler and a thick paintbrush.

Just a little further along I reached the best sign I think I have ever seen in my life: "Brownies, 1 mile!" I do not know at what speed I launched myself away from that sign, but I have no doubt it was the highest rate of acceleration I could have produced without the aid of a trebuchet, or cannon.

I arrived at the second sign, finding a cool box adjacent to it, with its lid secured shut with a chunk of wood. I opened the box to discover two freezer bags containing chocolate brownies. I helped myself to one bag and replaced the other. Sat upon my sled, I savoured the finest chocolate brownies I have ever had, gorging myself and enjoying an unexpected delight. After my day's exertions, food had never tasted so good, and none is ever as good as that which is unanticipated, delicious and so hard won.

There was a trail heading up the riverbank here, and, even better, a snowmachine had clearly passed by very recently. A quick check showed that it had come along the Quest trail from the direction of Eagle. I could not know for how far the trail proceeded, but it was possible this would be the best trail I had, for however long it lasted.

I decided I ought to check out the possibility of the cabin being close by the top of the riverbank, so headed up to take a look. There was a large fish rack near the top – a type I have seen on occasion elsewhere along the river. I continued on to the start of the woodland.

The trail was certainly fresh, but, for all I knew, it could be a mile or two to the cabin, if indeed it was along there. My main desire for seeking it out was that Mike had written down that a really good family lived there, and I would have liked to meet them. Still, I deemed it to be in my best interests to return to the trail.

The snow had now stopped, but I did not know for how long. I had the gift of a broken trail, offering me a chance at the best progress of the day. To stop now and lose this trail to more snowfall, or wind, would be to flirt with potential disaster. I had to make use of it, ideally until the trail left the river close to Eagle.

There was a portage area called Calico Bluffs, and some miles on from there the homestead of an Andy and Kate, where Mike had recommended I stop for a beer and somewhere to spend the night. It was a nice idea, but a total of 33 miles (53 km) from Mike Sager's was out of the question, due to the conditions up to now, and my exhaustion. But just to get off the river at Calico Bluffs would mean great progress.

* * * * * * *

As I proceeded along, with the sled not sinking so deeply into the snow on the broken trail, I accepted it was still tougher than I had encountered on any previous day, but so much easier than anything that had come before it today. The trail hugged the riverbank to my left, and there was a large island a few football pitch lengths (300 metres) off to my right. My GPS would have had me go through the middle of it, rather than this longer route around, but this was the way the trail led this year, presumably because of some jumble ice, thin ice, or open water.

It did not snow anymore that afternoon, but I found myself regularly checking my Suunto watch and my handheld GPS to give me a broad idea of how long, and how far, I had to go, before the river crossed to the far bank at Calico Bluffs. With the overcast sky I sled-hauled through the gloaming, before the night quickly fell.

Ordinarily, I preferred to refine use of technology on these trips to the bare minimum. I like to switch off from it all, experiencing both detachment from modern technology, and a closeness to the wilderness, the natural world around me, and a more traditional way of moving across the land. When progress becomes tough, and distances harder to judge because of the more challenging trail, so I feel impatient to know how well I am doing, and how far I have left to go. In times like these, I fire-up the technology to give me that more continuous feedback, but it does breed detachment. I feel more as though I am racing, tuning in to location, objectives and pace. I reconcile all this contrast to my standard *modus operandi*, with the reflection that the alternative focus provides a change as good as a mental rest. Little comfort is gleaned from this, because I do not entirely believe it, and it really does make me feel dirty.

The trail led off the river to my left, cutting across land sections for the first time since going into Circle. Since then I had only been on the river and islands, with the subtle exception of the cabins close to the riverbank. Now the path led me through sparse, fairly open woodland, along mostly flat trail, stretching out into the darkness.

I limited use of my headtorch to help preserve the batteries. Another reason I like to limit use of a headtorch is to improve the view. With a headtorch it is difficult to see beyond the beam. The world becomes a white blot, lit up in whatever area the headtorch is pointing towards. Without the headtorch, the whole world is in view; there is depth, there is substance, there is still a world to see, even in relatively low light conditions with an overcast sky.

When the night sky is clear, the starlight and moonlight are reflected from the white snow on the ground, on the trees and on the hills. The only practical use of a headtorch is to detect the reflective strips on trail markers; making it easier to see where the trail leads into the distance.

The way was easy enough to feel beneath my feet. One aspect of my surroundings drawing my attention was any line where a trail might have gone, whether because I could actually see tracks, or there seemed a straight line between trees. In such a sparsely populated area this was harder than in close woodland, but I seemed to spot potential trails well, and would often flick the headtorch on, just to check there was not a trail junction.

I feared strolling on along a random snowmachine track, missing a deviation onto the main trail, with the result that I would be miles off course before realising. Trail markers were extremely few and far between here, essentially because there were no divergences from the trail, but it nevertheless became disquieting whenever extended periods passed between markers. The route was not the same as on the GPS, which had stayed on the river.

The trail would lead me to open areas, perhaps ponds, swamps or creeks, and I would use the headtorch to help detect trail markers further off. Confident of my direction, I would return to darkness, continuing onwards. I took some open areas to be possible creeks leading onto the Yukon River, and the final trail before crossing to Calico Bluffs, but each time I was mistaken, and the trail rediscovered land for me further on. My tiredness grew.

With another section of open and meagre woodland, I came into view of hills again, having seen nothing but flat lands surrounding me for miles. With the hills I believed I must be back at the river, but was soon routed-off beyond them, and still no sign of the river. I was getting through the distance, which was a positive, considering the morning's nightmare. Whereas then it was moving 100 yards and collapsing down onto my knees, now I felt that I was at least making solid progress again. I turned on the GPS. I had 8.5 miles (13.5 km) to the river. An hour passed along the trail and I checked again; 6.25 miles (10 km) remaining.

The GPS gave me straight lines, whereas the trail weaved around. I moved on and I rechecked. I took a break at what I took to be a creek, before pushing on into the darkness. At least it was not snowing, and the trail remained broken. Of whomever had broken this trail I knew one thing, and that was that I loved them; deeply and disturbingly. What a day it would have been without them. Three and three-quarter miles remaining. Three miles. Two miles. One and three-quarters.

The trail brought me back to the river, finally, and I breathed a sigh of relief. I had not been stuck on a random snowmachine track after all. I could see where the trail led across the jumble ice to an island, and would then continue on to the riverbank beyond. There lay Calico Bluffs, and somewhere soon would be the portage through it. I reached the island, and the space between the island and far riverbank, and the trail took me left, between the two.

Just beyond the main riverbank were a few cabins, but the bank was too far from the trail, and too high, for them to be worth investigating. I hoped the trail would lead from the river soon, to pass through the homestead. I scoured the riverbank for where the portage began, but was left wanting. The trail continued to parallel both island and bank.

Considering my efforts to reach this area, I was frustrated at how long I remained on the river, and without signs of an exit point. I eventually reached it after a further half an hour or so, and began working my way along a trail through dense woodland. I wanted to make progress towards Andy and Kate's homestead, but knew I could not visit them tonight. I would not reach them until close to midnight; far too late for a casual visit. Any self-respecting Alaskan would have shot me on sight, before setting the dogs on me, and shovelling-up whatever remained for compost.

The trail continued through the woods, over undulating, sometimes fairly steep, ground. I found a gap between the trees to my left, and stamped the snow down to create my campsite. I withdrew for the night inside Hines G.H.Q. for the first time since before Circle City, and it was a relatively warm, pleasant night. So tired, I easily fell asleep, thinking about how close I now was to Eagle, how grateful I was that someone had ridden through since the snowfall, and hopeful that it would not snow again.

* * * * * * *

The next morning it took a few hours to reach Andy and Kate's; my proximity to the homestead given away by what seemed like a million furious dogs, all taking issue with my impending arrival. There was a good number of cabins, including one apparently under construction, and the welcoming sight of smoke rising from at least three chimneys.

Following a short walk around, I determined that Kate and Andy were elsewhere, with fresh snowmachine tracks leading along the trail towards Eagle. One of the smaller cabins was filled with camera carry cases and photography equipment, so I suspected others had been staying here, but there were no signs of people. The dogs had calmed down now that I was walking around without the clattering pulk. It felt such a shame to have missed the human occupants, so I headed on; only about 12 miles (19 km) remaining now to Eagle.

The trail continued through the woodland before ejecting me back out onto the Yukon River and turning right. The clouds had cleared and the sky was looking as brilliant as ever. Walking along the river, some sounds came from beyond the bank, and I perceived someone was out and calling to their dog, but could not see either them or the dog, and I carried on. Civilisation was close at hand.

Although it was not quite the time for a break, the view of the azure blue sky, the glistening white hills, and the crystalline, sparkling white snow, was simply too much to not fully appreciate, and I took 10 minutes to lie back across my sled, simply basking in this magnificent view. Heaven washed over me, and for every second of every minute I bathed in my own, personal paradise. It was wonderful. It was bliss. Yesterday had seen me endure through hours of hell, and many more hours of sub-hellish hardship – purgatory, if you will – but today I lingered in this paradise. I savoured it completely.

I moved on, passing some cabins up to my right, knowing I was reeling Eagle in. There were hills lining the river further on, and somewhere just beyond that I could see where Eagle lay. With the sounds of dogs howling from across the river to my left, I took another break to enjoy some food, ahead of the final slog into town.

Before I had the chance to finish and move off, the air was filled with the familiar sound of a snowmachine, approaching from behind. An older track lay to the side of the trail, which could be used to get around me. The snowmachine conveyed a male at the front; his young son riding behind him. Attached to the snowmachine was a large skimmer, with a woman standing at the back of it.

We all had a chat, and they advised me of where I could spend the night in Eagle. We soon established that these were the folks who had broken trail for me the day before. I shared with them the tale of my tribulations, and the reality of my unerring love for them. They had followed my own trail here, passing by my night's campsite, and had been expecting to see me. Even hearing that felt good, somehow.

They had indeed visited the cabin I passed but had not seen. I was informed I really should have continued along that trail, for just another couple of football pitch lengths (200 metres) into the woods, and I would have arrived there. Still, I had made a good day's progress instead, and was now almost infesting Eagle.

I waved them off as they headed onwards, towards town. Cabins lining the side of the river came into view from some miles away, and I found myself racing the sunset, not that I minded arriving after dark. It was late afternoon now, and the northern winter sun was making a good dash towards the horizon. This was a longer day than I had anticipated, care of the long and tiresome slog the day before, which had not actually added-up to as many miles as I might have liked. Still, it could have been so much worse.

I headed up a fairly long slope to arrive at the end of town. There were Quest markers continuing up a hill by an airfield, but as musher facilities would be closed I did not follow them directly. I abandoned the sled next to a car that had not been moved for weeks, considering the amount of snow on it and lack of tyre tracks, and went off exploring. I strolled to the airfield just to check where the markers would lead, but did not find anything of substance.

In town I found the B&B my new friends had alluded to, but nobody was there. I had the phone number but no reception. Eagle was a mobile phone black spot. I strolled around for a while, and decided I would probably be camping again, which was a bit of a shame, as I was keen to have an extended rest here to properly experience the place. As with so much of this journey, each place and every person was most likely a 'once in my lifetime' experience, because I might never repeat this journey again.

I discovered the post office, which was left open to allow people access to their mailboxes. The building was heated and I was very tempted to just camp in there for the night, but decided to give myself another turn around the centre of town, before making any rash decisions. A snowmachine driver went past, with a few more following-on, who then stopped about the length of a humpback whale (15 metres) away. I overheard one tell another that I had come up from the river with a sled, and I hailed them. This was a good move.

It transpired that it was Andy – of Andy and Kate's Homestead fame – who had gone past me. The remaining five were young filmmakers, who had spent the day on American Summit (my next climb, directly out of Eagle), and were staying at Andy and Kate's; Andy being their guide. After allowing a moment or two to recover from the unmitigated thrill of meeting me, in the flesh, they took the opportunity to give me a bounty of their available food, including a bevy of quesadillas, and suggested I knock on someone's house to use a phone for the B&B. They had stayed there themselves. All in all this was a good meeting.

Within minutes after their leaving, I had made three new friends, when I knocked on a random door (and heard the cheery and welcoming response of someone yelling at me to go away). So after this verbal assault, they made arrangements, and I was swiftly collected by the B&B owner on her snowmachine, and taken to the large log home.

My first act was to set to work consuming the five quesadillas, together with a fresh soup the young family had given me, on the understanding I leave the rest of Eagle's good people in peace. They had offered me a beer but that had just seemed too decadent. Reflecting on this later I wondered why I declined that invitation. Politeness? Some misguided notion it was in my best interest? I was clearly not of sound mind – fatigue can do this to a chap, and may my tale act as a lesson for you all.

The cabin was not cheap, but it was superb value considering its size and general, brilliant luxury. There was a very good kitchen, and a shower which I took advantage of, during a pause from filling my face with food. There was a wonderfully comfortable sofa, and a double-bed. I relaxed on the sofa for a while before turning-in, reflecting on recent trials and triumphs.

In this section alone, since leaving Circle, I had seen the last of the dog teams pass, shared the trail with a large wolf pack, met locals, trail team, and park rangers, and triumphed through some of the toughest sled-hauling I have ever had to endure. I had slept in three cabins and in my tent once. And I had even been treated to a surprise chocolate brownie.

Tonight I enjoyed a hot shower, hot food, and a very comfortable bed, in an extremely comfortable cabin. I had made it approximately 382 miles (615 km) from Fairbanks, and around 165 miles (265.5 km) from Circle City. Ahead lay 150 miles (241 km), featuring American Summit and the Top of the World Highway, between me and Dawson City.

Chapter 14.
Eagle

At around the turn of the 20th century, Eagle village boasted a population of about 1500. Nowadays, even my pilgrimage was insufficient to push the current human total into triple figures. Despite this, Eagle was the largest town I had inflicted myself upon since leaving Fairbanks, with Central boasting only about half the number.

I was well-rested when I rose in the morning, had my second shower since arriving, and treated myself to a leisurely turn around town. The extent of Eagle, with several avenues around its centre, seems fairly large. As with many goldrush-associated cities, the population peaked around the time of the goldrush, and has been shrinking ever since.

The buildings themselves are of a similar design – and apparent age – as those found anywhere this far from the modern sprawls. Some of the buildings are late 19th century, and Eagle might have been frozen in time ever since. There is an old courthouse, museum, church, school, and shop.

I spent some time at a library, where I could get free Wi-Fi. Following some communications with home, I headed to the grocery shop to get stocked-up for the day, and to buy some snacks for the trail. At the request of the B&B owner, after lunch I visited the local school to torment the unwary children.

I was staggered that all the pupils had laptops on their desks. I had no idea precisely when each stopped listening to me and began playing games or watching videos on YouTube, but at least one lad was kind enough to Google me on his. The reward for my rather charitable presentation was a school dinner. No good deed goes unpunished, and all that.

Back at the cabin, I continued to gorge myself in an improbable effort to regain much lost weight. I had almost shrieked when I first saw myself in the bathroom mirror the night before. More than being overly skinny and still quite smelly – despite the invigorating wash at Kandik Cabin only a few days before – I was also quite distressed at the amount of dandruff. Without a comb for my hair, and not caring to make any efforts in that direction, dandruff had just sort of accumulated in a manner it usually would not. Two showers scarcely dented the issue.

It was around four o'clock in the afternoon that I left the cabin, to begin making my way out of Eagle, about 23 hours after I had arrived. I felt that it was a well-earned rest, and a good opportunity to see Eagle before moving on. Indeed, I think I had used my time well.

I headed up the road, taking a left and then a right, and was soon on the Taylor Highway, leading out of town. There would be mile markers along this road all the way over American Summit; the final unknown mountain for me of the normal Quest route.

Eagle itself was at mile 162 of the highway, although the first marker I spotted on the road was 160, with values decreasing as I went along. The road had a couple of inches of packed snow and ice over it, so there were no problems with getting stuck into the climb. Now heading through Eagle's outskirts, I approached a mechanics workshop and spotted a girl walking towards town.

She greeted me by name and wished me well on my way; one of the schoolgirls who had been in my presentation earlier, now going 'out out' for an evening with her friends. Another sweet reminder that this environment – as intimidating as it often is in its harshest conditions – is a place where people conduct their lives as much as they might want to anywhere else.

Children walk to school, people socialise and engage in sports, and they all live their #bestlives at least as well of the rest of us. Some might say it is better here. I like to reflect, after dipping a thoughtful toe into this civilisation, that if these folks can make themselves comfortable, so can I, if I put my mind to it.

* * * * * * *

The snowy, icy road, rounded a bend and continued up a short way, before ending abruptly in a layby area and a turn off. The trail continued, however; now a snowmachine track in the middle of the road, with deeper, untouched snow on either side. Signs were in place that the road was closed and there was no access to vehicles. Another sign made it clear that to proceed would be ill-advised, with much peril lying in wait ahead, and that was presumably for snowmachine users, or drivers heading through when the road is open. I doubted they received much foot traffic.

It was surreal to me, in that moment, to consider that this snow-covered route – The Taylor Highway – would be busy in a few months' time, with people driving along it to travel between Eagle, the Top of the World and the Alaska Highways. This highway was built in 1953, so relatively new. Before that there was an established road – the Valdez-Eagle Trail – which would have given access for people to reach the Alaskan gold fields from the Gulf of Alaska, although that was only completed in 1901, some years after gold was first discovered in central Alaska. Even that is fairly recent usage – a mere hundred years or so of history.

The Athabascan natives were using this route for thousands of years, as it – rather undramatically for my storytelling purposes – happens to be the lowest crossing point in the White Mountains. This was a useful link between the Gulf of Alaska and the Yukon River. Having left the Yukon River upon my arrival in Eagle, I expect to land upon it again in a few days' time, when I descend from the Top of the World Highway, and cross it to reach Dawson City.

Chapter 15.
American Summit

Having left Eagle feeling quite the centre of attention, the long climb towards the top of American Summit began steadily. Leaving in the late afternoon, I anticipated a low-key ramble of some 10-15 miles (16-24km), before setting-up camp for the night. It felt good to be making progress uphill in the gloaming.

A more leisurely Hines might have deemed it sensible to take a prolonged rest in Eagle, following my toiling along the river, with its deep snow, and anguished, kneeling exasperations and exhaustion. A more ambitious Hines decided that, what with a change being as good as a rest, having now left that river I could take a break by assaulting a mountain.

The trail was a little soft, but nevertheless deliciously easy-going, compared with how the bastard river had been after the gawd-awful snowfall. The filmmakers had previously informed me they had broken trail all the way to the summit, so as long as there was no fresh snowfall or high winds, the trail would remain. A 10-15 mile stint tonight would mean reaching the summit during the day tomorrow, rather than passing over at night.

It had been night time when I reached the top of Boulder Summit and Rosebud Ridge, and there had been a whiteout on Eagle Summit. I felt confident, beyond fear of any contradiction, that my progress over American Summit would provide me with a clear crossing and panoramic views. Well, a boy can dream.

I camped close to milepost 150, satisfied that 12 miles (19 km) was an acceptable distance from the centre of Eagle, leaving about 8 miles (13 km) to go to the summit, and 10 miles (16 km) before being back in the trees and descending on the far side. I slept off the trail and had an unfairly disturbed night.

I was positive I could hear an approaching snowmachine, coming from the direction of the summit, with its sound dulled by a bend in the road a couple of hundred yards further along. I was so sure of this, that I was preparing myself to reach up to turn on my headtorch, which I kept suspended from the tent's ceiling, in the hope of making my presence known before being flattened. But the sound came and went without getting beyond that bend in the trail. It dawned on me, sometime later, that what I was getting myself worked-up about was actually the sound of a growing wind, blowing up the valley and around the mountain. So much for my perfectly broken trail.

* * * * * * *

It was early when I packed everything away and began making progress towards the summit. Moving uphill, straight out of bed, is a good way of producing heat and feeling safe. The trail leading up American Summit was not easy, but nor was it arduous to any uncivilised extent either.

As with much of my progress since leaving Fairbanks, it rankled that I was working hard but that my speed was so slow. With the mile markers this was even more obvious to me. At best I would manage 3.5

miles an hour (5.6 kph), but mostly it was around 3 mph (4.8 kph) on good trail, and down to 2.5 mph (4 kph) on the steeper sections. It was a heavy sled and a soft trail, but I struggled to accept it; it frustrated me and I wished I could do more.

I felt fit, and the waif-like sight that had shocked me in the mirror the day before was evidence of how hard I had been working. I had progressed in spite of soft trails, fresh snowfall, patches of overflow earlier on, all these climbs and this heavy sled. Against the odds I was making progress, and I would still hold-off betting against me. So much I told myself, meditatively. Onwards, I climbed.

Familiar as I was with mountain landscapes, I expected the trees to become sparser the higher I climbed, and that eventually it would be open across the mountaintop. According to *The Guide*, I would be above timber for 4 miles (6.5 km), so 2 miles before and 2 miles after the summit itself, but the mountain actually became open much earlier.

Strong winds had created snowdrifts, obliterating parts of the trail. I was finding sections a couple of hundred yards in length where the trail occurred only in patches, with bumps of snow a few yards along and raised up more than a foot above the trail. The surface of these drifts was a hard crust of icy snow, but it was not quite hard enough to take my weight fully, and I would punch through, sometimes descending down to my knees. The going was getting tough again.

I held-off putting on my snowshoes until closer to the summit crossing, as between the snowdrifts the trail was fairly good without them. The snowshoes were an extra weight hanging off my feet, increasing energy expenditure, and, with prolonged use, increasing risks of overuse injury. I liked to save them for special occasions. You know; as a treat.

When the trail levelled out a little in the open, I could see the remaining climb up to the summit. The winds were strengthening; rising from strong to fierce to treacherous, with the air cold and biting; the trail sluggish and slow. From here it would be a long 4 miles before I was back in the relative safety of the trees again, and, before then, the conditions would worsen all the way up to the summit itself.

I took a brief break to eat some food, after which I strapped on the snowshoes (I deserved the treat), and pulled on my down jacket and goggles. I needed to be fully prepared for the environment I was stepping into, upon my final approach to the top, and for however long it took to reach calmer conditions during the descent. I ensured my neck gaiter and a Buff protected my mouth and nose below the goggles, and I pulled the hood up on my down jacket, ensuring it was a snug fit. The fur ruff would do its thing of creating a microclimate, protecting my face from the worst of the elements.

These manoeuvres, this preparation for stepping into extreme cold and windchill, are performed swiftly but deliberately. Each item of clothing is positioned exactly as it needs to be, and secured correctly. Once I am exposed to the worst this environment will test me with, I will not be able to remove my mitts to make any corrections to lapses made now, because frozen fingers and frostbite will come too fast, risking everything. Therefore, absolutely everything has to be exactly right, before taking that first step into what lies in wait. This is a ritual I have performed countless times before, and, as deliberate as my preparations are, there is also an automaticity to them; unthinking, relying on a trained and practised auto-pilot, and having the utmost trust in the equipment that my life literally depends upon.

As I moved-off, I felt that I was headed into the eye of a storm, knowing the higher trail would bring me to ever-more exposed and difficult conditions. The way was mostly lost here, with it becoming increasingly challenging to successfully discern the lines that had formed as part of the trail, and those which were simply ripples formed from mounting lines of snow and ice crystals, creating sastrugi, like wave-formed patterns in sand at a beach.

The summit elevation was 3652 feet (1113 metres), so on a par with a lot of what I am used to in the UK, but I would tend to avoid those climbs in the middle of winter, in deep snow, and in howling winds. Up I went; the wind growing stronger and the temperature dropping, seemingly with each step. Onwards, with deep snowdrifts more than two feet in height, snatching me down into them, as I fought to haul the sled through. The wind howled and I could scarcely identify the shape of the mountain at all, as I approached another mountaintop in a whiteout. Terrific.

Despite the struggle, and the need to get beyond the summit and down to relative safety, I managed myself well, and I took a moment to take a couple of photos near the top, in an attempt to later convey my predicament. I could only do so during brief moments, when the wind was busy drawing in a deep breath.

During the truly grim moments it was all I could do to keep moving; to keep placing one foot in front of the other with my head down, and such moments were not given to pauses for amateur photography. Over to my left, around the summit area itself, were abandoned cars, held fast in deep snow. It was a challenge to appreciate that I was sled-hauling along a highway.

As I descended to reach the four-mile-point (mile 138 of the highway), I realised, and with some disappointment, that this was not a steep descent into woodland, as it is coming over King Solomon's Dome on the Canadian side, but a gentler trail, leading back below the timber line only very gradually.

The trees that did stand early in the descent were small, meagre things, barely stalks compared with the grand pines lower down. It would remain a long, exposed descent, but at least a safe one. The nuisance that was my sled wanting to descend faster than me was realised yet again, but otherwise it was uneventful. The trail would undulate, with slow progress on the climbs, but overall I was descending and picking up the pace.

I had something like 35 miles (56 km) to go before reaching a bridge over the Fortymile River. From there it would be a notoriously cold river for 41 miles (66 km), before the next cabin (access to which was currently unknown), and then the reroute over the Top of the World highway to Dawson City. The goal for the rest of the day was to make solid progress towards the bridge.

* * * * * * *

Some miles further-on, I came across fresh snowmachine tracks, and the broken trail permitted my pace to improve further. Whoever owned the snowmachine was apparently a trapper, who had come along here to check their trapline, as the tracks always led off the main trail to pass coloured ribbons, which hung from nearby branches, signifying a trap close by. Whoever they were, my progress was faster for their coming this way.

The overcast sky cleared in the afternoon, leaving blue skies but threatening a colder night ahead. Occasionally, the trail would take me across a short bridge over a creek, and there would be a signpost with the name of the bridge or creek on it – many with fewer bullet holes than you might expect. The bridges would have names like Discovery Claim or King Solomon's, giving me cause to dwell still more on the great gold rush, and all the mines ahead of me. My mind rarely went long without contemplating the gold rush, and all those brave souls enduring to chase their dreams.

Close to the base of the mountain, the snowmachine tracks led off the main trail along another road, and that was the end of my nicely broken, happy trail. As I crossed a bridge and viewed the trail ahead of me, which led up a short and steady climb, the way looked nightmarish once again. This was deep powder which necessitated my snowshoes coming back on. I had been pulling the snowshoes on and off for much of the day, as I was challenged by varying degrees and depths of powder on the trail.

It was going to be a long slog for the remaining 20 miles (32 km) to the river. Darkness was falling, and, what with the work to get up and over American Summit, and the sub-optimal trail conditions I was now enduring, I would have to keep pushing on, with much effort, to reach a good campsite. I was also concerned that, now I was low in the valley, the temperature was feeling much colder. Onwards I went, into the cold night.

The trail brought me down to the level of various creeks. I passed an abandoned car to my right, and to my left saw rows of cabins within a mining facility. I deharnessed and went to investigate. Nobody else had visited all winter, just the occasional prospecting moose, presumably musing on how he remembered when all this was nothing but spruce trees.

The first cabin I could see looked good, but another cabin nearby bore a clear private property sign. I had to assume that if this was the case for one, it would be the case for all. Perhaps if I was in trouble I would persevere and try to enter one, but if the will of the owner was that they be left alone, I had to respect that.

As I continued along the trail, so I thought it would be better if there were a requirement that all such facilities built a rescue cabin for when the mine was closed. This would protect the main properties from misuse and damage, should anyone be in trouble and desperate for shelter. I later learned that such emergency cabins used to be the norm, and that perhaps it was misuse of these, which led them ceasing from being a requirement.

As the trail gently rose and then descended alongside a creek, so I became anxious that the way might remain low until the Fortymile Bridge, in which case I would be in for a particularly cold night. I took the opportunity, when the trail rose a few yards above creek level, to find a camping spot. I was still about 10 miles (16 km) from the bridge, but it was better to play it safe, than to put myself in a position where I was compelled to keep pushing through a cold night.

As I set up my camp, I was treated to my first really strong northern lights since the descent from Rosebud Ridge, right at the beginning. I attempted to take a photograph, but it was too cold to have hands exposed to get the settings right. I had managed everything except switching it to manual focus and setting to infinity. By the time I realised that still needed to be done, a switch in my head had been flicked instead, and I acknowledged there was no compromising. It was dangerously cold to have fingers out of my mitts, and now was the time to retreat to the warm safety of my sleeping bag.

I did not have a thermometer to hand, but one was not required to know I was in a cold spot. Upon ceasing movement, or removing my big mitts, I could easily sense how rapidly I was losing heat to the environment. It is that rate of heat loss, and the time it takes from pausing or removing garments to perceiving *The Cold* fighting to get in, that indicates the temperature. This was certainly below -31 F (-35 C), and most probably below -40 F/C. The impact of this now was discipline: colder temperatures force greater efficiency, to preserve warmth and to promote safety, but this is all perfectly manageable with the clothing and equipment I have.

The only difference between preparing to sleep on a cold, versus more clement night, is that when it is cold the procedure has to be as slick as possible. There is a more immediate need to undress whilst still giving off plenty of heat from activity, to ensure capture of this within the bag is maximised. On milder nights this is less essential, and I can be more lax, such as by placing my shoes beneath my legs outside the sleeping bag, rather than within it.

I zipped-up the sleeping bag, plumped up my mid-layer-jacket pillow, and settled in for the night. On this occasion, there was another part of the routine, which often occurred on the colder days, whenever a sizeable glacier had grown upon my facial topiary. Once within the sleeping bag, the warmth was sufficient to set in action a melt event, and I would spend a few minutes de-anchoring fairly sizeable icebergs from the facial fungus. These chunks I would fling down towards a bottom corner of the tent, where they would remain frozen, and I could eject them in the morning.

One highlight, which I especially looked forward to, and most of all on colder nights such as this, was my first bladder evacuation within the sleeping bag. I turn to the side, still all zipped-in and snug, and make use of a moderately-sized Nalgene bottle. I would 'enter' this, release the deluge, perform the most thorough post-urination shaking procedure it is possible to conduct, without actually flirting with masturbation, screw on the bottle cap, seal the bottle securely within a small drybag, and hurl it down towards my feet. On rare occasions I kept it close to my torso, but generally wherever I felt would benefit the most from the presence of bodily fluid, preserved at around 98F (37C).

I stirred during the night, when I perceived a casual moose strolling by, but it chose not to stomp me to death, and I was tired enough not to pay much attention to it. Its purpose along the trail was its own affair, and neither of us was in the mood to fraternise. Thrilled to still be alive, I drifted comfortably back to sleep.

Chapter 16.
American Summit to Clinton Creek

I awoke refreshed. My finely-tuned athlete senses warning me it was a cold morning, but nothing an experienced Arctic race veteran such as myself had to worry about. It is the cruellest aspect of a day, of course, when sleeping-out in an unheated tent in the Far North, to confront the bitter cold head-on. Feathers of frozen breath hung precariously from the tent canvas above my head, poised to break free with the slightest movement, to fall vindictively onto my unprotected, innocent, beautiful face.

Even with the tent zip open to vent a little, the moisture still accumulated and froze. In any other environment, the air would pass through the fabric, but here the canvas froze and lost much of its breathability. In such a confined space, any slight movement I made caused my sleeping bag to rub against the tent fabric, dislodging the ice and water droplets. Gingerly but steadily, I dressed and scrambled out of my sleeping bag and tent.

I released the chunks of liberated beard ice from the end of the tent back into the wild, noticing one chunk exhibited tones of red. My throat must have suffered with the cold. For those interested in why this happens, the short answer is because exercising at -40F/C is mad. I mean it is really not an intelligent thing to do.

Cold air at -40 meeting the lungs – nestled happily and doing their thing at +98.6F (+37C) – gives quite a shock. Add to this the high breathing rates due to exercising, with perhaps up to 22 gallons (100 litres) of this colder-than-ice air attacking the respiratory tract every minute, and it should be no surprise damage is done.

Oxidative stress increases dramatically, and the respiratory tract dries and becomes physically damaged, exhibiting considerable inflammation, and with the unpleasant effect of blood getting into the airways. At the time of writing, it is still unknown whether the respiratory tract scarring is reversible, or if it becomes a permanent feature (as much scarring that occurs around the body is indeed permanent).

It should be apparent by now that I do not engage in Arctic shenanigans because I am an intelligent individual. People might occasionally mistake me for an intelligent chap, and, as I have never been one to fly in the face of public opinion, one hesitates to correct them. I do this sort of thing because I mostly enjoy myself out here. But, too much of a good thing can have its consequences, much like alcohol, drugs, and Gloucestershire cheese rolling.

Preparing to set off that morning was, regrettably, the work of many prolonged and exaggerated moments. For one thing, I had the extra step of fastening-on my snowshoes, which was an especially drawn-out and frustrating faff now, as a couple of clips had broken, meaning I had to manipulate the straps to ensure everything was secure. Once moving, I would want to maintain a high work rate to generate heat. Stopping to make corrections to items not properly put on in the first place – especially as mitts would need to be removed – was a real problem.

American Summit to Clinton Creek

With the snowshoes on, I secured the sled harness, pulled on my mitts, and set-off along the trail. It was indeed a cold morning, but I did not think it to be much of an issue. Striking out into the cold white yonder is what this sort of exploit is all about.

My morning's routine had been longer than usual because of the snowshoes, but otherwise no different. I was used to fingertips being cold for 10-15 minutes, once the mitts were first on, but, 30 minutes since moving-off, I still could not get warmth into them. I flexed my fingers, repeatedly squeezing my hands around my trekking poles. I changed hand positions again and again, doing all I could to generate more warmth, but it was not working. I usually waited an hour before stopping to take a break for breakfast, but this morning I lasted 40 minutes before having to stop to examine the state of my hands.

I came to a stop where a climb flattened-out, and removed my mittens. It was the fingertips on my right hand that had felt cold, and I removed my liner glove – the first time I had done so to check on the health of my fingers all trip, so well had I managed everything until now.

On the fingertip pads of my thumb and middle finger were the tell-tale white, waxy, thickened signs of frostbite. For a moment my world skidded and shuddered to an abrupt and terrifying stop. I became angry, fast, which did not seem to help my immediate situation as much as I might have liked. I needed a moment to work out what to do, accepting that this had happened whilst wearing my mittens, so there were no additional layers to pull on.

I used the second that followed the first panic to declare loudly, in clear voice, and with vehemence, that I was, in fact, an arse. With that settled, I fumbled with my harness – my freezing fingers hardly working in my favour – struggling to take it off. With two hands and much more time and effort than should have been required, I painstakingly worked the clips and got myself free of the harness

I marched back to my sled and worked similarly hard to unclip my food bag. Everything was painfully slow, and despairingly difficult, with the frostbite setting in.

With these Olympic feats of manual dexterity achieved, I thrust my right hand into my pants and sat down. With my left hand I was taking my food to eat, placing the hand close to my armpit, within my jacket, when not actively shepherding food into my mouth. With my right hand I just searched out the warmest parts of my genitals and played with myself, mostly in disgust, which happened to be the only way I knew how to play with myself anyway.

Ten minutes later and I decided it was time to get going again. I checked my fingertips and they were looking much better. I would give them some more time along the trail to see how they responded. I replaced my mitts and moved on.

It was an angry, disappointed, frustrated, self-loathing Hines who continued along that trail. As far as I could tell it was 'game over' now. It would be all I could do to get myself safely to Dawson City, and would not be able to risk going on from there. But as Dawson City was still over 100 miles away, I could not really entertain anything much beyond this day.

Calling for medical help was not a serious option. I could make the call via my SPOT tracker, but I would then be waiting around for the Thunderbirds or whoever, and all I could tell them would be that I had mild frostbite, and was worried that to continue would cause it to worsen. And I did not know for sure that it would worsen – it might improve. Calling for help would be crazy and a waste of resources, for a condition I ought to be able to manage myself.

I had used an earlier model of these mitts from the same manufacturer at below -58F (-50C) and been fine. Then I had had my hands exposed for even longer on one occasion, and actually felt my hands cold for the first time in this environment, with ice crystals forming in the synovial fluids of my thumb joints. Then, wearing the mitts again, and making progress whilst moving my hands and fingers vigorously, I had rewarmed them completely, preventing frostbite from getting a look-in. Why had they failed now?

As the trail led up a long, very gradual climb, so I came to learn of a pain I have never before experienced. Fingertips on both hands had frozen, to the point where blood flow into those tissues had stopped, and fluids within the cells – including nerve cells – had frozen through the formation of ice crystals. Now those ice crystals were melting, leaving damaged cell membranes in their wake, and, even though this was occurring on a microscopic scale, the pain from the reawakening nerves was intense, exquisite and exceptional.

The pain began its adventures as a subtle sensation of warmth and tingling, but this was merely a precursor to the main show. From this mild state of affairs, Pain springboarded and soared to reach new heights. The enlivening sensation was akin to a strong flame burning through those points on the fingertips, and there was nothing to be done but endure it.

Well, there was nothing 'useful' I could do, that came to mind. I certainly whimpered and winced and might easily have sobbed a good deal, but I mean to say I could not actually diminish the sensation. It was the fingers coming back to life. Now this was happening I had to maintain it – to allow them to refreeze would be disastrous, causing considerably more damage, and reducing their capacity for a full recovery.

I suppose painkillers might have helped with putting a cap on the exhilaratingly painful side of events, but one avoids being dramatic. Besides, many painkillers have anti-inflammatory effects, and, as this is part of the healing process, I welcomed it to some extent. Medication for frostbite is largely to promote blood flow, whilst opposing clotting. Without such drugs available, movement and monitoring was the best I could do. Excessive inflammation would be bad news, but unless that occurred, there was no benefit I could think of in limiting the natural processes.

I have suffered very superficial frostnip before, but never frostbite. Frostbite is nothing to be proud of. It is not a sign of being in an extreme environment, but of making mistakes in equipment and/or self-management. It was an error and a sign of incompetence; absolutely nothing to show-off about. The fact that it could not have been that cold made the sting of shame even worse. I have experienced colder for longer and been fine. What had I done this time that was so disastrously wrong?

Following a descent towards a bridge, I passed by an area offering accommodation and outdoor pursuits, clearly for summer use. A little further on there were some industrial buildings, then nothing for a while. As I approached the Fortymile Bridge, there were a few cabins to my right, smoke billowing from a few. These were large workshops for small construction or other industrial operations, and I did not trespass.

I am sure that, if my fingers had not started to recover, I would have been crashing through and appealing to the staff for sympathy. As it was, I just needed to get to Dawson. I crossed the bridge, looking down to the river to see the trail, with tracks leading in both directions. I proceeded onto the river, passing a few markers during the descent, but was abruptly without any once upon the river itself.

I headed along in the direction that made the most sense, but kept an eye on my GPS at regular intervals, to ensure I was not inadvertently headed back to Fairbanks. For some reason I was highly doubtful about the direction I was going in. Perhaps it was the absence of any trail markers, or maybe the thought of the mistakes that had led to the frostbite, which dashed my confidence so much now.

It remained cold along the river, even in the middle of the day. This section of the Fortymile River is a known cold-spot, due to it being through a narrow canyon, ensuring minimal sunlight ever reaches the base of it. I would be on the river for another 40 miles (64 km) before reaching the cabin at Clinton Creek, and the turn-off for the highway. It all felt very bleak.

It was colder here than when the frostbite had first appeared. The problem with the frostbite was less the risk of losing skin off my fingertips, or the condition worsening to endanger the fingers themselves, and more about what it meant for my general safety and efficiency along the trail.

I was finding it incredibly challenging and labour-intensive to perform simple tasks, such as unclipping my harness, and manipulating the zips on my clothing and kit bag. These physical difficulties, coupled with the risk of frostbite deteriorating, were enough to put me off accessing my food and water, which increased my risk of hypothermia, secondary to dehydration, and all manner of other problems, including simply becoming overworked and losing the ability to make good decisions.

My mood, at this juncture, might have veered towards a low ebb, but I had reassuring resources to hand. I have always been a good, dependable Boy Scout. *Be Prepared* is my motto. For every trial I face, I have a solution. For my frostbitten fingertips and failing mittens, I had chemical hand warmer pads. These nifty little pads need only to be removed from their packet, and shaken around for a few minutes, and within about 10 more my hands would be roasting, all normal functioning restored, and I would plod onwards, as safe as houses.

It was with some regret that I realised they did not seem to be working. Nothing had happened within the first 10 minutes of using them, and, more than half an hour later, nothing continued to happen. I have used hand warmers on past adventures – when I did not really need them, but just for the luxury of the things – and they had always warmed my hands up a treat. I had been carrying packs of them around for years and never bothered using them after my first race up here, because I wanted to know I could use my clothing correctly instead.

I did not know why they failed to work now, but, being the always prepared Boy Scout, whose motto is *Be Prepared*, I naturally carried spares. It was with me the work of a moment to switch over the first pair with a second pair, and I progressed on, poised to feel my fingers saved from falling over the edge.

The second set did not work either. It is at moments like this, when one gains solace from the reflection that these are simply the times that try men's souls. These hiccups exist to make one feel menaced and plagued for belonging to the species of Sapiens. It is from these depths of self-pity that one finds the solutions that nobody else would have thought of, and one's spirit is elevated to one of feeling the master of one's genus, and the engineer of a brighter destiny.

Whilst drawing blanks as to what the exact solution to my crisis might be, I was content I would get there with sufficient time and a good run-up. My ignorance was not quite blissful, but I felt armed with a sort of unqualified optimism; the sort that manages to keep the rest of the truly stupid operating on a day-to-day basis.

A particularly ripe idea was almost certainly fermenting in my subconscious already, just waiting to be of the right fettle, before unleashing itself upon my magnificent brain proper. With this optimism now washing a warming glow all over me, I progressed along the trail, expectant of great things developing within.

* * * * * * *

I saw the occasional cabin or other mining area, sometimes pausing to gaze longingly, pondering whether I might be able to access them, but the walks across powder, and the likelihood of them being locked, or posted as private, would be too great to counter the loss of time. I looked to see if there were people, or signs of people, and, when there were none, I continued on. Relaxing in a nice warm cabin, enjoying a brief break, would have been a welcome escape from the reality of the cold river.

In the late afternoon it was still light, and the full moon was already high in the sky. There was a small cloud to the side of it. The moon and the cloud took similar amounts of space in the sky, but what struck me about the cloud was that it was not fully white, but a spectrum. Sometimes I get the illusion because of my sunglasses, but as I looked without them, so it remained, albeit fainter. I checked back on it from time to time, treating the cloud to an accusing look that it was playing silly-buggers. Very pretty, but odd.

The trail wound its way along the flat, narrow river, bend after bend. The moon remained above the hills with the cloud to its side. As the evening progressed, so a second cloud appeared in the sky, and to the opposite side of the moon, as if mirroring the first.

Both clouds were spectra, and a thin line of grey cloud arched over the moon, from one cloud to the other, apparently connecting them, and looking like a vast baby's cot mobile, just for me, and it felt apt. There had been at least a couple of times today when I could have thrown all my toys out my pram. And I could do with my mother right now, too. In the meantime, and in her absence, which I suspect she would be grateful of, I would just have to be content with crying hysterically, and occasionally shitting myself.

It was late evening now, and the sky had grown dark. I stopped and looked up. The moon was at my 2 o'clock above me. The clouds were still there. The line of thin grey cloud connecting them was now a light silver, and looped around in a vast circle entirely above me, as if a crown over the Earth. It was an enormous moon dog; the largest and most impressive I have ever seen.

Orion was rising beyond the moon, low above a low hill, and a line of green northern lights spanned across Orion's Belt, and appeared to connect onto the moon dog by one of the clouds. It was all astonishing. I paused for a moment, standing and gazing upwards, awestruck. As I continued along the trail, so I kept looking up, in amazement. It is such a fine, remarkable privilege, to be wowed and awed, taken aback by the surprises of nature in adulthood.

As I moved along the night-time trail, I scoured the riverbank to my left. The trail varied between 3 and 7 yards from the bank, and the bank was only a couple of yards high, but mostly vertical. It was late and I wanted to be off the river to sleep. All day had been an exercise in attention to my fingers, constantly thinking about them, squeezing the trekking poles, being overly protective, and acting as if it was -58F (-50C), when it could not have been much colder than -40. I would later learn that this was considered the coldest section of the whole trail.

I would usually only wear mitts in the morning and late at night, when it was coldest. Today I wore them all day, even when I had warmed-up so much my hands had begun sweating because of it. As far as I was concerned, my fingers could not be warm enough. I would do everything I could to promote healing, until they really were healed.

Sweating is not a problem as long as it is managed, and that means not allowing clothing to become wet. My mitts could be dried-out easily enough, if need be, but really the vapour from my sweat could be lost to the environment, without getting my mitts wet in the process.

I came across an area of riverbank, with an opening in the trees and a flat area further back, where I could potentially camp. The route up the riverbank did not look too severe, so I decided to give it a try. What followed was not something that could have been viewed by anyone with a weak heart, or a humourless temperament.

What ensued, was several minutes of me scrambling up a riverbank as high as myself, with no discernible progress being made. There were arms and legs frantically waving at the bank, but no actual upwards progression of the body. Even when I did occasionally manage to get myself up and off the river, the sled would unsportingly drag me back down onto it. Clearly he and I were not seeing eye-to-eye on this whole 'getting up the riverbank' aspect of the expedition.

With much expenditure of efforts, considerable panting, and an even more considerable and painful loss of any remaining dignity, I eventually managed to haul myself, and the sled, up to the top, but it was after easily 10 minutes of struggling in the snow. As I headed into the small clearing, I was confronted with a small, dilapidated log cabin, in a state of truly remarkable disrepair.

I walked up to it and was able to go inside without breaking anything. The doorway was on the left side of the cabin, along the long front wall. There was a porch which was falling apart. The floor within was covered in some sort of plant material, like seed casings, and they were up to a foot deep. I had struggled to open the door against the weight of them. There was a platform for a double bed on one side, and a single bed with a mattress on the other side. Between was empty space.

There was one table and one window. Next to the table was a wood stove, but it was full of holes and had fallen apart. Even if I could negotiate the various parts into some sort of order, there was no firewood anyway. The ceiling was low, although, in fairness, that could have been an effect of the stuff on the floor raising me up.

Without a source of heat, it would have been a colder night if I took a bed. I brought my things in and set up the tent on the floor, as bizarre as it seemed to be erecting a shelter within a shelter, but it would be a little warmer.

Whyever the seeds (or whatever they were) were there, they created a fantastically soft and well-insulating mattress. Being inside would also mean no disturbances from large, lumbering wildlife, and protection against any wind. I climbed into my sleeping bag and removed my gloves, for the first time since checking my frostbite in the morning. It was too dark to look at them now, but they felt better, and I fell asleep easily.

* * * * * * *

The following morning, as I sashayed from my night's bijou timber residence out into the snow, I was relieved to be feeling that my fingers were once more my own. I believed that I had snatched them back from the cold, and revitalised them to some considerable extent. I was gazing upon them and marvelling at this during my morning's *al fresco* dump by a tree.

   I continued gazing at them, whilst wondering whether willpower alone might be sufficient to continue their recovery, and why did I have to be feeling so constipated on the coldest mornings? Swaying gently in the cool breeze were my dangling genitals, and this morning was another cold one for all of us. I cannot claim that they held any definite expression, but they were giving-off a singularly incredulous vibe.

   My descent down onto the river was fast and perilous, and, with this spirit of adventure, I commenced my day proper. My journey towards Clinton Creek continued, and, as it did, my mind naturally dwelt upon the state of my fingers. Although feeling much improved, the loss of circulation during the freezing meant that the tips were still white, and I had a long journey of recovery ahead.

The fingers had become cold again whilst exposed this morning, but this had not been followed by any fiery pain, assuring me they had not refrozen and subsequently thawed. I rubbed my fingertips against my trekking poles from within my mittens, in an attempt to promote blood flow, whilst feeling the materials against my skin – a good indication nothing was frozen. I would keep the mitts on regardless of the temperature, and let my fingers heat themselves better.

The river trail remained flat and fast for me here, and the previous day and night of colder temperatures had firmed-up the trail appreciably. I consulted the GPS from time-to-time, to get an indication of the distance to Clinton Creek, but the river bended so mindlessly that the whole enterprise felt fairly pointless. Hills on both sides were the noticeable feature. Although they were low and covered in woodland, it kept the river as a sink for the cold air to sit in. It would be cold all day.

A couple of hours of my laboured peregrinations passed, and I found myself amongst six trail markers, arranged equally on each side of the trail, and all in a straight line perpendicular to it. As I crossed over the rudimentary line, I acknowledged – with some degree of happiness and satisfaction – that I had now left behind me the United States of America, and entered into Civilisation. Or "America's largest national park", depending upon your point of view.

I was alerted to a consistency in the cold weather, through my on-board, beard-based weather centre. The length of icicles on the facial topiary were growing, and, apparently, on some overt mission to reach my knees. This was accompanied by an impressive thickness of glacial ice forming around my mouth.

I confess that I have never really managed to get face protection right. I do not enjoy having my mouth covered, such as with masks, because I feel hot and bothered in quick order. The best I have managed now resulted from butchering a neoprene face mask, which originally included a face covering below the eyes, featuring both mouth cover and nose protection, with material extending around the face and secured at the back of my head with Velcro. By cutting away the mouth part, I was left with the nose protection, plus a rather useful microclimate effect, where the air was warmed prior to inhalation.

I did not wear this rather fetching garment often, because I did not need to, coupled with the fact that neoprene – like many other materials – loses elasticity when it freezes, making it feel either too tight or too loose, but always rigid, frigid, and generally unpleasant. I put it on now, because conditions demanded it.

Regrettably, after maybe half an hour or so, I felt so warm I wanted to remove the article, but was unable to do so. Moisture from my breath had gathered and then frozen on a section of material below the mouth, freezing it fast to the ice already in residence on the beard around my chin. Clearly, when cutting away material to create the mouth hole, I had not gone far enough.

I unsecured the Velcro and pulled the mask away as best I could, but it was frozen to the beard, left hanging from my ridiculous face. If I failed to work it loose, I would be stuck like this for the rest of the day. Another half an hour and I realised my face was getting cold again, but by now the face mask was frozen rigid and completely unusable. Attempting to wrestle it into position was impossible, as it was about as malleable as a breeze block. I pulled up a Buff from within my neck gaiter, using that to cover my face.

The trick with the Buff is that you have to regularly turn it around the face, otherwise moisture from the breath freezes on it, and problems ensue. Every few minutes a turn of a few dozen clockwise degrees, and a fresh, dry section of material, is in front of the face. Meanwhile, the wet section initiates an expedition around the head, at the end of which much of the moisture has been wicked away, and it has mostly dried out.

Having known and perfected this procedure over many years, it was interesting to note that, just like the face mask, it was now fully frozen solid; also stuck to my beard. At some stage, ice on my beard would have melted, due to the insulation from the Buff, and that water permeated through a sizeable section of material, before refreezing once exposed to the air on the other side.

Perhaps it was because it was so cold, and I had not appreciated the need to increase the Buff-Head-Rotation frequency, that I now discovered myself in this position. To confide in you my current predicament: I now had a neoprene face mask and a Buff completely frozen to my beard, and there was nothing I could do about it until in my sleeping bag later. This was the triumphant and majestic image I portrayed to mark my arrival here in Canada.

I occupied myself, over the following hours, with delicately peeling away tiny sections of Buff, as I marched along. Some concerted puffing of warm air in targeted directions helped a bit, but I was unable to entirely free it from its moorings upon my beard's lower slopes. Should I find myself in the company of others this evening, I will be presenting myself as both an Englishman and a large disaster area.

A further inconvenience was the almost overpowering smell, which assaulted me whenever I put my frozen face closer to my chest, to suck water from my MSR water bladder. This action brought my nose in close proximity to my armpit, an entirely sound strategy for ensuring the bladder hose and mouthpiece were kept warm, and free from risk of freezing-up.

The odour that now accosted me, regrettably, was reminiscent of a once particularly strong cheese, which had been expertly tortured and poisoned by the Gestapo, before being smashed to death and left to rot in my armpits. Until this moment I had wrongly convinced myself I had suffered enough. Still, one has experiences.

Further along and there was a bottleneck in one section of the river, where the ice rose up in thick, open pans, and this was the first point I really had to take care with my footing, and trust in the trail. For one thing, I was hoping that the ice had not cracked open since the trail was put in.

I made it through the narrow canyon, popping out on the other side philosophical but unscathed. The river was only a few metres across here, and to my right was a tall cliff face, which the trail led around. The river extended out to its customary width, and I paused to view a large cabin across on the far left bank. Nobody was visible, and there were no plumes of smoke billowing from the chimney, but in any case I now had Clinton Creek in mind, regardless of whether or not anybody was there.

As the evening arrived, so I detected a smell of wood smoke from the adjacent woodland, over to my right. In the twilight my eyes searched, but no source became apparent. The occurrence of phantom wood smoke is a genuine annoyance for me. So many times I could have sworn I smelt wood smoke in the air, only to later find that I was several miles from any potential source, and almost certainly it was my mind playing tricks on me. On this occasion though I was sure, almost beyond any real doubt, that I really could smell smoke. I saw no cabin in the woods, and no route into the woods from the river. If it was there, it was hiding. Onwards.

As I moved along the right side of the Fortymile River, I saw hills ahead and across the river from me, more woodland, and possible sites for cabins, not that any came into view. It was curious how in places the river appeared to be on a slope upwards, or, in the present case, downwards, when there really was no such slope. I suspect it was all a trick of the mind, and I felt a little sorry that my mind and I were losing touch like this.

My passage conveyed me across the river, and continued on, as was its habit. As the track rounded a hill it then split, with one trail continuing on along the river, and another gently rising and leading up the riverbank. All around was darkness, so there were no real clues as to what lie up there. My GPS indicated that the route went up and then back down, but I was aware that, due to the reroute from close to here, the GPS was now, like me, somewhat out of its depth.

The mapping on the GPS seemed to indicate a bridge further down, close to the town of Fortymile, but I could not be entirely sure. Although there was a road on the GPS, I did not know for absolute certainty that it was the one I wanted. I would investigate in the light of day, and for now my curiosity led me up and off the river. My main consideration, on taking the unknown route, was whether it would be a wasted upwards effort, but Clinton Creek was around here somewhere, and I did not want to risk missing it.

I passed by a collection of vehicles, caravans and RVs, and various old buildings. All was dark, all was quiet, and I followed the trail. I soon arrived at what I took to be the main cabin. There was light inside and smoke rising from the chimney. The signs were good. I knocked on the door, and was greeted by a gentleman named Earl. From Mike's instructions, this meant the woman I could now see was Sandy, and I was therefore at Clinton Creek. Three huge dogs accosted me outside upon my arrival, and they also belonged here.

What followed was wonderful. I was welcomed in, told that I was expected, and given a warm, wet tea towel, to begin the process of de-icing the beard. This took frustratingly long, and multiple tea towels gave themselves up to the cause. It was something like half an hour before I could remove the frozen Buff and face mask. I was assured that I had looked quite entertaining as I appeared out from the cold. With a cleared face I was granted food and drink. Earl and Sandy opened their home to the mushers, and they opened it to me, and I was full of gratitude.

Chapter 17.
Clinton Creek to Earl's Trailer

Earl and Sandy's log home was impressively large, comfortable, warm and cosy. Rooms led off from the main, open plan living space and kitchen. Large windows overlooked the frozen river. Tonight I would even have a bed to sleep in.

Various items of clothing, my sleeping bag and some of my drybags, were hung up above the stove. Some familiar queries were raised here regarding my equipment. The first was about my trail shoes. I was also asked about my hydration strategy, and, having clearly explained my tried and tested method of keeping a water bladder next to my baselayer, was confidently informed "That won't work up here".

I turned the statement over and over in my mind, wondering if, in my fatigued state, I had missed something, or turned over two pages of conversation at the same time. I believe that statement – as I reflect back upon almost a decade and thousands of miles of history of that bladder's usage and effectiveness 'up here' – will leave me baffled until my dying day, and, potentially, up to a fortnight after that. Still, one strives to learn new things daily.

When first entering the cabin, I had been struck by the sight of a large fur, stretched-out on a wall, which was so great that my initial impression was that it was a bear. The grey-blue fur, and the presence of a long tail, gave away its true nature. I had never known wolves to be so vast. I was informed that Earl had shot the animal down on the river, where it had been calling his dogs down, forcing Earl to dispatch it before it could slaughter his companions for an easy meal. The taxidermist had taken his largest wolf skull, split it longitudinally, and padded it out quite a bit, to make it fit into the head. It certainly would have been a character-building experience to meet this wolf out on the trail, in his wild and eccentric youth.

One point of import was learning now that the race finished in Takhini this year, rather than Whitehorse. This shortened the distance to the finish, although the re-route over the highway, into Dawson, compensated for it a bit. In any case, it all seemed a moot point as, on account of the frostbite, I now expected to finish in Dawson. My dream of reaching Whitehorse, or, indeed Takhini, had been dashed.

My fingertips were still fairly pale and cold to the touch, with the safety issues lingering throughout the last two days, with efforts to unclip and access items made difficult, due to a loss of manual dexterity. What I feared, in particular, was a refreezing event, which would cause considerable further damage, making it unlikely the tissues would ever properly heal. That was the sort of scenario that would turn my whitened fingertips black, and it would be a tougher career as a writer if my fingertips had to be removed. I mean, if I did not produce this Literary Gold for you to read, what on Earth would you be doing with your time? Crime, perhaps? Precisely my concern.

I was permitted to use a laptop, and set about updating friends, family and sponsors. The frostbite made typing a painful affair, although the subject I was typing about smarted my pride a fair bit too. The soft, sore pads on my fingers were made to feel worse with the impact on the keys, however gentle I attempted to be.

I let people know I would be calling it a day at Dawson City. I sent a separate message to Polar explorer chum Charlie Paton, who had been included in the group email to everyone else, and to express my hope he did not consider me too much of a bell-end for all of this. He soon responded, acknowledging how crushed I must be, but reassuring me that to stay the course would be reckless, and that the trail would remain for another year. It was good to hear. It helped. I *wanted* to believe him.

****

In the morning, I was treated to a generous breakfast and a delicious black coffee. Earl reinforced the fact that their home was there as a safe refuge for travellers, and, should I want to stay another day, this would be fine with them. I was conflicted about it, as I ever yearned for the call of the trail. But, the extra recovery day in the warm cabin would be useful. For one thing, it had been -36C (-33F) outside that morning, which was cold enough to put the fingers at risk if I made mistakes. It subsequently dropped to -50C (-58F). The day of rest would increase my chances of reaching Dawson City safely.

Earl shared a story with me, about a local from Eagle, who had taken his snowmobile along the river to Dawson some time before. He had lived around here for many years, and was experienced at winter travel, but when his snowmobile broke-down he was unable to get it going again. He died of hypothermia shortly after. I think everybody here knows to take emergency equipment with them on winter journeys, but sometimes people use the space for something else, or simply expect not to need it that one time.

Earl spent part of his day preparing to head-off in support of Tim Oakley's expedition; driving dog teams from Hershel Island to Eagle, to commemorate Amundson's trip. Tim had visited Eagle shortly before me, and similarly given a presentation at the same school. Earl would be teaming-up with Mike as snowmobile support. Such a small world it was, especially up here.

Earl was elsewhere when all the dogs became agitated at something going on across the river. Sandy and I could not see what it was, but the dogs were clearly ill at ease about something on the far side. I could not think what would bother them out here in the winter, except perhaps wolves. I cast an eye across to the blue wolf on the wall, and looked back to where the trail led up on the far riverbank, directly where the dogs were aiming their growls. Nothing.

Later on, I checked the weather forecast for Dawson City, and areas further along the Quest route. The consensus was that temperatures were going to increase considerably. Temperatures over the coming week were set to rise above -20C (-4F) at night, and later that week to -15C (5F), with daytime temperatures approaching zero. I allowed myself a little hope. If it really was going to be that warm, maybe I could continue to the Takhini finish line after all, so long as the conditions held. *There was a chance.* There was *Hope*. I did not convey this in a message to anyone yet though. I would wait until Dawson before making further decisions.

I spent the rest of the day conversing with the Clinton Creek inmates, with various topics we had mutual interests in, such as clean energy and technology, and some where our views differed, such as on gun crimes and alternative medicine. I also heard that a true Yukon legend – Larry "Cowboy" Smith – had recently sustained a serious hand injury, requiring an involved process to get him to a medical centre, from his remote and isolated base at Fort Selkirk.

Earl and Sandy were both from the U.S., and moved here some years ago, buying over 160 hectares (400 acres) of what was once a thriving village, built around an asbestos mine. Now it was all theirs. My time here passed in pleasant company, and I was glad I had stayed.

* * * * * * *

The next morning, I set-off from Clinton Creek, shortly after Earl struck-out for Hershel Island. I headed down to the river, across, and up onto the far bank. A short section through woodland brought me out onto a snowy road. Reflecting on the dogs' behaviour the previous day, I kept my eyes peeled, and nose hulled, for fresh tracks and scents, but nothing hove into range. Whatever it was yesterday, they had stayed within the woods and not crossed the trail.

Clinton Creek to Earl's Trailer

I turned right, passed an abandoned car, and began a gentle climb. I had 32 km (20 miles) to go today to a trailer, which was about a kilometre from the highest point on the Top of the World Highway. Gently does it; giving myself every opportunity to make good progress, whilst pausing to rest in the safest places, relatively speaking. I could have bailed at Clinton Creek, on account of the cold fingers, and I accepted that pushing-on was flirting with risk.

I was no longer struggling to work clips and zips, or access food or water, so the fingers were operationally fine. All I had to do was ensure they did not freeze again. The trailer I was headed towards belonged to Earl, and it was there as an emergency shelter, good enough to look after anyone in need for a day, or so I was told. It was a good target to aim for.

The trail led through fairly open woodland, and the theme for the day was steady climbs. The trail was soft and the going fairly hard, but at least I was keeping warm. The trail would undulate in parts, but the average was definitely up. I was feeling physically refreshed from my stay at the creek, and knew I could expect a fairly short day today, even with the slow trail and long climb.

There were trail markers, which were always a reassuring sight, even though there were not offshoots from the main trail to confuse my navigation. It felt good to be heading up into the mountains again. As fast as the river was for progress, the higher ground would be warmer, and the views of the land far more impressive. Not that I had any complaints about the river, of course, other than that it had tried to kill me, and had made me look like an arse on at least two occasions; first through exhaustion in deep snow, and second through frostbite. I console myself it was being sporting rather than malicious.

As the trail took me higher, so there were patches where it had been blown-in, making the going harder. Still, I was being rewarded for my efforts by the most magnificent views. I was surrounded by mountains as far as I could see, and, although they were relatively low (around 1000 metres or so), they nevertheless looked wonderful, captivating, and a rare privilege to be amongst.

There were a few clouds to be seen, but mostly there was a joyously blue sky. Winds would pick up around the occasional bend in the trail, but, overall, the temperatures were mild and I enjoyed good progress. With the clean, fresh air, the blue sky and the glistening snow, working my way up that mountain felt immeasurably good. I was feeling positive and confident again, and experiencing a deep happiness with myself and the world around me.

At some point today I would pass the halfway point of this year's Quest route. The temperatures were set to rise for a week, beyond which I knew not what they would do. Perhaps that week would be enough to take the fingers out of Harm's way entirely, permitting me to safely continue?

This was not simply a matter of bravado or ambition. I adored the section of trail between Dawson City and Pelly Farm. The trail would take me over King Solomon's Dome and amongst the Black Hills, through active gold mining areas, and to Scroggie Creek cabin. I have very fond memories of this section of trail, and it would be a shame to miss out. I love the family at Pelly Farm, and would regret not seeing them.

From the farm it would be easy river (if the trail was not rerouted along the mountain road) to Pelly Crossing, and gentle undulations to McCabe Creek, beyond which was a long woodland slog to Carmacks. From Carmacks the route featured chain lakes to Braeburn, and from Braeburn less than 100 miles to the finish line, through yet more astonishingly beautiful, open landscapes, and short sections of closed woodlands. My mind raced over the trails beyond my vision, as I imagined moving swiftly along the familiar route.

Most of all though, it was that initial section to Pelly Farm that I was interested in, and, if I made it there, I would be almost three-quarters of the way to the finish, so might as well continue. As much as there would be relief to end the hardships upon arrival in Dawson, I was in my element out here, and disliked the thought of the journey coming to an end at all, let alone when there was still so much wonderful trail to enjoy.

As the trail led around a bend to the right, so I saw another track heading-off to my left. The mountain that track led around was a beautiful sight, and from here I could certainly enjoy the view, even if not approach it, without a substantial detour. This was a mining road coming away from my own route. It always felt surprising to see road signs out here, in the middle of a remote winter mountain landscape.

As my route proceeded to the right, so I encountered deep snow. In places the trail hid beneath snowdrifts more than a metre deep. Only the top few centimetres of the markers were visible. Often, the depth of snow was less off the trail than on it. Once more I was grateful for the buoyancy of my snowshoes.

It was a slog through the soft, deep trail. By the afternoon, most of the climbing was complete, and I was working my way around a ridge at about 1000 metres. I could see the line of the highway for kilometres ahead, as it skirted mountaintops, disappearing behind some, and then reappearing in front of others. I was trying to ascertain the highest point, to gain some indication of where the trailer would be. The ridge was exposed far-off into the distance, with trees very short, few, and far between, and woodland-proper much lower down.

I rounded a bend and saw a flat space ahead, which I took to be a parking area during the summer, either as a viewpoint or simply for the sake of having a rest area. The trailer was positioned in the centre of it. From the outside I could see this was a standard, small trailer, maybe a few metres long, a couple of metres across, and a couple of metres high. There was a door somewhat less than the usual height. Looking from the front, on the right side towards the top was a small window, currently covered with what looked to be corrugated aluminium. The exterior walls were all corrugated metal, shining brightly in the deep blue evening light.

I deharnessed and headed within. To my immediate left was a homemade wood stove, fashioned from a propane cylinder. Suspended from the ceiling above the stove was a mesh, used as a drying and storage area, with a few pots and pans on it. In the centre of the opposite wall was a small worktop. On this was a gas stove, and some plastic containers with cookies, sachets of hot chocolate, and other goodies. Hanging from the wall was a battery-powered lantern. Wood was stacked-up for the stove, and there was enough for a week up here.

Against that opposite wall was a raised bed area; a little wider than a standard single bed, if a little shorter. There was a pillow, a mattress, blankets and a sleeping bag. Beneath this were a couple of boxes, one with newspapers, and the other with freeze-dried meals. There was even a pair of slippers. Just below the ceiling on the opposite wall was a shelf containing a few books and magazines, some toilet paper and some kitchen roll. The walls were covered in plywood, and there were a few centimetres of insulating foam between this and the exterior wall. Along the walls, wooden strips had been placed with hanging points for clothing. It was an abode any chap-about-the-lumber-yard would have been proud to call his own.

I stepped outside the trailer, and raised the metal sheet covering the window, pinning the metal in place with a section of wood left by the door for that purpose. I got the stove going and it was warm inside in no time. I brought in my sleeping equipment, food and clothing, and set about devouring a few cookies and some hot chocolate, whilst cooking myself dinner. Earl had told me I was welcome to the freeze-dried meals, but I was happy with my own food, and prepared one of my classic stews, making use of a sachet of gravy I was carrying around with me from an earlier cabin.

I was staggered with the brilliance of the trailer. Outside the wind had picked-up, and was now battering the trailer's exterior, as the sun began to set. Inside was a haven of warmth, and a protection from the elements. It was a small – but perfectly-formed – sanctuary, offering additional and unexpected luxuries, in an already blissful world. I was astonished by it. I was only sorry Earl was not around for me to thank directly, for having the kindness to provide and stock such a generous facility.

I flicked through the hunting magazines, and soon gave up all hope for humanity, so decided to listen to some music instead. I was now carrying the iPod with a similar attitude to that of Tom Hanks with that one FedEx box he had to deliver in *Castaway*. I would carry it into the Yukon Quest office in Whitehorse, when I reached there, however I did so.

I was uninspired by the music collection, and soon again gave up all hope for humanity. I tried and I mostly hated the whole experience of listening to music. I was so used to the absence of sound, or exclusively the sound of the wind or the occasional raven, that it was distracting, and even overwhelming, to have a head full of music.

Indeed, I far preferred the sound of the wind buffeting against the outside of the trailer, the occasional howl of a high gust, and the warming comfort of the crackling wood stove. I felt a part of the world out here; immersed within it. By injecting the music into my ears, I was transported away from this land, and into the world I had chosen to leave behind, with all its materialism, distractions, and detachment from the real world; this natural world. Overall, I could happily leave the modern world far behind for this one. Coldplay, in particular, could do one.

Clinton Creek to Earl's Trailer

I struggled to sleep that night, but only because I had gotten too much heat built-up from the stove. I spent close to an hour trying to get it right, with the stove full but turned-down, and the door pinned open. Once the fire had burned down a little, I would just have to keep it going through the night, and it would stay warm enough. Tomorrow I should have about 50 kilometres, or less, remaining to Dawson. *I drifted away into an incredibly warm and cosy night's sleep, with dreams of the mushers...*

Chapter 18.
Earl's Trailer to Dawson City

The wind raged relentlessly. It was an assault to my senses, as it howled so loudly into my hood it was almost deafening, and all the while my face was being pelted by snow and ice crystals, scraping and tearing at my skin. A fierce blizzard turned the ground into a restless sea of blowing snow, flowing in waves over the sastrugi; obscuring clear view of the trail beneath.

The dogs at the front of the team were consumed by the waves of wind and snow, but they directed the rest of us through, somehow. All 14 dogs had awful diarrhoea, which had impacted their energy and speed for almost a week. I had to stop several times a day, just to feed and rehydrate them, so they had something fresh to blast out into the shitstream, during the subsequent couple of hours.

I was red lantern, again. The thought of just quitting was a constant, depressing, and disillusioning plague on my mind. At least then I could get the dogs home, so I could smell a scented candle for a change to this assault. The air smells so thick from their stench that I gag several times a minute. The soft snow and slow trail are worsening everything, as the dogs work harder than ever, then their guts let rip.

The mountain looms menacingly ahead of us through the blizzard. I cannot imagine getting through this. I have already been suffering more than at any other point in my entire life, and that mountain, with its treacherous crevasses, its glare ice, and its exposed scree, can make it lethal on a good day.

This was as far from a good day as it was possible to be, and a cold night would be upon us long before we could ever reach the summit. Nothing outside of war-time can be worse than this hell. I needed something to help me through.

I frantically take out my iPod and put in my sports-fit earphones. I try hard to ignore the hell around me, just focusing on the music for a couple of minutes. I suddenly cry-out in acute anguish and pain, as Coldplay makes me reflectively wretch then vomit more than those shitting dogs ever could. I am almost in tears of pain, letting out an agonised but pathetic howl, sounding like it came from a lone, geriatric wolf, trying to shit a hedgehog. Unable to take this fresh hell any longer, I pull-out the earphones and pointedly hurl my iPod onto the trail behind me.

My experience of the world now reset, I gaze upon my surroundings with fresh eyes and mind. Coldplay has reliably done its work. The present, living reality of the foul weather, the dogs, the trail and that mountain are a gift of life to me now, and I feel fully rejuvenated and equal to the tasks ahead of me. The thought of finishing this race has been turned from a nightmare into a dream. Maybe next year, when returning to this trail, and these predictable nightmare scenarios, I might similarly trust in James Blunt, to motivate and inspire me through the worst of it.

Stepping out of Earl's trailer in the morning, I spent a few minutes photographing the sunrise. Reflecting directly afterwards that these were not going to win me any National Geographic landscape awards, I returned to the trailer. The next task was to get my stove going, to melt snow for my day's drinking water. If I had a fast trail today, I could head down into Dawson tonight, but judging by progress so far, it was more likely I would camp somewhere just before it. Sandy had told me it was an undulating trail for about 30 kilometres, followed by a fast 15 kilometre descent into Dawson. I would soon find out. The trailer was a little less than a kilometre from the highest point on the Highway.

I breakfasted and headed outside. The propane-bottle stove was out when I left, and I dropped the window shutter down. I harnessed-up and headed-on. The wind was blowing in my face, but was not cold enough to be a concern, beyond what it was doing to the trail.

I passed a road junction, which struck me as odd, as I appeared to be in the middle of nowhere, but this was the point the trail up from Fortymile joined onto the highway from Eagle. The wind was blowing waving lines of fine snow just above the ground, which looked beautiful and quite captivating. I paused for a moment to watch it. No need to rush a pleasing experience, after all.

My gaze transferred across to where the route would take me; arcing around to my left, just below the top of a long ridgeline. Falling away to my left was a deep valley, all hidden from the rest of the world, and encased in deep snow, with trees scattered sparingly across it. The conditions were good, albeit with the wind a little disconcerting, and I felt entirely alone and at peace. I got stuck-in.

The trail was soft, with sidehill conditions from the snowdrift, creating patches where the trail could not be seen. As I progressed onwards in my snowshoes, so the way worsened, and I was no longer on the trail itself, but uphill of it. My route was along a highway, but any evidence of a major road was imperceptible.

Below the ridgeline, the wind had blown snow down to fill across the road, creating the sidehill I was now navigating across. I had to be uphill of the trail in parts, because the slope was sufficiently steep to cause my sled to slide downhill from me, and, in crossing snowdrifts, it was in danger of going off the trail and onto the steeper, softer slope below.

One good and surprising yank through the harness and I might have been dragged off with the sled, followed by adventures into all sorts of nameless terrors, dangers, calamities and general peril; and my limbs distributed in the snow across a wide area. By staying up above the trail, the passage was no worse, but the safety margin a little less marginal.

Up ahead, I could see I had only a few hundred metres before the way flattened-out again, as it turned a bend, offering protection from the winds. I was not free from danger just yet though. Where the snowdrifts had built up, so there were additional lumps and lines, much like sastrugi, or miniature dunes. On occasion, the sled would not only slide downwards but would turn over too, much like it had when traversing Eagle Summit. Each time I had to remove the harness was time I was not progressing forward, getting closer to the good trail ahead, and dropping out of the wind.

Each time I ceased to be attached to the sled, there was a risk of a gust of wind snatching it away from me, and hurling it down the mountainside. Sometimes, I would only make a few metres before the sled went over again. It was hugely frustrating, but there was nothing that could be done. I could even see when it was likely to happen, but was powerless to prevent the infuriating acrobatics. A few metres further on, and again the sled slides down the mountainside, with the wind flinging it over. Deharness, trudge back to the sled through the deep snow, right it, return to the harness, and repeat.

In one spot, now less than 50 metres from the good trail, the sled went over yet again, and here the snow had set to such a steep angle, continuing over the side of the mountain, that the risks of losing the sled were greatest. As I righted the sled, so it began to move off, leaving me to throw myself over the top and arrest the slide. I was tired from my efforts and frustrated. Now suddenly there was a real risk I was going to lose the sled down the steep slope, into the frozen valley far below.

As I knelt in the snow, leaning over my pulk, the relentless wind whipped-up ice crystals, scratching and tearing at my face. Was the wind planning to push me down the slope with my sled? I was secure while I was not moving, but the sled was trying to slide free, and all the while the wind howled, and the ice crystals battered my face. The treacherous winds caused a ground blizzard, which I was now firmly subjected to, and my vision in either direction was obscured by the raging snow.

The situation got the better of me. I shouted out and swore as loudly as I could, partly to feel better for doing so, and partly to get some adrenaline on my side. My knees were buried deep into the soft snow at the side of my sled, with my body lying across it, and I had to move myself sideways, a few centimetres at a time, moving slowly on my knees towards the good trail.

With perhaps 30 metres remaining I dared to get off my knees and stand, and, using the plastic conduit that protected the ropes, I pushed the sled along instead of pulling it; walking at the side to push it back onto the main trail under some sort of control. My progress had been too slow and careful for me to be overly tired from my efforts. Still, I looked back across at the trailer, realising it had taken more than an hour to accomplish scarcely a kilometre-and-a-half. I momentarily reflected on that hour, where the situation had deteriorated from bad to appalling, to nearly ending me. I shrugged reflectively, as I consoled myself it was probably just going to be one of those days. One has experiences.

Sidehills and snowdrifts continued, but were nowhere near as bad. Where the trail looked firm, I removed my snowshoes to give myself a rest from their weight and inconvenience, only to be further annoyed and frustrated at the time lost in removing them, then having to replace them soon after, whenever I realised how deceptively soft the trail actually was.

I arrived at a distance marker, which also confirmed my lack of progress from the trailer. The distance markers were now in kilometres, spaced two kilometres apart. The trail remained high, still undulating at around 1000 metres, and continued to be soft for another hour or so of work. When the trail hardened, I was relieved to be out of snowshoes, and attempted to maintain a good pace without them, even where it softened again.

I reflected that, despite the moments of exquisite terror and abject hellishness on the trail, they were a fair price to pay for the privilege of experiencing this pristine, icy paradise, alone in the mountains. I accept there are those who think more warmly of a quiet beach on a sunny day, caressed by crystalline waters, but I have tired of such places in a matter of hours, whereas here I have not grown tired in weeks. I have the ongoing concern of my healing fingertips, and every day I must work against overuse injuries at the first sign of a flirting niggle, but I am persevering in my own private heaven.

The day was the perfection of a winter's day in the mountains. The sky was perfectly blue, the air now cool and still, and the views outstanding. Indeed, these were beyond doubt the most beautiful scenes I have witnessed anywhere along the Quest route, which is itself the most beautiful trail I have ever experienced. I felt most privileged to be here this year, when we had the re-route.

I walk, I think, I ponder, and I sing to myself, very, very badly. I am in my heaven and I am loving it. I gaze all around me at the mountains near and far, and here am I at the top of it all. I reflect on the good friends and family members who might enjoy these moments with me – not the singing of course – my singing is the sort of thing Dante was grateful he never had to endure. I pause to take photographs, and I relax upon my sled to take breaks every few hours. Progress improves dramatically after the extremely slow start, and I am confident I will see the lights of Dawson, as I stop tonight, to sleep.

* * * * * * *

I was feeling good about the world. My fingertips were on the mend, and I had trifled with some extremely offensive trail conditions without disaster. I was now confident I could take my two days' rest in Dawson City, and should attempt to continue on to Takhini. Granted, I would be viewing the weather forecasts, and having doubts if I thought there was too much peril afoot, but I suspected I was now racing the coming of spring; so warm it was set to become.

In the early evening I looked out towards a mountain range, where I believed I could see King Solomon's Dome, and I wondered if I might be up there for a sunset. I have been up there for a nocturnal bitch of a blizzard, one sunset and one twilight. As it is around 50 kilometres (30 miles) outside of Dawson, and all uphill, I would be struggling to get up there whilst there was still light, but it was a good objective to have. A chap could dream.

Further on and the number of snowmobile tracks increased. These were not only the tracks of trappers, of whom there were only ever one or two, but of folk out here riding recreationally. I passed a small mining area where the tracks proliferated. I was getting close to town now. The distance was greater than what I had anticipated. Considering the beauty of the Top of the World highway, I would have been happy with plenty more kilometres to pass.

I arrived at a point where the trail continued, but the road had been ploughed adjacent to it, revealing spots of dirt and grit. The ploughed road was mostly faster, as it was down to the ice, whereas the trail was soft snow, but to travel the road meant to encounter materials that could damage the sled. I risked it and danced around the stones and grit as best I could, eventually surrendering to the less risky, safer, softer trail instead.

A rest area revealed itself to me where there was a campground, although not operating at this time of year. The descent into Dawson City had begun now, and far off I could see a few lights. There were also the red beacons on some of the mountaintops; a familiar sight during my nighttime descents from The Dome.

Adjacent to the rest area was a wooden structure, in the spirit of the goldrush shop fronts, and beneath a sheltering roof was tourist information, including a map and details of ferry crossings. The area was protected by three walls; the fourth side being open. This was here to be of some amusement when the campground and road were fully opened. I reached the structure by clambering over a snowbank, after which I set my tent up on the wooden floor in the middle, and settled-in to sleep. I was as good as in Dawson City now, and two days of rest would be my reward. It was still a long way to Takhini.

* * * * * * *

Packing everything away the next morning was, with me, the work of a moment. Another moment and I had charged up and over the metre-high snowbank, and back out onto the road. It was a long and winding road, but it was downhill, and easy kilometres towards Dawson. At the side of the road were adverts on billboards, or miniature cabin-fronts and similar, advertising hotels and businesses in town. All carried the same goldrush theme.

As the trail took me around a bend, I came into view of Dawson, and, even though the sky was overcast, dull and grey, the colours of the buildings in town looked magnificent. She was a delightful sight to behold, with the Yukon River frozen before her, and the frozen Klondike River wrapped curvaceously around her side. Soon I passed an area where signs stated the road behind me was closed, like bookends mirroring those I had passed on leaving Eagle, now so many days before.

The road was ploughed here entirely, and I took to the pavement as vehicles came to pass me by. There were residential areas here, and a golf course, and I was passed by at least four cars. I waved to the drivers and they waved to me. At the base of the road there was a closed campground to my left, and a small parking area to my right. The road continued onto the river, where an ice road led across to central Dawson City herself.

It was at this point that I was ambushed by Harvey; a dog musher who wanted to share tales, ask thoughtful questions, and offer valuable advice. For example, he informed me the road up King Solomon's Dome was ploughed now, which would risk the integrity of my sled, but the injuries could be avoided by constructing new runners from willow.

I saw in Harvey an older brother; there to look after me and shape me into the man I thought I knew I could be. However, there comes a time when a chap must step away from the loving care of a doting elder sibling, and make what he can of himself alone. In this instant, for example, what I really wanted to do was cross the river and get to my lodgings for the next two nights – I was being beckoned by promises of a hot shower, the attractive flirtations of a soft bed, the majestic call of a bison burger, the seductive whisper of Yukon beer, and the siren song of hotel laundry services.

I had endured and enjoyed approximately 885 kilometres (550 miles) of long slogging to reach this point, yet I could not fully relax and accept my success until the harness was off, and I was relaxing in my room in the Downtown Hotel.

From where I now stood, I could just about lob a brick through the hotel window. I let Harvey know I would be thrilled to catch-up with him later on in the bar, over an invigorating and reflective beer, and I struck out across the river, along a trail adjacent to the road, over some jumble ice, and into my hotel.

Chapter 19.
Dawson City

Soaking myself in a hot bath was blissful, although, upon reflection, the bathtub itself may have held different views. I could discern as much by the look the overflow hole was giving me, as I scraped-off so much smelly grime and filth. I did not linger to the point of shrivelling, but the bath felt like a good break and mental reset, just the same.

I had shot a glance in a mirror, and not been impressed with the sight of the withered wraith which I detected looking gormlessly back at me. I was exhibiting myself as a shadow of my former self. And still, Takhini remained a long way off. I took immediate steps to address this calamity, with gluttony.

Later on, I capitalised on the hotel's laundry facilities to wash my clothes, and was mocked by Harvey and other friendly folk, for sitting around wearing waterproofs indoors. Having such a minimalist and select wardrobe, these were my only options, whilst every other item of clothing I had was cleaned-up. The consensus from others was that they had all been there, and, as much as it was always entertaining to see and to mock, it was also a common practice for many in these parts.

I went for a walk around town, which brought back warm and fuzzy memories from previous trips, and I revelled in it all. Dawson City was so often the place where my journeys were naturally concluded, and so it was almost the case once again with this one. I had now seen all of the Quest trail, but, with a promising fingertip recovery, and with warming temperatures, I was beginning to feel equal to the task of seeing this expedition through to the very end.

I bought some snacks to enjoy in the room, from a small supermarket nearby, formally sorted out my entry across the border into Canada, and I relaxed for the afternoon. In the evening I ate well and drank a little. A bison burger, and a couple of refreshing Yukon Brewing beers, were very much the order of the day, in the Downtown Hotel's 'Sourdough Saloon'.

I made friends with some staff and visitors. I brought delight to the lives of a couple on holiday from Vancouver; Zac and Mirtha, when the former asked what songs had been going through my head, and I informed him it was, by now, mostly Flight of the Conchords. He found this news hilarious and joyously unexpected. They ordered some food, which looked delicious, and I ordered a plate of what they were having. I later walked them back across the river, to where the sky was less polluted by the lights of Dawson, and where they stood a chance of seeing some aurora, should it make an appearance.

* * * * * * *

I treated myself to a couple of breakfasts the next morning, before heading off for another jaunt around town. I wanted to take some photographs, but, most importantly, to check the river, to see it was safe and that there was a trail. Although I could not spot trail markers, there was a clear track, and that was enough. I headed to the library to send some emails and make some WhatsApp calls. I informed various contacts that the weather forecast looked good enough, for the next 10 days, for me to be continuing on. As it happened, the temperatures were set to go above freezing in the middle of some days.

I visited the local parks service offices, chatted with the staff for a while, and got the number of John 'Mitch' Mitchell, who had co-ordinated the rangers who put in the Quest trail on the Canadian side. He confirmed the finish at Takhini, and that the trail from Pelly Ranch to Pelly Crossing led along the mountain road and not the river. This generally meant a slower pace than along the flat river, but if conditions were against a river trail, so be it. I have had nightmare experiences along the Pelly River in the past. I was told that markers were not due to be taken-up any time soon, and that, where they were absent, it would remain the only packed trail available.

My day was spent relaxing, eating and chatting with folk, including Harvey and another new friend, Rod. That evening, in the bar, I was compelled to declare some classic words to the barkeep: "I suppose it's about time for me to have a Yukon Jack. And stick a toe in it".

The history behind the Sourtoe Cocktail is that, once, a chap dared another chap to take a shot of his drink, containing an amputated, frostbitten toe. This then became 'a thing', with people sending in their own amputated toes, which are kept in salt and brought out for the ridiculous game. As the bar staff asserted, "You can drink it fast, or drink it slow, but your lips must touch the toe."

This particular toe once belonged to a Norwegian woman, who had suffered an unfortunate lawn-mowing accident. I have done 'The Toe' once before, but it seemed wrong to pass through on such an auspicious occasion, without doing it again. Another bison burger and beer later and I turned in for a fairly early night.

It was a curious feeling to be in a hotel room, with the obvious comforts of a proper toilet, a shower, a television, central heating and a vast double bed, bedecked with a smorgasbord of pillows. I slept well but really I longed for the trail. The Quest mushers and their teams get a minimum of 36 hours of rest here, and I had decided that I could honour that before moving on. I had lost a considerable amount of weight, and wanted to top-up as much as I could, before attempting the next 700 km (430 miles), or thereabouts, to the end.

* * * * * * *

Breakfast in the Downtown Hotel took a surprising turn the next morning. Adhering to my usual tradition in public spaces, I latibulated in the furthest, most tranquil and secluded spot, steadily combobulating over my jentacular nourishment, when Brian Wilmhurt – Quest musher – hove into view. I put down the dictionary, loosed my moorings, and bestrutted over to grace him with my presence.

Brian and I had actually met the year before at Scroggie Creek, not that I expected him to remember this. I feigned apology for the disruption to his companions, as I proceeded to pump Brian thoroughly for information, on whether or not he had been up on the Dome recently, and/or if he could provide intelligence on what conditions were like.

At this point, one of the other chaps – armed with an offensively British accent – enquired as to whether or not I was the chap hiking the Quest trail. I conceded thus, and was promptly introduced to Tim Oakley, The Kiwi Graham Burke, their guide Wayne Hall, and a local imbecile, toward whom I bare no ill will, beyond that which was entirely deserved.

This was the 'In Amundsen's Footsteps' expedition team, who had visited Eagle before me, and who Earl was support for. How wonderfully fortuitous! Tim invited me to take a seat with them. I pulled-up an inviting pew and we chatted over our journeys. These chaps were debating whether to leave today or tomorrow to reach Eagle Plains, beyond which the highway was closed, but might reopen by the time they reached it. They needed to get themselves, and their three dog teams and kit, up to Herschel Island to begin their 1130 km (700 mile) journey.

It was moments later that the local chap, the fatuous git, encouraged me to hope it would not get down to 40 below, because my feet would fall off. Until this moment I had hoped that, now in civilisation proper, I would not encounter the mindlessness and imbecility which had plagued my nerves previously on this trip. From Hope there now issued forth a strangulated cough, immediately followed by its unfortunate asphyxiation and violent death.

Sitting despondently in the wreckage of my Hopes and Dreams, my eyes glazed over and I adopted a lifeless demeanour. I fixed the feckless arse with a look of incredulity, which was naturally lost on him, and he persisted with his mission of infuriating me. I listened to his words without resorting to immediately chastising him, and instead allowed my mind to wander, transporting me elsewhere, into a dream of all the ways I would happily see this irritating blight tortured, ideally by those hard-working and dedicated folk in the special forces, or raccoons.

How could someone live up here, I pondered, seeing all they saw, year after year, and still imagine theirs was the only way of doing things? How can they be so instinctively opposed to the concept that there are alternatives, and so convinced that anyone who does anything differently to themselves must have no experience, and is therefore doomed to instant defeat? What a complete git.

I took a deep breath, committed my soul and sanity to the winds, and embarked upon an extremely tiresome charade. I explained to the village idiot that trail shoes are just fine, even below -50C, and they are very much what the hundreds of foot racers wear for their events up here, and always have done, with cold injuries to the feet being extremely uncommon. I gave an example that Brian was familiar with – that Yukon Quest in 2011, when we had temperatures fluctuating from -40C to -55C, between the Pelly River and Dawson City – where absolutely none of our feet fell off.

Faced with the prospect he had been mistaken, the ignoramus retreated to within the deepest, farthest reaches of his mothballed mind and found inspiration – proving clearly that the lights might be on, but only because someone had forgotten to turn them off, when leaving the building ahead of its dereliction – and he retold the tale of a German chap who had passed through Mike Sager's cabin some years ago, also in 'tennis shoes', and how shocked Mike had been about this.

The moronic waste of oxygen proceeded to laugh at his own comment, as if he was the authority figure on fast and light sled-hauling. I halted him in his tracks, assuring him that Joachim completed his journey from Two Rivers to Whitehorse safe and well, and that most of the rest of us do just fine too. Of course, it should not have been necessary to allude to this, considering how far Joachim had travelled to reach that point.

Then, of course, there was myself, and I had travelled close to 1000 km on the trip to this point already. How could someone fail so remarkably at processing the evidence of his own eyes, such was the severity of this cognitive dissonance? One day this chap will die and be buried, after which his cells will decompose and fertilise the soil and the plant life above, meaning that his mind will literally become the vegetable it is already yearning to be.

It was at this moment, when I was suddenly overcome with a profound respect and admiration for all those brave and daring heroes who have ever initiated pub fights. I am far from a violent man by nature, but I was absolutely certain that nobody could possibly be reproached if they were to break a beech chair over this cretin's head, or bean the fathead with a well-intentioned whisky bottle. Indeed, I am sure it would be doing him a great service, from which his reality might be altered, and a more philosophical, reasonable individual would be reborn from the carcass of his old, absurd self. I have no reason to doubt this is the result of all good, honest, fair, bar room brawls.

I decided to attempt a different approach with the local excrescence. After all, the aim of argument should not be victory, but progress (hat tip to Karl Popper). I pointed-out his giant clumpy boots, and suggested how nobody could get very far hauling a sled in the snow wearing those, which he seemed to understand. I could see he was catching on so I decided to stretch him further.

I explained that the risk of cold injuries was greater because of the time taken for feet to warm-up when wearing movement-restricting clumpy boots, compared with something quite light and flexible. Shoes like mine permitted me to move fairly fast for big distances, and the movement kept my feet warm. Because I was moving. If I was going to be standing around in the snow, big clumpy boots were a good option, but for sled-hauling they were not.

At last there was a quiver of hope, as the faintest spark of understanding flickered for a moment, doubtlessly in some previously unexplored region of his mind. He was all at once struck by an idea – which I naturally put down to beginner's luck – and he asked me what was the brand of shoes I was wearing. I explained that these were Salomon, but that that was not really my point. These were excellent trail shoes with an appropriate sole, and these were the sort of thing everyone else wore for the races, there being many other brands that can be similarly employed. He seemed to surrender his former position and acquiesce.

Anyway, all this proves was that, armed with my superior intellect and debating skills, I can win battles of wits against unarmed assailants all day long, but there is really not much sport in it. I can only take meagre pride in the triumph. In terms of sporting satisfaction, it is up there with shooting fish in a barrel, if they were really very big fish indeed, and if beforehand you drained all the water out of the barrel, and despatched the remains with a machine gun. Admittedly, I had not expected this journey to present me with such a target-rich environment, but one strives to learn new things daily.

With our meeting of the minds session now concluded, I made a move back to my own table, following a momentary pause to bestow an Englishman's curse upon him. I ruminated over our intercourse during my breakfast, back at my own, very sensible table.

Not long after, secluded back in my room, I prepared my equipment for leaving. I sent out an email, letting people know the condition of my fingertips had improved considerably, and, with warmer temperatures ahead, I had no real concerns about not making it to the finish. I emailed the Kruse family at McCabe Creek, to let them know I would pass through in about a week's time.

With this administration accomplished, I set myself another task. I took a pair of scissors to some baselayer leggings, and cut them into shorts. With rising temperatures, I had no need for a full baselayer during most of the day. When the night-time temperature drops, I will not be likely to strip down and pull on a baselayer. With much assertiveness and bravado, I had told myself that my legs were permitted to get a little cold at night, and this was entirely manageable. I could not, however, make the same bold claims regarding the collection of dangly objects, nestled adoringly between my legs. I have suffered mild frostbite in that region once before in my life, and that was once too often. A repeat would be to flirt with accusations of perversion.

I was a little sad to be leaving Dawson City. For three races it was the end point; a sign that some remarkable feat had been accomplished. Now it was scarcely over the halfway point. The trail behind had been all new to me, and what an adventure it had been! Despite the hardships, that reroute over the Top of the World highway had been a real privilege to me, amongst several hundred kilometres or so of other privileges.

What remained was familiar trail. I have raced it three times, supported events along it, and journeyed through sections of it multiple times on snowmobile. There is a section between Pelly Crossing and Pelly Farm that I have driven a tractor along. All this familiarity was a comfort to me. The trail and conditions are different every time. When I travelled on foot during the races, I was generally aware of conditions worsening with the journey north, whereas now I was headed south, towards an early spring, according to the forecasts. I harnessed-up as Rod took a couple of photos, then he walked alongside me to the end of the road, to see me off on my way.

After a couple of hundred metres, I took a route down onto the Yukon River, and soon after took a left onto the Klondike River. It was a bright, sunny day, and it felt warm. The snow was glistening in the sunlight, and I was feeling the familiar sensation of the pulk bouncing easily along behind me, atop the frozen river. Soon after I arrived at the Klondike Highway's bridge; a familiar sight, and the point where the trail took me up off the river, where it paralleled the road for a while.

Along the side of the Klondike Highway the local businesses are mostly motels, RV parks and fuel stations. I took a right turn onto Bonanza Creek Road, sticking to the left hand side as a couple of cars passed. It is a very gentle slope, and it will be a long, 40 km (25 mile) slog to the summit of King Solomon's Dome.

Chapter 20.
Dawson to King Solomon's Dome

Anyone who has read about the history of the Klondike gold rush will be familiar with Bonanza Creek, and, for me, this is as much an expedition along a trail, as it is a journey back through time; to a harsher period, as recounted in writings from Pierre Burton back to Robert Service, with a nod to Jack London and so many brilliant others. My mind swims with it all as I go. I am carrying *The Law of the Yukon*, *The Spell of the Yukon*, and other Service poems with me, printed out on a couple of A4 pages, tucked away with my map and route description.

> *It's the great, big, broad land 'way up yonder,*
> *It's the forests where silence has lease;*
> *It's the beauty that thrills me with wonder,*
> *It's the stillness that fills me with peace.*

I move on up the road, alone and making distance from Dawson, and into the mountains for the last time. This is usually a fairly active area, with mines at various points along the roadside. The road was ploughed, but there was still plenty of snow and ice on the surface, so no danger to the sled's hull. Rod drove past and jumped out to take a couple more photos, then headed back into town, having wished me well on my way.

I had enjoyed spending time with Rod, and with his wife, who worked at the Downtown hotel. I reflected on how pleasant it is to meet good people on a journey such as this. Mine had only been a fleeting visit to Dawson, but I had benefitted so much from it; the inspiring walks around town, the chats with good, interesting people, and the chance to rest, reset, and to start-out refreshed, feeling fit and wearing clean underwear.

I pass 'Dredge number four'; the last wooden-hulled dredge in the world. It is an impressive sight; a relic of this region's rich history, built for operations out here in the gold mines, more than a hundred years ago. It is a perfect reminder of the Klondike goldrush, as I head up through the landscape of the gold fields. It will not be much longer before the gold mines reopen for this year's operations. The trail continues on, winding its way up a flank of The Dome.

A little further and I pause to sit on my sled and take a break. It is an incredibly hot day today, practically blistering, at around -5C (23F). I am wearing my baselayer top, with the water bladder over that, and the down vest to help protect it, but there is no need for my usual vapour-rise jacket as a midlayer. I will only grow hotter as I get stuck into the climb.

The trail takes me across a creek and along an unploughed mining road, far smaller than Bonanza Creek Road, and then onto just a single snowmobile track. The Quest markers are still here. Most importantly, despite the heat of the day, the trail feels fairly solid under foot, and I feel confident of a strong climb to the top of The Dome. My objective is to camp on the far side of it, if conditions allow. I had left Dawson in the direction of Whitehorse, I was making strong progress, and all was all right in my world.

My memories of past journeys came flooding back. Of course, with the races I was always heading from

Whitehorse into Dawson, so now the memories came to me in a sort of reverse order, as if I was Gandalf or Merlin. 'This was the spot where I changed my socks that night after falling through the overflow...this was the spot where I fell through the overflow...this was the spot where I wondered whether or not I might fall through the overflow', and that sort of thing. 'This is where I was charged by a moose...this is where I charged a wolverine' (because I did not know it was a wolverine, because I had been hallucinating and thought it was something entirely safe and innocuous).

I had only ever travelled this section of trail in the darkness, and it was a pleasant experience to savour it during the day. I could see cabins and mining areas that had been merely shadows before, or even entirely invisible to me. So it was that I wondered if some features were new, or if I had simply raced passed them, oblivious, in the past. Granted, I had always been heading downhill, not only in the dark but at racing pace, with a feather-light sled and an attitude that in Dawson City breakfast, rest and a hot shower awaited.

It was a pleasant slog up into the hills, and I would often look back from one hillside to a previous one, surprised that the slope appeared steeper than it had seemed during the climb itself. Such, I think, was a result of the well-packed trail. The lighter sled and my improving fitness offered some contributions too.

The overflow I encountered on the climb now, was worse than any I had encountered on any previous year in that area; the result of a relatively warm winter. Occasionally, I pulled on my NEOS overboots, to give me some protection in case I fell through, but mostly I just pushed on without issue. It all adds to the excitement of the winter trails.

I encountered a particularly forbidding section of overflow on the final part of climb. It was maybe 30 metres (33 yards) in length, and as wide as the relatively flat terrain. It was not possible to negotiate my way around it – the mountainside was far too steep for that at the edges of the overflow, especially with the sled in tow. The ice had frozen onto the slope ahead of me, so I would be going uphill on solid ice, angled slightly in line with a subtle slope sideways too.

I would have had an easier time crossing it if I had my microspikes, but, as I had probably used those for about 10 metres of ice out of so many thousands of kilometres in the past, I brought my lighter Yaktrax, which would not have been up to this. I hugged the side of the trail where the ice was less firm, with my feet punching through a centimetre or two. This gave me sufficient grip to make my way across, save for a section closer to the end, where I had to step out onto the solid ice.

It was always at least a little character-building to cross overflow, whether the risk was getting wet or getting hurt. Accordingly, there was always a palpable relief, each time I made it across without incident. Whenever an incident did occur, such as a slip or a wet foot, I breathed a sigh of relief that it was not worse. Wet feet would dry out soon enough, while I was making good progress, and before it got cold at night.

Now I was racing the setting sun. The views of neighbouring mountains were beautiful, but I hoped for even better scenes from the summit. It would be good to be at the top of a mountain with sufficient light to take a usable photograph for a change, as during previous visits this had not been possible.

The trail led around to my left, and I passed through a familiar area. This was a parking space and lookout point with a couple of outhouses. All was just snow now, of course, but the lie of the land made sense, even though all I had was my narrow trail, the two wooden outhouses, and flat land to the righthand side.

I recall on my first trip through, after being caught in blizzard conditions on the summit. I had been tempted to use an outhouse as a shelter, but when I stepped off the trail I was up past my waist in a snowdrift. I had rolled back onto the trail, and within moments I was on the descent and out of the hell on the top. Unlike then, today I had a quiet night ahead.

I was above timber now, and the trail undulated for some kilometres, as it wound its way around the summit. It was sunset as I passed the outhouses, and twilight as I passed over onto a ridge between two higher points. Darkness fell as the trail brought me around the summit proper. An hour before would have been perfect for sunset views across the mountain ranges, and off towards the Black Hills. There were occasional patches of sidehill and snowdrifts, but, overall, the conditions were as close to perfect as I have ever had them.

Suddenly, a bright white flash of light filled the entire black sky above me. I froze in shock. I knew it was not lightning, as the sky was mostly clear and no storm clouds were in sight. I looked back towards Dawson, but there was no sign of what caused the flash. I continued on, perplexed, cautious, and wondering if it would repeat. I was more than a little concerned the source of the flash may have been closer to me than the lower atmosphere, such as inside my own head. It remained a possibility. A shooting star was possible, but I have never experienced one so bright, and lighting up the whole sky before. I moved on, baffled.

A short downhill stint brought me to a junction, Sulphur Road, which had been ploughed. This meant no more trail markers, and the appearance of the road left me unsettled and uncertain of direction, as I was used to seeing only a single snowmobile track. The GPS confirmed I was headed the right way, and the feel of the road and sight of the valley to my left helped to bolster my confidence. I did have Memory here.

Having begun to recover from the first bright flash of light, I was now in view of a flickering amber light across on the far side of the valley. It seemed to shimmer around a small area, perhaps a mine, and I was captivated by the sight of it. It was so bright and so unfamiliar, so I gazed across as if at any moment a penny might drop, and I would realise what it was. No pennies dropped, alas, and I looked on, baffled yet again. The best I could suspect was that someone had gotten a fire going outside, but I was far from convinced.

Soon after this great mystery had begun, I was stunned to see another amber light appear on a distant ridge. It seemed to explode out of the darkness, sitting atop the ridge as if an inferno had broken out. I paused, amazed, to watch it as it spread-out and grew before my eyes. It must have taken fully 30 seconds from the point of first noticing it – baffled – to the point I realised I was gawping at a moonrise.

Granted, I have never seen a moonrise so spectacular: such a vivid colour, like fire, and so rapid a rise up into the sky. It gave me a feeling of ambivalence, which came from being entirely in awe and grateful for the moment; of witnessing this incredible sight, whilst concurrently feeling a total arse for being confused by what the moon looked like.

Negotiating the sled down from the summit was achieved with questionable dignity. There was much Hines-Sled pirouetting going on, as the sled often tried to overtake; a game at which it often succeeded. I regained the position of lead dancer as and when possible, just to get the look of the thing right. In patches, the road was ploughed down to the dirt, and this was now welcome as a means to slow the sled, and to help keep it in place.

I arrived at the base of the mountain without incident or catastrophe, crossed another patch of overflow, and continued to progress along ploughed road, the occasional sleeping gold mine lower in the valley to my right. I knew this route from the opposite direction, and even paused to look back at the Dome, nestled there in the moonlight, reliving moments during the races, when King Solomon's was the final obstacle before that long descent into Dawson City and the finish.

The total distance from Dawson City to Scroggie Creek is a little less than 170 kilometres (105 miles), with Indian River in-between. Scroggie Creek would be a welcome stopping point on my way to Pelly Ranch, with about 115 kilometres (71 miles) between them. Historically, when racing, it would be two days between

Scroggie Creek and Dawson City, following a day and a half between Pelly Ranch and Scroggie.

With my slower, non-racing pace, I was estimating three days to reach Scroggie, and at least two to reach the ranch after that. I passed a section of trail where I had once seen a beautiful bull moose (tan hide, brown socks), canter away from me, after we had embarrassed each other close by.

I made a few more kilometres, hiking into the early hours of the morning, to capitalise on faster progress along the firm trail in cooler conditions. Indeed, both Harvey and Rod had recommended I focus more on making progress at night now, on account of the warmer daytime temperatures.

I set up my camp at the side of the road, in a spot I considered safe from any snowmobiles or other traffic. Now the road had been ploughed to allow access to the mines, I did not know what to expect. Might vehicles start driving through at any moment? The next day I hoped to cross the Black Hills; the toughest section of trail on the Canadian side, although thankfully not so bad from this direction.

Chapter 21.
King Solomon's to Scroggie Creek

The next morning, any casual observer would have detected that it was with a sluggish pace that I marched along the road. Now treated to the advantage of daylight, I could see clearly the extent of how well the road had been ploughed. Indeed, in places it had been cleared right the way down to dirt and loose stones. The predicament this invited was that the road now tore at the base of my thin, plastic sled, like a lioness shredding a recently ambitious big game hunter, impatient to get at his soul. In patches the dirt was present for dozens of metres. I tried to avoid it where I could, by weaving along over less stony ground, to limit the carnage, but I suspected that, sooner or later, it would wear through.

If the sled did succumb to such damage, I would patch it up as best I could, but a sled with holes would not glide well, would generate more resistance, and would be at risk of falling apart entirely. Worst case scenario would be to improvise a sled out of Harvey's willow saplings, or whatever else presented itself as new runners and frame. I was not really kitted-out for spasms of DIY, but could probably manage to create something workable, should circumstances demand it. I truly hoped they might not.

Even without the holes, the presence of dirt on the trail created a considerable resistance. It seemed unfair that the trail was still finding ways to slow me down, even though the sled was now so much lighter than when I had first begun, thanks to so much food having since been consumed.

It was to be a close-run thing as to whether I had sufficient provisions to reach Takhini, but now I was approaching outbreaks of civilisation. I would be passing shops at Pelly Crossing and Carmacks, and I knew of a good place to eat a burger and pick up a cinnamon bun or two in Braeburn. These points were all less than 150 kilometres (93 miles) apart. I could restock if need be.

The trail led me through a built-up mining area, and without stakes I had a quandary regarding the trail. I had moved through this area from a couple of different directions over the years, and there was a good amount of snowmobile activity off the road. I continued along the road whilst checking this against my GPS route.

I knew the road stayed close to the hills that bordered the mine, and would take me to Indian River. The GPS was not entirely with me on this section, but it soon came back into agreement, once I was a little further along. These times were always fairly tense. Had I paused to think about it, I would have appreciated that any forks or deviations in the trail were not going to send me too far adrift, and I could always pull on the snowshoes to cut across to the main trail if a little off course.

When I reached Indian River – less than 10 kilometres (6 miles) before the start of the climb up Black Hills – I was stunned by the amount of mining machinery. I had always arrived at Indian River at night, but at least once left in the daylight, and never seen so much. As I crossed a bridge over the river my mind reflected on past visits here – always a great place to get to – a flat, cleared oasis in the middle of nowhere, between Black Hills and King Solomon's Dome.

The trail took me up, undulating for a little way, and I paused for a break with a view back over Indian River, and to the pretty hills that bordered upon it. My passage continued with some fairly short and sharp bumps, before I arrived at a steady climb up through a mining area. I recognised this as the mine that lies at the base of the Black Hills.

This area always reminds me of an Austrian racer, Klaus, who had a hallucination near here that a fellow racer, Andy, was encouraging him into his tent, to get warm and share a hot chocolate. Had Klaus been more immersed in this hallucination, he would have been sitting in the snow, drinking a hot chocolate that was not there, in a tent that did not exist, talking with an Englishman who had already arrived in Dawson City. I had suffered with the company of my own sleep monsters from time to time out here, but mostly towards the beginning of my northern career, and had experienced them little since.

There were several hundred metres of overflow through the mining area. It looked beautiful in the evening light; a matte pale blue in contrast to the pure white everywhere else. In some sections, the glaciated overflow lay in large ponds, extending over hundreds of square metres on both sides of the trail. In others, the overflow was confined to a few tens of metres along the trail itself. It was only at the final section, where the overflow looked frozen hard, that I managed to come a cropper and a foot went through a little. It would dry out soon enough. In the meantime, I enjoyed the privilege of something new to think about.

It was early evening when I began the main climb, and I was off the wretched ploughed roads and onto the welcoming snowy trail again. It was a committed climb, but not the nightmarish experience it is from the other side. As I climbed, I could see the ridge where I would end up, and I was enjoying getting through it.

There is something quite unreasonable about going over mountains and along high ridges in the winter, in the late evening or at night, in the sub-Arctic, which brings me a self-directed nod of acknowledgement, for being the oddball I have come to cherish, or, at the very least, to endure.

This would be the last big climb of the route. Granted, I still had a handful of hills before Pelly Ranch, but this was an intimidating climb, and I looked forward to succeeding on this one. The trail itself was fantastic. My impression was that, whilst the trail was fairly well-broken on the Alaskan side, on the Canadian side it was actually packed-down, making it as hard as a pavement, even with the warm conditions. This was a reflection I later learned was shared by the Quest mushers: The Quest is very much a race of two halves.

From up ahead, the noise of an approaching snowmobile filled the air, and I soon saw the light. The rider came to a stop to engage me in idle banter. He and one other had been recording animal trails around the Stewart River, and had been staying at the Scroggie Creek cabin for a few days.

These obscure hobbies that pass as careers out here really are quite irritating, when one considers how the rest of us toil hard at the coalface of open plan offices and the like, working long hours after the arthritic canaries have been invalided out, whilst the Yukoners simply muck about staring at animal prints. I have been looking at animal prints almost incessantly on my journey, and nobody is waiting in Takhini to hand me a cheque for my troubles. We continued on our ways, with the second merry snowmobile rider soon passing me by too.

I had hoped to reach the top of the climb in time for sunset, but once again I just missed it. Nevertheless, in the clear starlit sky it was beautiful; the snow reflecting the light, and the visibility still good for many kilometres all around.

I was pleased the conditions were calm atop the ridge. This is a formidable section of Quest trail, not only because of the brutal climb from the south side (and fairly committed climb from the north), but because of the amount of time exposed on the high, long and winding ridge, before beginning the descent. I had forgotten how many kilometres it was, and, with my slower pace, it seemed to drag-on more than far enough.

I was heading towards the rising Orion constellation, then it moved behind me. I wove around the hilltops at around 1000 metres altitude, at times feeling that I was doubling-back on myself. It seemed like a horseshoe ridge, and I wondered whether it fully connected further along, and I would find myself going around in circles, or heading back towards Dawson. The tired mind plays these little tricks on itself, mostly just to pass the time of day.

There was a flash of light above, albeit on a smaller scale than when I crossed The Dome. It was a shooting star, striking across the sky. I have seen dozens of shooting stars in my life, and many on this trip, but I have never seen the white flash fill the sky before, and now I saw it on two consecutive nights.

This meteor was so large that it visibly split as it entered the atmosphere, with the main body continuing its white streak before disappearing, and the section broken-off fading momentarily, as it entered a higher trajectory, then coming through and burning up close to the parent rock. A peculiar occurrence indeed, but at least I felt my mind was in the clear about the white flash the night before, and on this count if no other. I spotted two shooting stars tonight.

As I progressed around the hilltops, so a wisp of green could be seen, where the aurora was just beginning a warm-up for its night-time performance. The show was building its efforts far to the north, giving the illusion it was rising up from the ground beyond the mountains, stretching closer towards me, and billowing out across the sky, from right to left, as I watched it. As I walked, so I gazed across at the lights. The constellations, the full moon, the aurora, and a gentle breeze, all ensuring this was an exceptionally pleasant jaunt along the ridge. Winter in the Yukon wilderness never ceases to impress me, lifting my heart and buoying my mind.

I was on the top for hours, heading along the trail, and wondering when it would ever begin its descent. As much as I enjoyed being up here, I enjoyed progress, too, and yearned to be further along the trail, closer to Scroggie Creek.

I was betrayed by the occasional short descent, which later turned to an ascent that brought me up onto the next hilltop. The going was not unkindly arduous, but it was long. There were patches of snowdrift and soft trail, but mostly all was fine.

When the descent proper did begin, I enjoyed a fast pace around a series of switchbacks, having to drive the sled into the snowbank to slow it down, in an effort to keep it behind me. I knew the views to be spectacular in the daylight, and even the metallic appearance of the slopes in the moonlight was enchanting.

I camped fairly high on the main descent; a relatively warm spot where I was at least guaranteed spectacular views greeting me in the morning. Additional progress might have been useful tonight, but I liked the idea of doing more to savour the journey, and it was going to be a quick descent from here in any case.

* * * * * * *

Because the gods are hilarious, the morning sky was leaden and overcast, giving me no expansive views to enjoy. Also, I think a moose may have passed me by in the night, judging by the tracks I saw as I was packing away my camp. Despite the flat light and lack of brightness and contrast, the views were still comprehensively epic on the descent.

There was little that could really dull my mood that morning. As I descended from Black Hills I listed to myself: 'Boulder Summit and Rosebud Ridge, Eagle

King Solomon's to Scroggie Creek

Summit, American Summit, Top of the World Highway, King Solomon's Dome, Black Hills'. All of the tough climbs were behind me now. Granted there would still be some hills, but they would be fairly low-lying and easy.

Jane Creek Summit lay between Scroggie Creek and Pelly Ranch, but that was an easy climb, and not high at all. Everything after this was straightforward. I thought of fellow racer, inspiration and friend, Andy Heading, who, like me, considered everything the other side of Pelly Ranch as 'lumpy' at worst. Of course, with a heavy sled every slight bump is in danger of becoming a terrifying ordeal, but the trail was good now, and the sled moved well.

From the bottom of Black Hills I paralleled a creek, and progressed through an active mining area. I passed through mines I remembered gazing across at many times before, including during howling winds at night, with the ambient temperature well below -40. Now it was all rather pleasant, and I was enjoying every moment.

My breaks were still 10-15 minutes in length, more for practicality than anything else. At 20 minutes I start to feel colder, and it takes a little longer to warm-up. Besides, I was enjoying the journey, and did not feel a need to rest for longer. I paused to take a photograph of an open section of mining machinery, where I had escaped the wind for a few moments on that previous, harrowing night, grateful I had never had to endure such nightmarish conditions since.

The trail was good, my only cause for delays being slower progress across overflow. It existed where I have never previously been aware of creeks, as they had always been covered in snow. I remained dry and that was the important factor.

The trail took me into woodland at the side of a mining area, with a creek to my left. Here I was confronted with some particularly nasty overflow. It was only 10 metres across, if that, but it was angled over the trail, so a slip would send me off into saplings and bushes, where I would doubtless experience a world of embuggerance as I attempted to extract myself and the sled.

To my right, the overflow was less well-frozen and deeper, but had the advantage of small 'islands' which saplings were growing from. The ice was flatter, and I would be able to wedge my feet against the side of the saplings, to prevent a slip down the marginal slope. I pulled on my NEOS waterproof overboots, regretting the lack of grip (good for slippery mud, useless on ice). I cursed myself for not adding some tungsten studs to the soles, which would have remedied this issue.

Crossing overflow in this manner was nerve-wracking. I was rushing a gauntlet where various risks competed for the most perilous, from the sled getting stuck (and it came very close), to water being deep enough to worry me with threats of a soaking, or else sufficiently glaciated that I might fall over. There was also the risk of saplings tearing my clothing, causing me additional irritation.

Reflecting back on these moments though, I realised they brought excitement to otherwise very straightforward and uncomplicated days. I was working fairly hard to maintain progress, but it was all consistent; all easy. The times when I lost the trail beneath snowdrifts on the higher ground, or the slopes threatened to carry the sled over the mountainside, when I encountered overflow, and when met with large, lumbering mammals and so on, all accounted for focused but relatively short-lasting anxiety, amongst roughly 1600 kilometres (1000 miles) of steady progress, and very low stress indeed.

I considered that, overall, my progress along the well-packed Canadian trail was such that I could see no barriers to my safe and timely arrival at the finish line, and permitted myself a little more pride and confidence that all was going well.

As I moved along the trail, I became aware of the sound of snowmobiles approaching from behind, which eventually caught up with me. I deftly leapt from the trail, like a springbok dancing over a cheetah, and brought the sled off with me. Five snowmobiles arrived, the rider of the first coming to a stop at my side.

Having seen a couple of lads on snowmobiles the night before, this was apparently something of a major highway. It transpired they were all heading to Scroggie Creek for the night, and they had plenty of food. These were all the right sounds. I let them know I anticipated arriving there at around eight 'pip emma', so would see them later. With this settled they all passed, heading out of view, the familiar smell of spent fuel hanging in the air for several minutes after. Even that was comforting, in a sort of diabolically familiar, shameful way.

As evening came I was still on-form to reach Scroggie by 8pm. The trail brought me in view of the hills bordering the Stewart River, long before the trail ejected me from the woods onto it. I knew it was about 5 kilometres (3 miles) from there. I remembered this point as where a fellow racer had performed a navigational blunder, and I had deharnessed to run after him along a single snowmobile rider's track, where the fellow had bizarrely chosen to leave the packed and obvious main trail. I would have been with him at the point he initially took that wrong turn, had I not at the time been taking an exhilarating morning dump in the middle of the river. Needs must and all that.

The trail skirted the far riverbank and an island. A cabin was in view further along, which I had never noticed before. I did not know if that meant it was new, I had forgotten about it, or I had previously been preoccupied with looking elsewhere. The latter seemed so unlikely, because it was hard not to look absolutely everywhere when walking along the trail, simply because that is what one does.

Evening passed and night came as I moved briskly along the trail. I did not bother with a headtorch, as out on the river there was sufficient starlight for me to see my way. The moon was yet to rise. I believed I could smell a wood stove burning, whilst still a few kilometres from the cabin, but I have been hurt before, and fought down the urge to get my hopes up that I might almost be there.

As I passed another island, I was frantically trying to recall previous passages along here from the opposite direction, trying to make sense of it all, and how far I still had left to go. I was moving fast, aiming for the 8pm target. I neglected the headtorch, not only because there was just about enough light, but because the beam would be noticeable from the cabin, and I rather liked the idea of appearing out of nowhere to surprise them. If they asked how I managed it, I would simply confess that I used *The Force*.

My passage led around the end of a long island, and I knew this to be the point where the trail cut across the river to the cabin. Indeed, as I rounded the island, I could see the light from Scroggie Creek, the smoke billowing up, and the mess of several snowmobile tracks between here and there. It was a tough climb up the steep and slippery riverbank, but I made it without too much exasperation.

I deharnessed and gathered up bags of kit to take in with me. The light from within the cabin was incredibly strong – a gas lantern turned up fully – and it placed much of the outside space in shadow; complete darkness. As I approached the doorway I did so from the side, rather than straight-on, so I would limit the amount I had to open the door to sidle in, and thus minimise heat loss to the outside.

I knew this cabin well, having spent time here on multiple visits. My name was on the wall three times, from two journeys on the 430-mile race, and then my visit last year, when supporting the Quest. The only reason it was not up for three races was that the cabin had not been built on my first pass through. The whole cabin is raised up on sections of tree trunk, not that I could see that in the darkness, with a few wooden steps beneath the wide doorway. I opened the door and greeted everyone, and received a cheery response as I moved to step up and inside. It was as I raised a foot to enter the cabin, that a disaster occurred.

****

The door of the Scroggie Creek cabin did not really close sufficiently well to create a heatproof seal. The result of this, was that heat generated by the wood-burning stove leaked out of the cabin, along the edge of the door. The heat rose up until it met with snow overhanging a few centimetres off the roof. There, the heat worked its magic and melted the snow, which dripped down onto the side of the wooden steps. Below the base of the raised cabin, beneath the point where heat escaped, the water refroze on the steps as smooth, black ice, invisible to me in the darkness. It was this ice that had suddenly consumed my entire world and outlook.

Unbeknown to me, I had placed my right foot upon that thick, sheer ice. As I took my left foot off the ground my centre of balance shifted, and my right foot slid over the ice. I could not grab anything as I was in darkness and my hands were full. It is said that everything happens for a reason. That reason is Physics.

After placing my foot on the side of that step, disaster should have occurred immediately. Instead, Disaster held-off for a few moments, sufficient to get His friends around to watch, so they could really make the evening of it.

Rather than plummeting directly to my doom, I achieved a tranquil state of equilibrium. This was not some fluffy spiritual affair, but a purely physical one. My feet led my legs arcing up through the air in a north-

north-easterly direction, at the exact same moment that my torso and head began to rapidly recline, in an opposing arc to the south-southwest.

In a moment of clarity, as my mind rushed to consider what lay beneath, I recollected the presence of a large chunk of tree trunk, used to split logs upon. It was this that I managed to break my fall over, care of a few ribs in my lower back. With this concluding my evening's demonstration of amateur acrobatics, there followed something of a lull in activities.

The fall itself, and the collaboration of my ribs with the tree trunk that followed, could have been quite nasty and fairly unpleasant. Instead, it was atrociously nasty, and exquisitely unpleasant. So that seemed to make the whole thing more worthwhile.

I was winded completely as I landed, back-first on the log, arse second in the snow. Once the well-placed sniggers and guffaws of the inebriated hyenas within the cabin died-down, I heard a voice ask if I was okay, but I was so winded that my 'Nope' was a breathless hope of reply, rather than an audible sound. Indeed, the fact that I acknowledged to them – and to myself – that I was not okay, spoke volumes to me, and I was quite puzzled about it for a moment. I strive to look on the bright side of all trying situations, but I recognised the current state of play to be something grim.

I lay sprawled across the section of tree trunk, the coldness and wetness of the snow now creeping through my clothing to my cold arse, meeting with the hot, stinging and shooting pains from my back. My heart raced and my breaths were fast and shallow, as I tried to avoid breathing deeply and moving my back. I gazed up into the darkness of the night sky, trying to acquire a philosophical outlook about the whole thing.

A large Swiss chap, Heinz, was first on the scene of the carnage, bursting out through the wide door, almost committing the thing to splinters. He was followed closely by a woman, Maggie. They both inspected me as I lay there feeling hurt, ashamed and embarrassed, which was as far as my ruminations had taken me.

Heinz asked if I wanted a hand, and I held up mine to request a moment first. Maggie supported my view. A few seconds passed and I decided that, as I was not getting any younger, I should concede to move, helped up by Heinz under Maggie's diligent supervision. I was led within, appearing now before the inmates like something out of a Russian novel.

Chapter 22.
Scroggie Creek

Taking a seat and making my apologies for the drama, I was soon handed a warming moose chilli. Sitting down in the warmth of the cabin, surrounded by encouraging faces, I felt instantly better, although purely in the psychological sense. My spirit was lifted, my mood was buoyed, and my arse was in a comfy chair. Any untold physical horrors were being played down on account of adrenaline, endorphins, and a hearty 'can do' attitude on the part of Denial – my closest ally when the unmentionable hits the fan.

Nevertheless, I was keen to establish the extent of my injuries. What I kept asking myself was, was it purely bruising to skin and muscles, or had I fractured some ribs? If broken, how bad could it be, and what did this mean for immediate health, and for the future of the expedition? I felt that it was unlikely to be more serious than these – I suspected that if a wayward rib had lanced an organ I would probably know about it already. Not that I could rule anything that dramatic out, but statistically it seemed unlikely. In terms of probabilities, I was probably going to be just fine.

What I was really thinking about – in terms of what was forefront in my mind – was how delicious the chilli was. Rod, who I now adopted as my personal physician, insisted this was the time for a medicinal beer, and I accepted his sage counsel without question. He was, after all, in authority here, and I had no place to question his judgement on these sorts of medical matters.

I sat there, incredibly grateful for all this support, even whilst feeling sore from my collision with the tree stump. I moved about a bit, experimenting with the placement and intensity of the pain, and accepted I must have given the soft tissues a good wallop, but there was nothing serious. It was difficult to move and get comfortable, but I adopted the least bothersome seated position and stuck with it. The food and a few beers flowed, but I needed to be heading off the next day, and was not in the mood to flirt with alcoholism just yet. Now was the time to rest and to heal.

My new friends would be heading off the next morning, to visit chums further along the Stewart River, as they were all currently enjoying a long weekend. A game of Scrabble was in progress. Two people – perhaps those I had met returning from here – had left their sleeping equipment and other personal belongings on the top two of the four bunks, which seemed uncharitable.

My new pals did not mind too much, as they had camp beds. There was space for me too, but when I heard that Heinz was a committed snorer, I decided I would set-up to sleep in a small, adjacent cabin – 'Buckbrush'. There was a single bunk and a small wood stove there, and it had been renovated a few years before by a friend of mine, and it would actually be quite cosy. I headed across to get the stove going and then returned.

Rod did his best to assert they had done something wrong to drive me out, and with that offered me another beer. They talked of many things, including an extension to the mining road all the way to the Stewart River, all for a single, private mine. Rod declared that this was bullshit. He also informed me that all the machinery at the Indian River mine was a product of Discovery UK television, hence the absurd and ridiculous level of overkill.

Despite the painful injury, which I could have well done without, it was a pleasant evening, enjoyed with the loveliest, kindest and most generous of company. Before leaving for my own cabin, I stood and performed a few movements to help self-analyse how the back was doing. It was very sore and uncomfortable, and I began to wonder if it was indeed entirely soft-tissue, or if I really had done a number on some ribs too. I headed-off to set-up my bed and restock the stove. I brought in sufficient wood from outside to get me through the night, and I brushed my teeth.

As I moved to lay down on the lower bunk (I knew full well I was not in shape to mount an expedition to the warmer, upper bunk), I met with the most exquisitely agonising stabbing pain, directly into my ribs. I was unable to take a deep breath, and became quickly consumed by sharp pains all around my back and the side of my chest, as I attempted to sit up. I did not scream, for such is not my way, but I came very close. I cannot deny that my eyes might have bulged, whilst a sound was issued forth from my mouth, which could accurately be described as somewhere between a shriek and a whimper.

Although I could move my arms without issue, as soon as I clutched onto the slats from the above bunk with my right hand – in an attempt to shift my body without wriggling my torso – so the pain returned. Indeed, I felt an unfamiliar, unusual movement in my back. It felt that several solid lumps were being drawn across my back below the level of my shoulder blades. At the time I naturally convinced myself this was muscle tissue in cramp or spasm.

I slept partially propped-up against the wall on the bunk, but, in truth, I did not sleep much at all. Breathing hurt. Moving hurt. My back hurt. A couple of paracetamol might have been helpful, as would a defibrillator on standby for my pride.

* * * * * * *

Unaccustomed as I am to spending nights in unprecedented, blistering agony, I met the new day with a spirit of ambivalence. I was somewhat thrilled to not yet be dead, whilst less than overwhelmed at the prospect of suffering through a day filled to the brim with Anguish, Pain and Torment. Wriggling free from my sleeping bag, and rising to splendid erection, I presented the world with a heart-warming – if at times harrowing – scene, of one man overcoming incalculable odds, to achieve an ambition the rest of the world had confidently proclaimed could not be done.

I did it though. I stood up, in my underwear, with only the smallest amount of groans, yelps, cursing, and crookedness. Triumphant, I dressed and left the little cabin, and – not repeating the previous night's misstep – managed to progress inside the main cabin, without pausing to throw myself at the floor and splintering my remaining ribs.

I was cheerily greeted by the cabin's inhabitants. Indeed, their gay merriment was the sort of stuff to churn a man's stomach, bringing on a sense of deep loathing and utter hatred. I attempted to crush their spirits by breaking the news I was confident I had broken some ribs. They correctly rushed to console me, nourishing my soul with the sympathies my attention-seeking and egotistical self so desired to leech-off.

Because fortune often favours the brave and imbeciles alike, I was lucky to discover that Maggie happened to be a paramedic. Together with her husband, she took some of the strapping I carried in my first aid kit for joint injuries, and did an exceptional job of binding my ribs. She took her own tension bandage and overlaid this over the first. I was in pain but at least it was less and I felt more secure; better able to move.

Being fully knowledgeable about the healing patterns – and best course of treatment for fractured ribs – you will recognise at once that binding them is contraindicated. As you yourself might have once informed me, this is because the binding can make breathing harder, with casualties less likely to cough when required, increasing their risk of pneumonia. However, the need to make progress along the trail necessitated a more secure package.

Maggie offered to take me back to Dawson on snowmobile for medical attention, but the thought of sitting on a snowmobile, or even lying in a skimmer, was terrifying. After a painful night of lying still, I knew too well that bouncing around would be an agony too great to consider; up there with testicle-kicks, papercuts and childbirth – none of which I was keen to endure.

My scheme for the day was to do as little as possible. I wanted to stay inside somewhere safe, warm and dry, to give my body a chance to show any signs the injury was even more serious than Melodrama suggested. If it was, I would surrender to better sense and initiate a medevac. If gangrene took possession of my torso, or if both legs dropped off, or my kidneys swelled and exploded out of my body, I would probably concede to call for a lift. Otherwise, I would walk out the following morning.

My next port of call would be the Pelly River Ranch, and as these reprobates here knew those miscreants there, I requested the former notify the latter that, if I had not shown-up to infest their shores in three days' time, to send out the Thunderbirds – or at least one of the clan on a skidoo with a salmon sandwich – to snag me and haul me the rest of the way in.

I did not yet feel justified to pull the plug on the journey. A friend of mine, Charlie Paton – the chap I had emailed about my frostbite – had broken ribs during a crevasse fall in Antarctica once, and had dusted himself off and continued. If I ever wanted to look him in the eyes again, I would need to crack-on and finish this thing. I wanted to finish it too, but there were natural doubts regarding the safety of doing so.

The other cabin guests were generous in the breakfast they fed me. Heinz left me some moose sausages, to help get me through the day. The animal had been hunted by these chaps, and the meat was about the healthiest and most delicious one can be fortunate enough to enjoy. I was sworn to secrecy as to the location where the hunt had taken place, as these chaps thought other chaps might stampede to the area, if they ever got wind of what fine animals inhabited the place, simply begging to be shot in the face and have their guts turned to sausage casings.

Rod offered me some beers but I declined, just as I had mistakenly declined to join the others in having a shot of Baileys in their morning coffee. I liked these people immensely. I liked their style and their way of doing things. I liked how they chose to spend a long weekend out of town.

The merry band packed away their things and headed off. I moved my own stuff over from Buckbrush cabin and settled in for a sore, frustrating, and extremely long day. I watched the others leave along the Stewart River, and I harnessed-up and went for a short plod in a circle in front of the cabin. My conclusion was that my ribs hurt regardless of whether or not I was towing the sled, and, as the greatest pain during walking was due to breathing – and I would probably be doing quite a bit of that anyway, as was my habit – I ought to continue. Tomorrow. Just to err on the side of caution and let the healing get started in earnest now.

****

I sat in a comfy chair, contemplating my existence and next moves. I would have enjoyed a good book to read; there was a limit to how many times I could check the photos I had taken. I have always enjoyed and savoured cabin life, but alone and without distraction, the novelty soon started to wear-off. This situation was at least partially due to my feeling sorry for myself. The weather was not helping either.

When I raised myself out of the chair – another act of inspiring heroism – I gazed out of a small window adjacent to the door, to look at the world beyond. A thermometer placed on the wall outside mocked at me that this was a hot day. The temperature at midday in direct sunlight was 10C (50F).

I looked out at the trail leading from the cabin, cursing the blue sky for the first time, and cursing my injuries confining me to this dosshouse. I could sense the snow melting away, the overflow thawing and river ice opening-up. If temperatures rose over the coming week, what would be left of the trail – how much exposed dirt to slow the sled and tear holes in it? How much chance for foot injuries, with warm and wet feet in the day, becoming cold and wet at night? I felt an urgency to get going, but Caution advised me to give myself this day.

The heat did not bode well, and I felt even more that I was racing the coming spring, but held back to give it a full day's head start, after which I would be going at a very sore and sluggish pace indeed. A thousand kilometres (620 miles) and now this, just when all the toughest sections had been completed. So close to the end and yet still so far, the injury and climate combining to make my chances of success seem even more distant than ever.

I spent the afternoon eating and reading a book left behind by the chaps who had abandoned all their kit here. I would have preferred a good book, but in a crisis I can be forced to suffer whatever is lying around. I wandered around and took some photographs. Inside the cabin I wrote my name on a section of wood, as is the custom, and read the graffiti of others. So many stories in one small cabin, sitting here by the Stewart River.

* * * * * * *

I was apprehensive about what would happen if I took another fall. All it would take is a moment of carelessness on a patch of glaciated overflow, and fractured ribs, clinging on by the outstretched arms of single bony threads, would be loosed from their moorings as if from a crossbow, lancing all my internal organs several times each, before leaving me to die in the cold, wet snow, of a sucking chest wound.

As Luck would have it, I knew there happened to be a considerable amount of overflow coming up. There always was in this area, but this was the worst year for it I have known. Considering the warming temperatures, more overflow was likely to appear too. With Optimism as my constant companion, I harnessed all my brain power to convince myself another fall was not at all likely to happen.

It was in this moment that I suddenly experienced a spasm of logic. I realised that I would almost certainly be absolutely fine. The only thing to stop me from completing my expedition was the absolute worst case scenario. And, after all, how often does the worst possible scenario ever get realised? Upon reflection, the answer to that question is just the once, I suppose. However, I ignored that, simply considering that the probability of it happening was so low as to be laughably absurd and improbable. I would be just fine.

Indeed, with already so much pain on breathing and sleeping, and the acceptance these were necessary factors of life, the thought of sitting in a café in Whitehorse – even my favourite café, the Java Connection, drinking delicious coffee whilst revitalising my tissues with soup and sandwiches – experiencing all that pain breathing anyway, when I could be experiencing it on the trail, sealed the deal for me. I could quit and be a truly sore loser, or I could persevere and stand a chance of giving it my all, either accepting defeat if it was forced upon me, or else savouring an even sweeter victory.

As Rod had told me, because I would be writing this book I was committed to finishing now, the tale would be all the greater for it. I accepted the truth in this, although, to be perfectly honest with you, I would have been at least equally happy to have snuck through this whole course without peril, pain or incident.

There were still more reasons to continue. My good friend, Pete, at Braeburn, had a beer waiting for me, and I looked forward to sharing his company for a while, whilst savouring that beer. He had taken a photo of it for me and posted it on my Facebook page, just to make the point, and it had had a very strong motivating effect on me. It meant something; it conveyed the spirit of something worth making happen.

This was not about turning up 'by any means', but about marching myself across snow and ice, to arrive at a friend's cabin to enjoy a privileged moment with him, and I wanted to earn that moment. The thought of a bottle of 'Lead Dog', from the Yukon Brewery, was a pretty good carrot to dangle in front of me too.

Scroggie Creek

The first time I met Pete was in the adjacent Buckbrush cabin back in 2009, before this larger cabin was built, when he was assisting another Mike as race support. Back then, I was on my first journey to Dawson City, enjoying my first encounter with the Yukon Quest trail. Mike had greeted me here as if I had already finished, appreciating it was 'only' about 160 km (100 miles) left to go. True enough, most people had scratched from the race long before here, and nobody quit between here and the end, unless they really did have a calamity.

* * * * * * *

The day passed at an excruciatingly slow pace, mostly spent with me feeling like an arse. After the exquisite discomfort of the previous night, I was now apprehensive about sleeping. I could not bear the thought of trying to sleep on a hard bunk. I had experimented with the plan during the evening, but it was far too uncomfortable. If anything, I was in more pain today than last night. Instead, I would sleep in a large camp chair, left here for the Quest.

I recalled chatting with Quest and Iditarod legend, Lance Mackey, as he sat in this same chair in front of the wood stove, while I prepared his food and drink during the 2015 race. When he was ready he drifted off to sleep, forsaking the available bunks, and remaining poised in the chair. Now it was my turn to sleep in it, propped-up into a corner by the wall and a bunk, my feet raised on a stool. It made for a surprisingly comfortable night's sleep, and I would be sorry not to be taking the chair with me out on the trail. I drifted off, contemplating whether or not the next day might be the making or breaking of me.

I did have reservations about what lay ahead. Back on the trail I would not be able to clamber comfortably into my tent, and, even if I could, I would struggle to find any comfort to sleep. If I could not get into a position to sleep for the night, would I be forced to march on, exhaustion growing, until something really serious went wrong? This had been in my thoughts since my stabbing pains during the previous night, and was one of the reasons I had chosen to take this day for rest. Tomorrow, whatever else happened, I would march onwards towards Pelly Ranch. I had committed to so much already, and now I could commit to this.

Chapter 23.
Scroggie Creek to Pelly Ranch

Once again thrilled at surviving the night, I squared away my kit and left Scroggie at around 8 o'clock. Accessing my sled bag to pack had involved squat and lunge-style movements that any expert personal trainer would have been proud to observe. My back remained upright throughout, with all the movement going through my legs. Bending or otherwise stooping threatened my state of comfort. My favoured facial expression was wincing. Sounds featured occasional groans, whimpers, yelps and sighs. Meanwhile, my internal monologue focused mostly upon cursing.

Every step was distractingly painful, but only as a result of my breathing. I consoled myself that hauling the sled was not directly stressing my body all that much, compared with, as examples, a day working as a scaffolder, or engaging in professional gymnastics. The muscles of my core and torso had long been trained by this expedition, and had grown used to the stresses of hauling a sled, which started-out far heavier than it was now. The lower portion of my ribs, where the fractures were, were going to oppose any twisting or bending actions, which meant a slower pace to limit stresses through those tissues.

All this made for a slow start, but it was a start, and that was the key. Whenever I arrived before even the shortest of bumps in the trail, I had to pause and very carefully edge my way over, as I thought this best to save sudden jolts through the harness. What hurt the most was the occasional slip, or slight descent through soft snow, where my body would brace itself in reaction, with such tension causing acute stabs of pain, often accompanied by an involuntary yelp and another curse, either at myself or the universe more generally. Such instances occurred where minor avalanches had swept several centimetres or more of fresh snow across the trail. I had no illusions about the delays to reach the ranch, in consideration of all my previous stints along here, but I would get there. Probably.

The trail led along the base of hills, low down and adjacent to Scroggie Creek itself. There was overflow on the creek, staining it with hues of green and blue. The sky was clear and the hillsides were sparkling and beautiful. I could not help but notice the lack of snow on the trees, another sign of low snowfall (at least since heavy winds shed the snow that was previously there), and the coming spring. The warmth was also responsible for the mini-avalanches. During four previous travels along this section, I had only seen one of these, and now there were a multitude. In places, low hanging branches caused me to stoop, and this was not an elegant manoeuvre.

I could not take my breaks sitting atop my sled, as was my normal fashion, due to the discomfort of getting up again, so instead took some weight off my carcass by propping a trekking pole or two underneath my withered and bony arse. This sufficed in a crisis.

As I crossed another small avalanche area the sled tipped over. I inspected the base of the sled before righting it, noting the scratches and a couple of holes that had formed. This was the scarring from the ploughed roads. It raised the question of how much worse this would get, and whether the sled would make it all the way to the finish, or if I should replace it somewhere (or bodge new runners). It seemed a little unsporting to replace it, and I took a few moments to place some duct tape underneath to help limit further damage. The tape would get wet and need to be removed before littering the trail, but it would help for a short while.

Setting it right was not a pain-free experience, but I was learning to accommodate and limit problems. Every time I did experience pain, I silently thanked Maggie and her husband, for the fantastic effort they did of binding me up, because I knew I would have been so much worse-off without this. The sled only tipped over twice that day.

The trail brought me down onto a creek, which was entirely overflow for about 50 metres. It was a steady and deliberate crossing to where the trail rose again. I do not recall ever being so concerned about falling over. Further on, the trail rose and fell a little here and there, but these were gentle undulations. Halfway to Pelly would be the little Jane Creek Summit, and I would reach that tomorrow, or so I expected. It was another warm day, but my slow morning pace was conducive to coping with this.

By the afternoon, I felt my pace had quickened a little, which was reassuring, even though it was still far from my normal speed. I knew people would be watching my SPOT, wondering why I was making such a meal of things. Maggie and the others would reach Dawson tomorrow night, and contact Dale to let him know what had happened. Nobody else would know until I could send an update from the ranch.

The occasional rabbit or squirrel had run across the trail, but mostly there had been wolves, their numbers hard to judge where they walked in each other's prints. Night fell and I wondered how far I had really managed. 40km? 30km? 20? I kept pushing on, and by around 10 o'clock was hopeful I would soon come across a suitable location to sleep.

I was moving along with an upwards slope to my left, in densely wooded forest. To my right, the hillside fell away with a steep drop. I was looking for an inviting spruce tree, where the lower branches were fairly high, and the slope to reach the base of the tree gentle but not flat. I was apprehensive about whether I would find enough respite from the discomfort to actually sleep, but this was being pushed to the back of my mind, with the front focused on more practical solutions.

I made use of my little folding saw to cut down branches, building up a good mattress at the base of an encouraging spruce. Holding down branches as I cut through them was sore on the ribs, but mostly just mildly irritating, rather than painful, like drivers who switch lanes in front of you without indicating and then brake; or like lukewarm, lumpy custard.

I arranged the mattress so I could prop myself up against the tree trunk. I laid my foam insulating mat atop the spruce mattress, to help protect the sleeping bag. I used my down jacket and clothing bag to further facilitate the propped-up position. This system was not perfect, as during the night Gravity, that utter bastard, kept pulling me down into a flatter, less comfortable position.

Sleeping was not pleasant, punctuated as it often was with exquisite stabs of pain, but these only occurred if I moved. If I stayed still I experienced a much duller, growing pain, which was easier to sleep through. Nothing lasts forever, of course, and I appreciated the pain would subside over the coming days, as the ribs healed.

Following a day that was physically challenging, and acutely painful for fleeting moments, I reflected on the forbidding nature of the warmer weather, coupled with the serene beauty of the blue skies and the glistening snow, with signs of the Yukon's wild inhabitants ever present. I was grateful for the sleep when it came, and, in a rather focused and deliberate manner, considered that tomorrow would be another long, full day, along this section that I have always previously completed in under a day and a half.

* * * * * * *

I did not linger long in my warm and cosy sleeping bag; happy to get moving and to be more in control of the discomfort. It might have been unwelcome pain, but it was *my* pain, and I was taking ownership and whatever control of it I could. My pace as I set off was on a par with what it had been the previous evening; not as brisk as my usual speed, but a fair improvement on the previous morning's. I could not help but consider it a shame that something had come to slow me down, here where the trail was otherwise so fast.

Something else that came to slow me down was a need for a morning pause to drop some surplus weight, which I had already been carrying with me for far too long. As I crouched down at the side of the trail, my arse exposed to the elements, and my balls swaying calmly in the breeze, I regretted that I had allowed myself to become so horrendously constipated. During shorter events this was never an issue. The extended journeying period, with limited fibre-rich products in my diet, resulted in an inadequacy to permit this time to pass more fruitfully. In future adventures I would have to do better. Childbirth could never be as painful as giving birth to that brick.

It was midday when I began the gentle climb up Jane Creek Summit. At the top I paused for a while, to soak in the view and take a few photographs. Not wanting the sled to attempt an overtake during the descent, I set-off while dragging the sled into a snowbank, which ran alongside the trail, thus slowing it down and keeping it in its place. I dared not remove the harness and send it off ahead, not knowing how much effort might then be required to retrieve it from whatever patch of deep snow it landed in.

At the base of the hill was a short section of overflow, but with an uncharitably steep metre drop down onto it. I gave it my best to keep the sled under control, but it turned over. Regardless, I hauled it across the ice on its side, leaving the overflow on the far bank and getting a good metre or so, before deharnessing to right the sled. None of this caused me any greater pain than the now low-level soreness I experienced with deep breathing, or the even lower level discomfort that was there as I moved along. Healing was well underway.

As I moved to turn over the sled again, I scrutinised the scratches and holes underneath – they had not gotten any worse, but the tape was now hanging off the back of the sled, needing to be removed. I would have to dry-out the base of the sled to have any hope of the tape sticking.

Considering that Jane Creek Summit is approximately halfway between Scroggie and the ranch, it did not bode well that it was early afternoon by the time I was making my way along the trail away from it. I would not reach the ranch until later on the next day; a new record slow.

The day was warm. This was a constant reminder that the snowy trail would be softening more and more, with every hour that passed. One benefit of the cold was that it was so easy to vent heat away from the body, and to feel really cool and fresh. It is then easy to adopt a high work rate, whilst maintaining a comfortable body temperature. Now I was wearing minimal clothing and my tongue was still hanging out, as I panted along like a knackered old dog. Occasionally I would take a handful of snow into my mouth, just to help feel cooler.

The land flattened-out and opened-up. This allowed for views of more distant woodland, and the low-lying hills around me. Far ahead, beyond my sight, lay the Pelly river, and, just before that, the ranch.

Along the trail I encountered tracks that were unfamiliar to me. There were still plenty of wolf tracks too, but these new ones were different. For one thing, they were larger. They were round tracks, like those of a lynx, but lynx tracks were much smaller than these. There were two sets, one larger than the other, and apparently parallel to each other, as if a mother and adolescent had been walking together. That it belonged to a carnivore seemed obvious, but I was perplexed as to which. These two animals made use of the trail in the same direction as me, and the tracks were fairly fresh – less than a day old.

A long patch of overflow caused a couple of jolts as a foot slipped, reawakening a dormant soreness, but it subsided as soon as it came. I made it across the overflow without further incident. The big tracks had taken their own route.

By the evening, my pace was approximating something more normal for me, which I took with great relief. I was determined to make solid progress to Pelly Ranch. I was also enjoying sled-hauling in the late night and wee-small hours, when it was cooler, and the trail firmer. By about 10 o'clock I was certainly tired enough to sleep, but I knew I was approaching the ranch. I checked my GPS and saw that I was about 18km (11 miles) out, as the old crow flew.

I sped up, giving it my best as a time-trial. I enjoyed the thrill of working hard with self-imposed targets, feeling the cool night's air on my face. The night-time trail was satisfyingly colder, firmer and better for progress. The starlit sky caused the snow to be bright enough for navigation without a headtorch, and I relished all of what my senses perceived.

The area was woodland with some occasional, mild undulations, but not at all steep, and mostly it was flat. Thanks to the firmer trail, I felt as though I was flying along. I checked after an hour and saw I was a little over 12 km (7.5 miles) out. I had been working hard for that ~5 km per hour (accepting straight line distance was not the same as full trail distance), and I reckoned I would be doing well to reach the ranch by 3 o'clock.

The thought of the comfort of sleeping in one of the cosy armchairs was a definite pull. However, if I worked hard, reached the ranch, and was asleep by 4 o'clock, I would be woken a few hours later when Dale set about his morning chores. There was also the issue of waking the dogs with my arrival, which would doubtless impact how thrilled Dale might be to see me.

My preference – as it had been with my arrival at Dawson – was to promote enjoyment, health and so on, by maintaining a reasonable sleeping pattern. I could sleep well tonight, and head into the ranch for breakfast or, perhaps brunch, and that would suit me just fine. I considered this approach far more reasonable, as desirable as a comfy chair generally is.

The area I now moved through was dense woodland, and fairly elevated. I was on the lookout for an optimal camping area. I passed a snowmobile track off into the woods to my right, but had no idea where it went. I took it that most of the snowmobile riders were trappers; out to check their traplines.

Further on I came across a good-looking, inviting tree, with beckoning, come-to-bed branches, which I found entirely irresistible. Just before that, on the opposite side, I saw fresh wolf tracks leading into the woods, causing me to consider what I might awake to see staring down at me. Sleeping in just the sleeping bag, without a tent, did cause me to look something like a human burrito, but a knackered and fairly rancid-smelling one, so I had that treat in my favour.

I built up another spruce mattress, and took my saw to a small, dead tree, which I limbed and sawed in half, using two thicker sections to help prop me up against the tree trunk. I considered what would happen if I did wake to see a big ole wolf staring back down at me. An attack would be extremely unlikely, but, alone in the dark, the mind enjoys tormenting itself with these absurd fantasies.

I wondered what might happen, should a particularly desperate and sick wolf, burdened with excruciatingly poor taste, and no sense of smell, decide to look upon me as the last word in culinary delights. I suppose there might be some potential in explaining to the wolf that I was, as a matter of fact, about 1.86 metres tall, carried an impressively sharp titanium knife about my person, could punt a small mammal several metres (if occasion dictated this course of action), and could probably offer even a big wolf a good walloping, with the sections of wood I was now using as a bed frame. However, as I was stuck in my sleeping bag, with my arms effectively trapped until I could unzip myself, and any action on my part extremely restricted and awfully slow, I had to hope the wolf would weigh it all up and call it a draw, before shrugging the idea off and skulking away.

* * * * * * *

It would be a stretch to state that I slept extremely well. To say that I slept like a baby was still only true in the sense that I woke up crying twice, although reassuringly I did not soil myself. I had slept better than the previous couple of nights, so was convinced my health continued to improve.

When I did wake in the night, it was not to be consumed by wolves, or by very dangerous rabbits or whatever, but to the captivating sight of the aurora, dancing overhead. It had been a scene of privileged wonder, and I had been almost reluctant to close my eyes to it and return to my slumber.

Early in the morning, I packed my gear away and continued along the trail, which soon began its descent towards the Pelly River. It was a long, winding trail, and I was moving at a good speed, all things considered. There was a creek lower down, and hillsides and woodland. It was already shaping-up to be another warm day. I passed an area where at least one snowmobile had recently been manoeuvring.

I arrived at a familiar junction, where the route split for Quest 1000 and 300-mile racers, on the years when the race started out from Whitehorse. There was a place where someone had been chopping wood at the side, but I had no time to investigate – I was keen to arrive at the Ranch and spend some time with Dale.

I headed downhill. I was being led past woodland to my left, when I saw the black shape of a large wolf darting from the trail into the woods. When I drew parallel to where it had left, I paused, looking into the woods, but could not see anything but shadows. It is wonderful and daunting how animals can be so close, seeing me easily, and yet entirely invisible and imperceptible to my senses.

This is perhaps the only instance that really makes me feel detached from nature – my inability to be as immersed into its system as other animals, where they might be observing me yet I cannot detect them. If I threw a brick into these woods, it would probably bounce off two furious wolves, three irritated squirrels, a gormless moose and a disgruntled rabbit, all before hitting the snow. All I could perceive was absolute silence and still shadows, where apparently not a creature was stirring. And yet that big black wolf was in there, close.

I scanned the ranch as I approached, but there were no signs of activity. I deharnessed outside the main cabin and proceeded within. Discovering nobody at all I headed back outside and explored. Discovering nobody there either I returned inside. I cooked-up a couple of Heinz's moose sausages, delighting in how wonderful they were, and made myself at home. By 'made myself at home', I mean I tidied away some breakfast items from the table, tidied a few items away in the kitchen, and did the washing-up. After a little rest I went for a walk and to take some photographs. I loved this little spot; it was filled to the brim with great memories.

I knew my way around the ranch, because I had worked here for a week or so, a couple of years ago. This had centred around doing various chores, although Dale would have been quite happy if I had used the ranch as a training camp or writer's retreat. Sitting out by a fire next to the road, eating salmon sandwiches with Dale and his son, had been good times too.

Mostly, I had been getting fires going in the wood stoves. There was a stove in the main cabin, another in the workshop (where the tractor got to sleep when it was feeling cold), and another close to the cows' water trough. The latter was a necessity, because the water would freeze overnight. There was a pump for filling the trough with water via an underground pipe. It all made sense and it all worked with only a modicum of applied effort. The familiarity, and reflections on past experiences here, help me to feel instantly at home. I was impatient for Dale to show himself, so we could get down to the serious business of catching-up and talking BS. It was far too long since we last did that.

Chapter 24.
Pelly Ranch to Pelly Crossing

A young gentleman called Swiss arrived and introduced himself. That is how I came to know he was called Swiss. I am extremely perceptive like this. He was a good lad, who had stopped by during the summer, deciding then to do a week's work. Considering he was still here, on the verge of spring, I wondered which week it was he felt so determined to do. He invited me to make myself at home, which was lucky. Dale was bringing a bulldozer back along the mountain road, driving it at a walking pace, and not expected until after nightfall. Apparently it moved even slower than I did these days.

I made use of an unattended laptop to send out an update to my contacts about progress and 'other events'. I was getting information from Mike's wife, Jessica, about the final section, where the Quest trail deviated into Takhini. Another good friend, Murray, was hoping to see me finish, but it looked like he would be on the road as support crew for the 6633 race at around that time. When I had left Dawson I was expecting to make it before he left, now sadly not.

I liaised with a sponsor from the UK, Tom, who managed a brewery (definitely my kind of sponsor) and who was coming out to Whitehorse with a friend, wanting a few days with me on the Quest trail. It was an unknown as to whether I would arrive before them, on the same day, or if they would need to improvise a strategy to meet me on the trail.

Pelly Ranch to Pelly Crossing

I attempted to help Swiss with some chores, and later he made us both dinner. At around 22:30 that night, he headed-out to locate Dale, and to haul him in. I had already turned-in for the night by the time they returned. There was a room with a couple of bunk beds in it, and I took the largest of the bottom bunks, loaded-up with the available bedding from the other three beds, and managed to prop myself up well with pillows. Each night was becoming more comfortable than the one before.

* * * * * * *

Seeing Dale in the morning was an absolute delight. He started out by giving me the cheerful news, that, the previous night, I had passed within about 100 metres of a cabin. My last night on the trail could have been replaced by a night in a bed, in a gloriously warm cabin, with a wood stove burning away. Although I had spotted the snowmobile trail, I had taken it that it was a trapper, and did not consider there would be a cabin anywhere close. Oh well, it had not been too bad out on the trail, and I had had the privilege of seeing the northern lights, whilst enjoying not being eaten by an unsympathetic wolf.

Dale had endured a long and cold night out on the road, and would be back out today for a few more hours. My plan was to wander down to Stepping Stone, a checkpoint on the Quest trail a few kilometres away, on the confluence of the Yukon and Pelly rivers. The route from the ranch to Pelly Crossing lies in the opposite direction, so if I did not go for this excursion, I would be missing-out on those few kilometres of trail, and one strives to be a purest. Also, it would offer me the opportunity of seeing how it felt on the ribs, to be walking without the sled.

I showed Dale some photographs I had taken of the large, round footprints, and he informed me they belonged to a couple of mountain lions. He seemed less than thrilled at where the photographs were taken, not being too far from the ranch. It turned-out they had moved into the area to hunt deer, although cougars were so rarely spotted that many doubted their presence this far north at all.

In the right, honourable and utterly delightful fashion of folk just like Dale, he progressed to narrate the stories of previous sightings and encounters, painting me the picture of wilderness out here, and bringing it all to life. I was a sponge for all of it.

I later looked-up incidents of mountain lion attacks on people. The cats are huge and can be aggressive, but attacks are extremely rare. My perusal of the available literature led me to the conclusion that one should behave differently with cougars than with other predators.

When one sees a bear, for example, the available options include staying very still, playing dead, laying down a rucksack (or similar items of interest) and backing slowly away, and that sort of thing. It gets a little more complicated, because the actual response is sort of led by the bear, in that it helps to understand if the bear is acting defensively, such as to protect young, or aggressively, such as out of peckishness.

The person confronted with an advancing cougar, by contrast, ought to behave more like a town drunk; shouting and waving arms about, throwing objects, and generally being loud, boisterous and aggressive. Running away will likely initiate the lion's 'hunt and kill' instincts. Playing dead will let it know you are providing no threat at all, and they are welcome to head over and get stuck in.

Realistically, this is all rather moot. Perhaps you, like me, simply cannot get enough of Attenborough and his padawans. One thing that really stands-out as a theme, when engrossed in the narrative of a big cat hunting its prey, is that the big cats are fiendishly stealthy. They tend to sneak impossibly close to the antelope, only in the very last millisecond presenting itself, right up there in the antelope's business of munching grass. If the antelope is forewarned by its colleagues, and makes a dash for it, it stands a chance. These antelopes are incredibly fast and athletic. If a cougar were stalking me, I simply would not know about it until the absolute last moment, and, lacking the speed and agility of even a quite elderly and arthritic antelope, I would expire in a moment.

With this being the case, the only cougars we are likely to see, are the ones that are not particularly interested in lunching on us. In this event, launching projectiles at a cat that is minding its own business is probably on a par with those bored zoo chimpanzees, which pass their time flinging their own excrement at the zoo keepers. Anti-social, is what I mean.

I prepared some non-cougar-related safety equipment, and struck-out for Stepping Stone. It was a

5 km (3 mile) trail, or thereabouts, and it was almost all flat river. I walked along the Quest trail from the house, leaving the ranch and passing some disused cabins, here from an outdoors enterprise that folded, and I entered woodland bordering on the riverbank. A little further and I headed down the bank onto the frozen river itself.

Today was shaping-up to be incredibly beautiful. I roamed beneath a light blue sky, with low-lying mist caressing the hillsides on the opposite riverbank. A heavily-wooded island, some kilometre or so in length, began almost at the point I entered the river trail, but close to the far bank, and extending along in the direction I would be heading. There were still trail markers in place, and the river ice here had frozen about as flat as a snooker table.

My path was extremely well-packed, and had not been lost to any snowfall or strong winds. It seemed that the snowfall I had suffered with, on the Yukon River before Eagle, was a fairly isolated affair, and then again on American Summit, but nothing further south along the Fortymile River, or beyond. Here in Canada, the trail had been untouched by recent snowfall – a disaster for my sled where the roads were ploughed – but otherwise excellent conditions.

The route along the river became more wonderful the further I walked. I was in no rush today. The mist cleared and any lingering clouds evaporated. The snow crystals glistened, presenting to me a soft blanket of the purest jewelled white, beneath an azure sky. The hills, the sky and the river looked like a winter paradise, and, indeed, to me it was. Could I ever tire of such views?

Yet people tell me the summer is the time to be in the Yukon, and that the autumn is the prettiest. Being out here on days such as this reminds me just how much I want to build a home here someday. Each visit causes me to fall in love with the region even more, with any hardships simply feeling like a rite of passage.

It had become apparent to me that the soreness I felt when hauling the sled was not reduced now I was without it, confirming to me that the sled was likely not causing me further damage, or interfering much with healing. Wandering alone here in paradise, any pains seemed to melt away, into some closed-off closet in my mind. I was absorbed into the stunning beauty, and absolute peace and tranquillity, of my surroundings. What a day to take a stroll along a frozen river!

I reflected on what I was carrying with me. I had a couple of small drybags containing my mitts, survival kit and some food. It was only going to be a few hours of travel, at most, with the Stepping Stone cabins halfway, but I felt a certain sense of satisfaction that – even though I had left my sled behind – I still carried sufficient items to take care of myself, should there be a problem requiring me to stay out for an extended period. The Boy Scout in me lived on.

Up ahead, I came into view of the cabins of Stepping Stone. Here was a long stretch where the river had been angrier when it froze, near the confluence with the Yukon River. The jumble ice was such a contrast to the flat ice the trail conveyed me across. Further on would be Fort Selkirk, which I have only visited once and on a snowmobile, where Cowboy Larry Smith, Yukon

Legend, resides. It was his snowmobile I was riding at the time.

I exerted some effort to carry myself up the riverbank, grateful I did not have the sled in tow. At Stepping Stone there is a bevy of cabins; some older than others. There are solar panels and there is a church. At the checkpoint I read a sign that all were welcome, a statement not supported by the evidence, as the cabin door was padlocked shut. I stood near the top of the riverbank, gazing across at the jumble ice, and to my left towards Fort Selkirk. Such a warm and wonderful day.

For most of the trail back, I was the only presence detectable, and I took a shot of my footprints leading in both directions. Further on, I took some photographs of an old lynx track, before heading back up the riverbank and along to the house.

Later that day, Dale and I were reunited at the kitchen table, passing the time by talking top-notch, high-spec BS (as was our nature). We chatted of mechanics and driving adventures, of Larry Smith's recently exploded hand, and of local medical emergencies. Dale was only too pleased to disregard the inane comments of sourdough pretenders, and their ignorance of The Ways of The North. He regaled me with stories of children walking to school in plimsols, and hunters and First Nations folks wearing their thin mukluks.

I was welcomed to stay as long as I liked, but felt compelled not to make the expedition too much of a holiday. I also needed to get back so I could meet with Tom, and to finish before the conditions worsened in the warmer days. A disadvantage was that I would not get to see Dale's son, Ken; a wonderful young lad in his early teens. Ken was at school at the time, but would be coming back to the ranch for his spring break, arriving the next evening, well after I expected to have left.

I have fond memories of Ken riding out on a snowmobile to check-up on me, when I was first racing here. I think he was seven years old the first time. When I had been staying at the ranch some years later, he and a friend of his had come out with me in the middle of the night, even though it was getting on for -40, because they both wanted me to point out the Leo constellation. Ken also approved of my cooking. Overall then, I considered Ken to be a good egg, and I was sorry to be missing out on seeing him. I hoped to meet Dale's wife, Sue, in Whitehorse, where she worked during the week.

Dale and I chatted away the hours, and I did feel a pang of regret that I would be leaving so soon after I had arrived. To me, Pelly Ranch was a wonderful haven of loveliness, in a heavenly land. The family who live and work here are some of the nicest, most generous, and interesting people I am privileged to know.

Before turning-in for the night I checked my emails, only to discover my mother had suffered a minor emotional fit after reading about my ribs, requesting in no uncertain terms that I stopped playing silly buggers, and called it quits immediately. I was staggered that my own flesh and blood should have taken such a negative view of things. My father emailed at around the same time, declaring that 'I'm proud of you' and 'You can do it!', and all that sort of abounding positivity and encouragement. I believe these two emails perfectly represent the contrasting maternal and paternal perspectives towards the maturing offspring. Although, in all fairness, I did read between the lines that father was the worthwhile side of at least a few good beers when he read my message and penned his reply.

Mother's email was later followed-up with a second and final email, informing me she had every confidence I was doing the best I could to take care of myself. I might have felt a pang of guilt and selfishness over her two messages, and what I was apparently doing to her.

* * * * * * *

Dale had gone out to commence his morning chores as I finished squaring away my kit. It was approximately 50 kilometres (31 miles) to Pelly Crossing, along a mountain road that mostly paralleled the Pelly River. The yomp to town was along the gently undulating, lightly meandering, winding road.

I said goodbye to Swiss, wishing him well on his future travels, and I harnessed-up to head over to Dale, interrupting him as he waited upon his cows, serving them their hearty breakfast. Dale confided that I could have done more to let them know when I was headed their way, learning of it as he had through the grapevine.

It was at this late hour that I shared my doubts about the trip; not knowing for sure until I reached Dawson that I would have a punt at this final section. It was my fear of failure, in front of those I held in the highest esteem, which had caused the Wi-Fi waves to be silent on the matter.

Dale reminded me of the case of the German, Joachim, who had visited the ranch many times during his races, and again when he solo hiked most of the Quest trail before me in 2010. Since then he had never returned. Dale was hoping the same fate would not befall me, to which I earnestly rejected his hypothesis. The ranch and its inmates were an oasis of wonder and loveliness, which I cannot long endure without.

I was already toying with the idea of a bike trip from the Arctic Ocean, at the top of the Dempster Highway, south to Vancouver, and I could easily see my way over here. With this news of yet another Hines infestation at the Pelly River Ranch, we bode each other farewell, and I set-off on my way. It was Melancholy who accompanied me away from the farm buildings, replaced a little further up the farm road by one of the dogs.

I knew the first third of the farm road fairly intimately. It is the only section of road anywhere in the world that I have raced along, been driven along, driven cars along, and driven a tractor along. There was a general trend upwards at first, taking me higher above the river, after which were only gentle undulations, and nothing at all uncivilised. This was a ploughed road around hills, not over them.

Indeed, the major resistance to progress came wherever the road had been ploughed down to the dirt, which occurred for many hundreds of metres in all, which did its job of tearing away at the hull of the pulk. I continued my habit of turning to check there was not a bear clutching to the back of it, being dragged along, such was the incredible effect of the greater friction to my progress.

I had one car pass me, and I exchanged a friendly wave with the driver, and he passed back some minutes later. At a high point in the trail, I could look down to the Pelly River, and the jumble ice was indeed looking rough, for all of the river I could see.

In the evening, I was heading down a slight decline when another car hove into view. I shifted to the side of the trail to wait for it to pass. There was every chance, if I kept moving, that the sled might have slid out to the side to embrace one of the car's wheels.

A wave came from the passenger side and I realised it was Ken. The driver pulled-up next to me, and Ken and I exchanged a few friendly words. For the sake of not embarrassing him, I did not announce the very obvious growth spurt which had occurred since I last saw him a couple of years before. As they continued on their way, I wondered whether or not I should have asked how far to Pelly. One seldom receives the information one wants to hear in these circumstances, and, when one does, it is vitally important not to actually believe it. I plodded on.

As night began to fall, I got my first glimpse of the lights of Pelly. I took a break, sitting on the snowbank, before continuing on. There were no trail markers, but I mostly knew my way along the residential roads into town. From the side of the highway, I took the Quest trail down onto the river, across, and up the far bank. The Quest trail itself led up on the opposite side of the bridge, but from there it went through an area where I would have been on roads and pavements, whereas the side I took offered a snowmobile track.

Pelly Ranch to Pelly Crossing

The petrol station-cum-supermarket was closed as I passed, but I was in no real need for more supplies. I had enough to make it to the finish, just about. If I took more food it would have been as a treat, rather than need. I rejoined the Quest trail a few hundred metres further along, on the opposite side of the highway. The trail led off along a road, then a woodland path.

It took me a while to get my bearings, not least because my GPS seemed to be sending me along a parallel route, which was an anomaly, rather than a real path. I had had to investigate it though, then trusting my judgement with the path, until trail markers reappeared. Soon after I was on a familiar, fairly long, steep series of climbs, bringing me up onto higher ground. I looked back and down towards the lights of Pelly, now some kilometres behind me. I would camp soon.

Despite an abundance of trees, the branches I tested seemed too rigid to make a truly comfortable mattress. I slept in my tent that night, relieved that I could manage it without too much discomfort. The night was colder than previous ones, and I benefitted from the additional warmth of the tent. That being the case, I also accepted that I preferred sleeping out more exposed; I liked the feel of the free-moving air on my face, and of being able to look up to the stars, with the occasional surprise of stirring in the night to briefly wake and see the aurora. There now remained a meagre 380-kilometre-ish march to the Takhini finish; my confidence was growing once again.

Chapter 25.
Pelly Crossing to Carmacks

The next morning I was accompanied along the trail by Mild Trepidation, later handing the baton over to Sweating Anguish. I knew I had at least one formidable section of overflow to negotiate. I recalled crossing a particularly unwelcoming patch of the stuff in 2009, and that had been my first encounter with the Living Nightmare. If it was there this year, to the same extent, it would give me an area some hundred square metres to cross, with no options to go around.

It was an overcast, flat day, which meant dull, lifeless surroundings. I reflected back on those clear, sunlit days of my past, where the snow sparkled its clean, bright white, with long shadows cast not only from trees and hills, but by the smallest saplings, mounds of snow, and even within animal tracks. The land boasted its beauty, its depth, and its texture. Today's monochromatic scenery lacked all that good stuff, appearing before me quite dreary by comparison. Overcast days are always harder because of this, so I occupied my thoughts with the dreams of yesterday's clear skies.

The trail led me through gently undulating woodland, ejecting me onto large, flat areas, devoid of vegetation, which I took to be lakes, until I saw grass sprouting up through the thin shroud of snow. There were lakes along the trail too, but the land between lakes and woodland could be any manner of marshland, swampland or grassland.

Pelly Crossing to Carmacks

As I crossed one lake I saw a whole pack of young children out playing. One young lad approached to ask if I had ever ice fished before, and I conceded I had not. That being the extent of his interrogation I presumed I was free to move on, and continued on my way.

Back where the trail contained no children, I came across patches of dirt and grass. These were not overly frequent, but they occurred, and were a reminder of the meagre snowfall this year, and the midday temperatures now consistently above freezing.

In the early afternoon, I arrived at the worse overflow I have ever encountered, and it was not where I was expecting it. My way was through a narrow corridor, created from a path bordered by tall saplings, arcing steadily around to my left. The overflow filled the way for more than 50 metres. The overflow was glaciated, and angled down a subtle slope. Further to the left it was open water. The whole thing looked appalling. To the right was a flat open pan of only partially frozen water, but at least it was not treacherously glaciated.

I pulled on my NEOS overshoes, striking-out on a route to the right of the trail, directly adjacent to it, rather than on it, where I could use some brush for purchase. It was a very slow, extremely careful process. On each step I needed sufficient grip to pull the sled passed any saplings, and to be braced in case it slid down even the slightest angles across the trail. When it did slip down, I needed to produce sufficient force so I could move forward with the sled moving at an angle, or across the open overflow lower down. Sometimes I would get lucky and the sled would move back up, through the saplings, and into its rightful position behind me.

Initially, my feet went through the ice a couple of centimetres or so, giving me stability and some security. On occasion, a foot ventured further, with water close to the top of the boots, with me hurriedly raising the foot and replacing it elsewhere. Because of the presence and density of the ice, feet do not always fall rapidly through the upper ice crust, but can descend very gradually and steadily, as the ice beneath is compacted. It is a crème brûlée top with a slushy centre.

The worst patches were a couple of sections, a few metres in length, where my feet did not break through the surface, but the ice was still angled, presenting a good chance of slipping. I tried stamping down on the ice to break through, but it was too thick. I tried slamming my poles down as hard as I could, but they did not get into the ice either.

I placed all my hope on reaching a standing dead tree, a couple of metres ahead, producing my best anti-slip, slow motion lunge, and grasping it with a grateful, outstretched hand. Using my new BFF as an anchor, I slid myself up to him, hugging him lovingly, with gratitude and emotion.

Scanning ahead, examining the remaining ice, I wondered whether the section across the trail to my left looked any better. It looked wet, and I could not have reached it anyway with ease. I was saved by the path ahead being flatter, and I had the protection of some low brush to plant my feet on or adjacent to. I made it off the ice with some considerable relief. It had taken more than 10 horrifying minutes to move about 50 metres.

The trail wound its way along, and I was soon traversing the much larger overflow pan I had been anticipating. Here the overflow was less glaciated, so there was better purchase, and, most importantly, it was thick and flat. I succeeded across all the overflow that day without falling over, or getting my feet wet, which was always the goal. The path led up from the overflow, onto more undulating trail through woodland, with tufts of grass, and patches of dirt, here and there.

I could see low-lying hills up ahead, as well as over to my right, but the trail would not take me up to them. My path was low and easy. The overcast sky persisted through the day. Now, in the middle of the afternoon, I was wondering whether I could reach McCabe Creek before it was too dark. I did not know if the resident Kruse family had received my email, alerting them to my impending arrival, and I did not want to be dragging the sled through their private property in the darkness, unannounced.

The Klondike Highway was my companion, on and off, for much of today. The highway itself was out of sight, but there were moments when the occasional vehicle would pass by close enough for me to hear it. I was approaching civilisation, and what some folk – despite its modest population of around 28,000 – called 'The Big City'.

I kept glancing across to my right, searching for indications of where the trail would lead me down. There would be an electricity junction, from where the track paralleled the road, all the way to McCabe creek and the Kruses. I could see the electricity pylons and lines, but the junction station eluded me for a while.

As my path turned right and began descending, so I came to see some large wolf tracks along the trail. I followed these all the way to the junction station, where the wolf had become preoccupied, leaving the remainder of the trail untouched. The trail would go on for several kilometres, before leading me beneath a bridge to the far side of the road. Perhaps it was the straight line of the trail that did it, but this section always seemed uncharitably long. The trail was fairly soft, by Canadian trail standards, which contributed to a sluggish pace.

The sun was just setting as I arrived at the long driveway to the Kruse homestead. I was disappointed to see a sign that their farm was for sale, but I could not argue with folk wanting to move on to pastures new. As I approached the farm, I inadvertently put some horses ill at ease, and they ran to and fro in their pen, making a racket, in some efforts to avoid being too close to yours truly. I found it challenging not to take this sort of boisterous rejection personally.

Having deharnessed outside the main house, I poked my head within. I was both expected and welcome. The last time I had done this, many years ago, I had interrupted this good family at breakfast. This time, having learnt my lesson, I interrupted them during their dinner. Their hospitality had lost nothing over the intervening years. I shared their dinner and was treated to a welcome cup of tea.

Our conversations were of the trail, the Quest, of medicine and of the future. I loved that the beauty of the Yukon was something locals like these never tired of. The wood stove was already on in their workshop, and a large double mattress put out on the floor for me. The space was used as a race checkpoint for the Quest, and for the footrace, so I was on familiar ground, so to speak.

* * * * * * *

The next morning, I once more poked my head into the Kruse household, to thank them for their hospitality, and to wish them well. One of their dogs accompanied me down onto the creek, which helped me recover from the previous night's emotional bruising from the horses. I was impressed with myself when the little fella understood my communications with him, consenting as he then did to my request, and headed back to the homestead without me. I had observed a few fresh wolf tracks, and would not want this adorable little fellow at risk.

Wolves like to call out to dogs, and dogs – presumably feeling rather flattered by the attention – tend to fall into the trap of rushing out, into what they must imagine will be some unbelievably fantastic orgy. Naturally, most dogs are no match for committed pack hunters like wolves, and become an easy meal. Although sometimes the wolves do just fuck them.

I struck-out across the creek, where the ice had been fractured, and it appeared to be thinning and fragile. I was then onto the Yukon River again, for the first time since leaving Dawson City. Considering its vast breadth back by Circle City, here it is quite narrow, and will be narrower still at Whitehorse. The ice was jumbled, and the trail led me across to the far bank, from where I was on woodland trails. I am sure this section of trail is different each time I am on it. I suspect it is a matter of the quality of river ice, as to how much distance is covered on the river, and how much in the adjoining woods and hills.

Travelling during the day was easy-going. The trail was a little soft, but mostly fine. Less than 7 kilometres (4.4 miles) later I was descending back onto the river. It was a chaos of jumble ice, and a short river section led me into woods further on. Despite the overcast day, the hills bordering close to the river looked impressive, or perhaps more impressive because of the formidable, grey skies, with minimal light reflecting off their dark, metallic rock faces.

The trail continued through woodland, and along gently undulating ground. I was close to wolves in this section, although I did not see any. There was an abundance of wolf tracks, all at least a couple of hours old. Their excrement was fresh enough to smell strongly though, and in one area I paused to look around into the woods, due to an almost overpowering smell of what I recognised as indistinguishable from wet dog. They were close, but skulking out of view. Maybe one was watching me, but too shy to poke his head out for more formal introductions. There might have been a whole pack in there, and I would have been none the wiser.

I was back in woods for most of the rest of the day. This would be a long slog to Carmacks; around 70 kilometres (43.5 miles). I wanted to arrive tonight, so I could make use of a shop early in the morning. I would enjoy some different food and a general stock-up, but mostly I needed duct tape. The repeated contact with dirt and grit had worn a larger hole in the sled's hull. It was becoming a little tiresome to be emptying out snow

Pelly Crossing to Carmacks

blocks from the pulk, whenever I stopped for a break. I found a broken Quest marker that I could use to shore it up on the inside, using duct tape to hold it in place.

The conditions on the trail were good, and easier than they were in my memory of previous visits. I think that because it is a long stint through woods, it can seem monotonous, and the little undulations feel tougher in the night. Also, I usually camp along this section, due to my racing habit of avoiding sleep at the checkpoints.

Nighttime through the woods is mentally hard work. The world becomes a dark and narrow corridor, where moving along can seem like treadmill work – it is repetitious and a drain. For whatever reason though I was not having that experience on this adventure. I seemed to be enjoying everything, and even more than I expected to, considering its familiarity.

From the last river crossing, it was about 30 kilometres (18.5 miles) to Carmacks. The woods spat me out onto a ploughed road, and there would be no more markers into town. I began to see the lights around Carmacks from a fair distance off, and the topography became a little lumpy. Mostly, when leaving Carmacks, I considered these short climbs and descents to be no more than undulations. Now the going seemed harder. I wondered whether it was the night, the dilapidated sled, and my fatigue, all weighing on me. In good conditions, during the daytime, I do not perceive anything remotely hill-like at all. It is a hill for the tired mind alone; otherwise it is a straight, fairly flat shot.

The only time this portion of the trail ever seemed tough, coming the other way, was when it was under a few centimetres of fresh snow, back in 2009. Then I had met with six racers who had all quit, on account of being troubled by these fairly tame lumps, combined with the snowfall. Later that day, still more competitors dropped-out, apparently due to fatigue from the increased workload, brought about by sled-hauling through the snow. Those of us who had worn our snowshoes through this section had fared the best.

So, now it was a longish hour on the way down to Carmacks, with much dancing around the sled on the descents. The trail was winding around to such an extent, that it was not long before I was disorientated, and wondering in which direction I was headed. Fortunately, there were certainly occasional points on the trail I recognised, including a spot where I had had my baffling altercation with the team that had scratched, on account of their bewilderment at snow in winter.

My evening peregrinations led me around hills, up some ups and down some downs, and with much dancing around the sled. I eventually hauled myself to the outskirts of Carmacks. The first area was residential, so cue much barking of disturbed dogs, although I then felt a little lost, when in quieter spots, and wondering if I had taken a wrong turn. I consulted my GPS for some much needed reassurance.

Carmacks has a population nudging 500, but the town is spread-out along one side of the Yukon River, giving the impression it is bigger. The trail led me along a pavement and onto the river, which I mistakenly began to cross before picking up a trail back in the correct direction, as I tried to find the route that made the most sense and matched the GPS. The trail hugged

Pelly Crossing to Carmacks

the side of the river for a couple of kilometres, before I arrived in the central area of Carmacks.

I left the river close to the race checkpoint, which was a large recreation centre, and headed up to a petrol station, now closed, passing a hotel along the way. The petrol station-cum-grocery shop would be open in the morning. I headed across the adjacent Klondike Highway, and heaved self and sled over a roadside snowbank. There was a trail through the deep snow, up to some trees a fair climb up the hillside, which, the more I inspected them, seemed less like human tracks and more like those of a large ungulate. Nevertheless, I was committed, and reached an area of small trees and flattish ground, and set-up my camp.

It was about 3 o'clock in the morning when I climbed into my sleeping bag. Carmacks; I had now covered more than 1300 kilometres (800 miles), with less than 300 kilometres (186 miles) to the Takhini finish, or thereabouts. Tomorrow (well, later today), I would strike-out for Ken Lake, where I would hope to find a cabin that I probably would not have access to, but would be a good spot to camp outside nonetheless. I took off my socks and hoped that these and my feet might dry before the morning. It had been a warm day, after all.

Chapter 26.
Carmacks to Braeburn

It was a good morning; a civilised morning. Rising majestically up from, and out of, my night's compact, studio accommodation, complete with woodland garden and riverfront views, I packed away and descended to the petrol-station-cum-grocery-and-souvenir-shop. I did not hold back.

My steadily acquired nutritional deficiencies, accumulated during recent weeks, were remedied with a litre of V8 vegetable juice, and, with this, I also bought a couple of warm croissants, a hot black coffee, some sausage rolls, cookies, cakes, and duct tape. Breakfast of champions. I stood in the petrol station's warm entrance, drinking my coffee and getting outside of the croissants – the height of decadence – and enjoyed conversations with a couple of chaps who joined me to pass the time of day. One was on holiday from the US, and had been staggered by the warm weather. It was an easy assumption that the warm weather meant my travels were easy, and how wrong he was!

I was fantasising about -20C and below, when my sled glided merrily and oh so easily over the pristine, hard trails, smoothly frolicking along with a gleeful wag of its tail. This was far more preferable than the more recent state of affairs, featuring that sled being dragged heavily over mud, or torn apart by stones. And all that manual labour in warmer temperatures, with a higher work rate, making it harder to stay cool. I really should have a union. Oh, for those blissful days of -20C and below, with strong sunlight radiating from blue skies, and when it just does not get any better than that.

And, as for the smell emanating from my armpits, pervading a good fallout zone all around me, causing my eyes to water every time I dipped my head to suck-up some water from my hydration pack: *Good grief.* No wonder nothing was disturbing me out here. Even *I* did not want to disturb me.

Today was familiarly overcast, and, even before 8 ack emma, there was snow and ice melting from the petrol station's roof. I hoped the clouds were not conspiring to drop snow on me. There was a real risk of rainfall now too, which would be an utter nightmare for the trail. My shoes, now with holes wearing through a couple of spots on the seam, between the Gore-Tex and chassis, would also not fare well in freeze-thaw cycles caused by rain.

I scraped the sled back down towards the riverfront, staying on the road there and passing the recreation centre, before rejoining the Yukon River, by a bridge for the Klondike Highway. I was soon heading away from town. I paused to look behind me – on my journeys from Whitehorse it was always such a relief to see the Carmacks bridge, and to know I had arrived. Now I had the Ken Lake cabin, and the beauty of Coghlan Lake ahead, before the final race checkpoint at Braeburn. Even more importantly, it was now almost certain I would reach Pete's homestead, that bottle of Lead Dog, and Pete's wonderful company.

The trail soon took me from the river, through woodland, passed a familiar cabin, and across a lake. The woodland sections between Carmacks and Braeburn are some of my favourite of the whole route.

They contain very short, very sharp climbs and descents, presenting punctuated moments of terror, only a few metres up or down, with mostly flat, fast ground in between. During races, there were support staff positioned at the top of some descents, to warn racers, and to help gather up all the debris and limbs from the ensuing carnage.

I recalled a tough climb of some metres that had seemed close to vertical, which required much digging-in of feet and poles, and much panting, with plenty of alarm and general panic and dread involved in getting to the top. Now, doing it all in reverse, I deharnessed and sent the pulk on its way ahead of me down that precipice, still relying on my poles to help safeguard my own descent.

There was a short stint back out on the Yukon River, a few kilometres outside of Carmacks, following which I was back in the woods. My focus was on reaching Mandanna Lake, 35 kilometres (22 miles) from Carmacks. That lake offered six kilometres of trail, and the start of the chain lakes to Braeburn, and, as such a long lake, reaching it was an important milestone in the journey. I had usually camped this side of it, after departing from the Ken Lake checkpoint. Leaving that warm cabin to strike-out across Mandanna was always tough, as the end never seemed to get any closer, stretching-out ahead and the passage lasting almost an hour.

I felt so at home and so alive out here in the woods. Granted, I could have done without the aches from the ribs, but I was already feeling well on the mend. My main difficulty was the weather. It was so warm I was down to my Sub-Zero baselayer top. My Rab vapour-rise trousers had all zips open. I was also not wearing my gaiters. I was still sweating more than ever, despite the easy trail and much lighter sled. My breaks today were a little longer than usual, partly to aid cooling and recovery, but mostly to get through my stash of food from Carmacks, before it all froze.

My biggest clothing issue was my choice of socks. I usually wore a pair of Injinji socks, as a liner, plus a pair of thick, warm hiking socks. I had a party pack of socks on the sled, but none were cool enough for these conditions. I was only wearing one pair of hiking socks, without the Injinjis, but they were far too warm. My feet sweated, making both socks and shoes wet, my feet now moving around in pools of water. If I wore the thinner Injinjis alone, they would become instantly wet in the wet shoes, and make my feet sore.

The result of all this was that I was changing socks every few hours, with the hope that my feet would not actually get too sore, or blistered, before I reached the Ken Lake cabin. I really hoped that cabin would be accessible, and I could use the stove to dry my socks and shoes. If not, I had been informed I could access the cabin at Coghlan Lake, and I would reach that tomorrow.

I knew my feet would suffer unless I dried them, together with my shoes and socks. A cabin will be most efficient for this. Failing that, a fire will suffice, although I would take issue with the time and effort-commitment. Nevertheless, steps must be taken to prevent blisters and sore feet. Closing-in on an event finish line, it is all too tempting to waylay discipline, and to throw caution to the wind. I might be able to crawl to Takhini from here, but sore feet are no fun, and life is hard enough. One has suffered experiences.

The sweaty feet were such a bother I seriously considered walking barefoot. The main reason against this was not the discomfort of the cold snow (which I imagined would actually be balm and heavenly), but the likelihood of a foot meeting something pointy and unforgiving. I had chalked-up enough accidents already for one trip. I did not need to lance my foot with a cut willow.

As I walked, so I varied my foot placement on the ground, attempting to reduce repetitive stresses to the same area. My feet had some hot spots coming along, but I felt confident I could make it through the day without blisters-proper forming, and sort everything out in the evening. The alternative was to lose a few hours mucking about with a fire, and, against my usual advice to others, I kept pushing on.

* * * * * * *

I arrived in a burn area in the afternoon. I have seen many burns, but none quite like this, and so close up. Usually with burns the trees are decimated, whereas here the trees were only without leaves or pine needles. What gave it away as a burn was that every tree was charred black. Under the overcast, light-grey to white sky, with the white snow all about, the jet black trees looked eerie, ghostly; almost menacing.

The warmth of the day had left the trail soft. As I passed through the burn, a new track joined from my left, and new markers signified a race had passed through. It was dark when the path led me out of the woods, taking a 90-degree turn to the right, leading me along the high bank of the lake. I knew this spot well, having camped here on two of three previous visits. From here, I used to look back over the lake, checking for the headtorches of approaching racers, and, had I seen any, I might have decided to push further before sleeping.

This time there were bright lights on another part of the lake. As I approached the descent, I realised they belonged to a couple of snowmobiles, and wondered if it might be anyone sociable. Whatever their motives for being out by the side of the lake at night, the trail did not take me in their direction.

The conditions along the night-time lake were pleasingly cool. There had been some snowmobile traffic, so the trail was easy to find, or rather it had been. After a few hundred metres the trail was continuing in a straight line from where I entered the lake, towards the opposite shore. Another, fainter trail, became apparent to the left. I checked my GPS and saw the older trail was the one I wanted. As the snow was shallow, it was not too troublesome to move across to that other, wider trail.

It was the predictably long stint along Mandanna, but I tolerated it well, perhaps owing to my easily distracted nature, which was so removed from a racing mode, in which I am thinking constantly of the next section of trail further on. In the past, I have seen racers bivvying down on the lake, rather than pressing-on to the higher and warmer ground. I always thought it was madness; guaranteeing a cold night, and an uncomfortable start, compared with a pleasanter experience to be had within an hour of consistent effort. Still, the nighttime photos of tents or bivvies, illuminated on lakes or rivers, always had a pleasing look to them.

* * * * * * *

There were a few portage sections between neighbouring lakes, some taking me a little way up before bringing me down to the next lake. I could not remember what Ken Lake looked like, but knew it was close to Mandanna, and about 5 kilometres (3.1 miles) in length. I had identified Ken Lake on my GPS as fitting this description, and with the track hugging the shore to the right side. Once there my eyes scoured the riverbank, looking for the high rise to where the cabin was. All along the bank was burn – whether from the same fire as had hit the far side of Mandanna I did not know – but it had to end before the cabin, because the checkpoint had never been affected.

There were no obvious signs or markers up to where the cabin was, but a few old tracks gave it away. I planned to camp at the top if the cabin was closed; it was high up off the lake, so warmer than down here. I left the sled on the lake and headed up without. It was an intimidatingly steep climb, and if the cabin was in use and no outside space available, I would be heading along to the next portage off the lake. Lugging-up the sled and bringing it back down did not appeal.

All was clear, and, even better, the cabin was open. It was really open; the door and all the windows, and even the fridge door. Everything that could be open, was open. I later learned this was for the comfort and convenience of the local bears. The logic goes like this; if a cabin is completely open, a bear will come through an open door, poke around at everything until bored, before heading out through an open window. If the cabin is all closed, by contrast, the bear would smash through the locked door, and then leave via a section of wall, now complete with bear-shaped cut-out.

This cabin, like so many other lake cabins, is used as a fishing retreat during the summer. Once winter has arrived, the cabins tend to lie dormant, until there is access again after the spring thaw.

Bringing the sled up was unfairly tough, and it was sufficiently steep to threaten the real possibility of a slip pulling me back down. I took my sleeping gear, food and clothes into the familiar cabin, closed the windows and door, and got a fire going in the wood stove.

Having hung-up my wet socks and shoes to dry, it became apparent the flume was not working properly. I did not want to get too aggressive with it in the dark in case I damaged it. The fire was being kept low because of a build-up of smoke within the stove. There was some heat from it though, and I hoped it was sufficient to dry everything by the morning. I warmed-up a couple of sausage rolls, and finished-off the food I had bought in Carmacks. Foam mattresses were a welcome addition to my sleeping set-up.

****

The next morning, following some efforts, I managed to finally get the flume open without breaking it, which felt like a good deed. With that accomplished, the cabin was up to a cosy temperature in no time, and my still damp socks and shoes were finally able to start drying properly. I used the time to make diary notes and improvise repairs to the sled.

It is perhaps noteworthy that my level of angst for any late start along the trail did not wane with the days. Indeed, my constant awareness that the trail was deteriorating, created more urgency than ever. I did not leave Ken Lake until shortly after 10 o'clock, having remained to ensure my shoes and all my socks were thoroughly dry. I left the cabin precisely as I had found it, as is the custom, and hoped the owners would not object to my unscheduled stay.

I sent the sled ahead of me down to the lake, gathered it up, and struck-out for the far shore. This was a beautiful, blue sky day. Too warm, of course, but I was getting close to the finish now. It was only about 35 kilometres (22 miles) from the cabin to Coghlan Lake, with 8 kilometres (5 miles) across what must be the one of the prettiest lakes in the Yukon to the next portage, and the final 20 or so kilometres (12.5 miles) to Braeburn. The late start made me think I could well be stopping at the cabin on Coghlan Lake, rather than being more ambitious with the day's distance.

The cabin might be useful, if I needed to dry socks and shoes again. I hoped to avoid this possibility, by managing today with a pair of dry shoes and the Injinjis. Just before Braeburn was Pete's place, and I could not arrive there at an unsociable hour, nor into Braeburn, as everything would be closed.

The day was staggeringly beautiful, but uncomfortably warm at 5C (41F) in the shade. In the early afternoon, I took an extended break on one of the chain lakes. I had depleted my water supply, so needed to melt snow to top-up my 3-litre water bladder. This was actually the first time I had needed to do so outside of a cabin. Yesterday I was drinking what I had bought in Carmacks, and today I had begun with close to 3 litres, exhausting the supply within a few hours.

Melting snow is a time-consuming process. It takes a lot of snow to produce a small amount of water. I was using an MSR titanium pot, which, filled with snow, would produce only 100-ml or so of water. The trick was to keep adding snow to the warm water, only emptying the water into the bladder when the pot was close to full, and adding some snow to the bladder at the same time. I had to assume 4 more days on the trail after today, so I could not burn through fuel at a higher rate to quicken the melting process. After about half an hour of basking in the sun, I was ready to move off.

The beauty of the day did not diminish in the afternoon. Every view was captivating, and I soaked it all up. The whole experience had layers to it; the visual landscape, the soundless air, and the enlivening sunlight on the skin. So much felt as though it was achieved from such a simple occupation. I was, as ever I was, walking through my own heaven.

It was early evening when I arrived at Coghlan Lake, and, when I did so, I enjoyed the sight of wolf tracks along the trail. These were big animals, based upon the size of their prints, and they had been running along this section. Sled dogs are run out here too, but these prints were too large for dogs. I knew there was a wolf pack that had its territory in this area, and now I knew they were not too far off.

A little further on and the pack had gone off in a different direction to my path. The Quest trail did not go too close to the rise to the Coghlan lake cabin, but I could see the way up clearly, and headed across to it. I deharnessed and went up to explore, following the tracks of a large wolf who had visited ahead of me. At the top of a long pathway, stretching up from the lake, was the first cabin. The whole area was a plateau, with only a couple of trees. A larger cabin stood a little way further along, and a main lodge building close by, with an outhouse to the rear. There was a bench seat looking out over the lake, and a picnic bench.

It was such a perfect location; the flat cliff faces of the hills running along the east shore, the flat land and low hills on the farther west bank, and to the south. The cabins were all locked up, but, having reached this high point, I decided I should stay, rather than continue and search for a campsite beyond the lake.

It was a shame the cabins were closed. I later discovered this was due to misuse – a common theme in so many wild places, where littering and so on leads to problems for all later visitors, as well as for the owners, of course. There was a large sofa on the main cabin's veranda. It made for an extremely comfortable bed.

I hoped the owner would not mind a respectful visitor quietly stopping here and leaving no signs. I still found it more comfortable to sleep without the tent. I pushed my down vest to the base of the sleeping bag, where it could help keep my feet toasty and warm.

* * * * * * *

I enjoyed a wonderfully cosy night. In the early morning I headed past the first cabin, on my way back down to the lake, and checked a thermometer hanging outside it. It was -25C. It was incredible to me that the temperature could swing more than 30 degrees, between the cold of the early morning, and the warmth of the day.

The cool chill of the morning air was even more noticeable down on the lake, where it was likely at least a couple of degrees colder. It would not be stretching the truth to remark that my pace there, when passing through a hill's long shadow, was somewhat brisker than the going average. Upon reaching beyond that shadow, now in the morning's bright and brilliant sunlight, I paused for a few moments, savouring the sensation of warmth upon my frozen features.

An already formidable beard glacier had formed, during those initial minutes in the shade, and once in the light I began shedding an icicle or two. This is the magic worked by direct sunlight, even in temperatures far below zero, where ice can vapourise without even making all the fuss of melting first. I stood there, scarcely half an hour since leaving my bed, basking in brilliant sun. It was still cold, but what I experienced was a feeling of radiant warmth upon my rosy, adorable cheeks. I was, in point of fact, experiencing both the sublime *and* sublimation (a little physics gag, for the nerds to roll their eyes and groan at there).

The trail led up a short climb into woodland, looping back to a view of the familiar hill bordering the lake. I selected an appealing suntrap for breakfast, and basked in the morning sun as I ate. I did not know exactly how far I had left to go to Braeburn, or if I would spot the road to Pete's homestead before reaching it, but at least I should be there in a few hours.

Once moving again, I met a couple of chaps on snowmobiles, one of whom was a local conservation officer. They were out looking for people illegally hunting or trapping. Although I am not a fan of confrontation, I suspect the job of bobbing around the beautiful Yukon wilderness on snowmobiles, protecting the sweet and innocent wildlife, and beating poachers half to death with dead halibuts or badgers or whatever, was the sort of work many would find rewarding. Find a job you enjoy doing, and you will never work a day in your life, and all that sort of thing.

The trail continued through woodland. There were also a couple of lakes to pass, and a pond, but mostly it was woodland for today. The trail led me from woodland to an open area, bordering the side of a ranch. I was beginning to think I might have missed Pete's, but in the early afternoon I came across a sign on a trail marker, which was even more stupendous than 'Brownies 1 Mile'. 'Mad Dogs and Englishmen' was the legend, and an arrow pointed along a road off the trail, with empty bottles of Lead Dog beer planted in the snow to guide me along. Ah Pete; what a guy!

The sled dogs gave Pete plenty of warning that I was coming along. He met me outside and we headed into his cabin, where I was duly fed and treated to a coffee, followed by the restoring bottle of Lead Dog, which I had been so looking forward to for almost 1500 kilometres. It was easily one of the best beers of my life. Pete and I chatted away, whiling away the time, and, I hope, enjoying each other's company.

I apologised for my pungent stench. I suppose I might have tried to reassure Pete that it was at least 100% natural and organic, which is the sort of meaningless drivel to disarm duller minds than his. Natural and organic – yes – but then so is chlamydia, although marginally less pleasant, whilst still satisfyingly-earned. Earthquakes, tsunamis and asteroid impacts are quite natural and organic too, but if you think they are forces for good, just solicit the views of any passing dinosaur.

Following the Lead Dog restorative, and accompanying philosophical banter, I found myself reluctant to move on. Pete had previously offered me some sleeping space for the night, but I had arrived early, and was compelled to continue on towards the finish. It was less than 2 kilometres (1.3 miles) to Braeburn Lodge. I had been looking forward to one of their burgers and massive cinnamon buns for a few days now. With some foot-dragging and hesitancy, I bid Pete farewell and pushed on.

As I arrived at Braeburn lodge, some minutes later, a familiar car turned-up. My good friend from Whitehorse, Murray, had been monitoring my tracker, and had driven out to meet me. So fortunate for us both that I had pushed on from Pete's!

Inside the lodge I ordered a burger, requesting half to be wrapped for later on the trail. I enjoyed my hot meal with a cold can of ginger ale, and took a small bottle of the same for my next break. Murray and I chatted for a while. It was superb to see him. Times spent with old friends, and new, were highlights of my otherwise solitary journey.

Before leaving, Lee – one of the owners of the lodge – gave me the option of spending the night there, but I remained keen to make up some more kilometres towards the finish. Murray told me there was a home nearby, where another mutual friend would have welcomed me, but the trail continued to draw me onwards. There was a cabin a little more than 15 kilometres (9.4 miles) from the lodge, and another shortly after (but off the main trail).

Just before I left, the other owner, Steve, arrived, and was told of my feat. Steve characteristically dismissed this with a comment that I should have taken a fat bike, just as Jeff Oatley had done, and I conceded his point. A fat bike would have made for a faster journey, but I regretted nothing in the nature of my own adventure. There is something special about traversing this sublime landscape on foot, hauling a sled, and it offers different challenges, and different high-points, to journeys on bike.

Chapter 27.
Braeburn to Takhini Hotsprings

"All men dream: but not equally. Those who dream by night in the dusty recesses of their minds wake up in the day to find it was vanity, but the dreamers of the day are dangerous men, for they may act their dreams with open eyes, to make it possible."

T. E. Lawrence

The late afternoon passed into evening, and, by the time I had harnessed-up and left Braeburn lodge, darkness was falling. A winding trail through the woods brought me out onto Braeburn Lake, and it was about a kilometre to its far side. It was a clear night, and the starlit sky was striking, with a faint wave of green-tinged sky to the north. I paused to drink in the sights, before climbing up a tall bank, leading off the lake.

This would be a wide route through the woods; well-travelled during the winter. The tall spruce trees presented me with a passageway through them, with a wide channel of starlight overhead. I walked along the trail gazing up, spotting two shooting stars pass overhead on either side.

I was keen to churn up the kilometres along this section, because the corridor of spruce threatens to become relentlessly monotonous. I planned to progress well through the cool woods tonight, and to take my time during the next warm day.

The trail began to open out, and I could see hills further away from the trail. It was hard not to feel privileged, as I gazed at my surroundings, all alone and in the dead of night. Starlight was reflected back in the snow, shadows were cast from patches of trees, and the hillsides presented a dramatic, metallic silver on their rock faces. It was a cool night, allowing for a good pace, which I would struggle to recreate so easily in the warmth of the day. I was still feeling buoyed from spending time with Pete, Murray, Lee and Steve, and I now had one hell of a big cinnamon bun in my bag.

As if I was not already feeling that my cup of happiness floweth over, the sky behind me erupted into the best aurora I have ever witnessed. It began in both the northeast and in the northwest, and it snaked across the whole sky to meet-up; this tall, deep and broad green curtain, swaying and dancing above me.

The aurora spread, from one vast curtain of green light to three, with so much activity it crossed above me into the southern half of the sky; the white snow now reflecting a dancing green. It was magnificent. The ballet of light up above was poorly reflected in the movements of the wayward drifting sled-hauler below, as I repeatedly tripped over my trekking poles, and my own feet, whilst distractedly looking around and trying to soak it all up.

I hauled late into the night before setting up camp, just before 3 o'clock in the morning. The long day had been glorious, and I had revelled in my own personal paradise for every moment of it. I had sled-hauled close to 30 kilometres (18.5 miles) since leaving the lodge, which I considered to be not a bad night's work.

Moving at night when it was between -20C and -25C (-4F to -13F), was vastly more pleasant than around 5C (41F), and more in the middle of the day. The trail was better in the cold, the air more pleasant, physical effort less, and the aurora a wondrous luxury.

I climbed into my sleeping bag, and finished off the now cold, but still delicious and revitalising, half a burger. I also enjoyed the remains of the cinnamon bun, which had lasted longer than expected, even considering it was the size of a small English village.

* * * * * * *

I did not know the precise distance to the finish line. Whitehorse was less than 160 kilometres (100 miles) from Braeburn, and Pete had reckoned the Takhini finish was a little over 112 kilometres (69.5 miles). That sort of fitted with what I had imagined. The distance between Braeburn and Dog Grave Lake was about 56 kilometres (35 miles).

I estimated that I was about halfway to Dog Grave, as I set-off the next morning. I reflected that the Yukon Quest trail was usually considered to be a little more than 1600 kilometres (1000 miles), and that whatever was lost below 1600 kilometres by finishing in Takhini, was probably compensated for, to some degree, by the diversion over the Top of the World Highway, in hardships if not in actual distance.

It was another beautiful day. Everything came alive in the sunlight. My daytime breaks were long and leisurely. The views were spectacular. So many times I have rushed through here, travelling at night and missing out on this epic scenery. I was absolutely making up for it now.

The trail was, more or less, flat all the way to the finish from here, forgiving a few very gentle gradients. When these rises did appear, I would usually be rewarded by stunning views out through the woodland, to distant hills and mountains, or across frozen river valleys. In the bright sunlight, with the blue skies and sparkling snow, I was experiencing paradise every bit as much as my night-time jaunt. I relished in it and drank it all in as I went. Instead of sitting on my pulk, I would often take my breaks sitting down in the snow, lying back against the sled and basking in the sun.

I arrived at a small public access cabin, at about 3 o'clock in the afternoon, approximately 20 kilometres (12.5 miles) from where I had camped. It was a small cabin, comprising a bunk bed and a stove, and not much else. Outside was a picnic bench, which I made use of whilst I relaxed and ate a bit more.

Leaving this cabin, I passed another soon after, by a lake. A couple of chaps had arrived there on snowmobiles, and had shown an interest in my passing by, though I was too far off for conversation. I wondered if they were out hunting or ice fishing, or just enjoying time on the trails.

It was another 6 kilometres (3.7 miles) to Dog Grave Lake. I arrived in the late afternoon, and the views across the lake to a mountain on the far side were spectacular. I deharnessed and scanned around for a cabin I knew was not there. There was an outhouse, but not a cabin, which confused me. I followed animal tracks of moose and lynx, and human footprints, to a lookout point for the lake. The early evening light made the snowy mountaintops reflect pink. I made use of the outhouse – a wonderful toilet without a door, but facing the wrong way to really capitalise on the available views.

A flat area, overlooking the lake, would suffice as an early campsite for tonight. During the footrace, a large wall-tent would be positioned here as a checkpoint, and it was a good area that I had never really managed to enjoy before, as I had always arrived in darkness, and only once left in daylight, and then at a good pace, needing to make up for lost time.

There were a couple of half oil drums, used as open stoves for barbequing on. I got one of these going, and set up my camp nearby for the night. Wood had been stacked in various places, which I suspected was the work of the race support staff, when they had set up the checkpoint. The drums were adjacent to a picnic bench.

I hoped I was doing the right thing. If it was more than the suggested 112 kilometres from Braeburn to the finish, I would have a long day tomorrow, arriving at the finish late or, at worst, having to camp before reaching it. Murray had told me a couple of people would be there to see me finish, provided I arrived at a sensible hour, and I very much liked the thought of a warm welcome in Takhini.

I savoured the views from my picnic table, whilst enjoying the warmth of the fire. I took my shoes and socks off and dried them out. I also set to work defrosting a small vitamin tub which Pete had given me, containing 'Spirit Dog' – distilled Lead Dog beer – which

Yukon Brewing had started to make, and which Pete suspected I might enjoy.

I had been impatient to try it, but it was worth the wait to have it here, in these spectacular surroundings, making for another perfect moment. I made my diary notes, ate plenty of food, and savoured the Spirit Dog, which tasted delicious. I rose the vitamin tub in a salute of gratitude to Pete, that brilliant Arctic Galahad, and was only sorry he was not here to join me.

Before retiring for the night, I got another fire going in the second drum. My tent was close enough to enjoy some warmth, but not so close it was being showered in embers. I had stacked the wood above the drum, in such a way that it would fall into the stove, as the wood lower down burnt through, giving me a good few hours of heat. It was another wonderful luxury. I went to sleep warm, cosy and dry, albeit with some small apprehension that my next day could easily be a long one.

* * * * * * *

I did not linger in my bed in the morning. I emerged from my petite bachelor pad, which boasted quiet lakeside views, and fully air conditioned *al fresco* toilet, to pack everything away and launch myself off along the trail. At night, this section had seemed like a rollercoaster of short and sharp rises and drops, and steep turns. By day, the winding, undulating trail seemed far less significant by comparison, although I was not now racing to a checkpoint, which doubtless impacted on the experience too. The trail led through woodland that became more and more open, and soon I was walking in open lands, and admiring the views of hills further on.

It was another serene, peaceful, beautiful day on the trail. I savoured my final day there – every moment of it. In spots the snow gave way to patches of dirt and tufts of grass. I was still taking time on my breaks to empty out the snow that accumulated in the sled, but at least now I was confident the sled would make it to the finish, without its state worsening too much more.

The occasional patches of grass and dirt still added their resistance, and mostly this reminded me that spring was well on its way. I took my time on my breaks, enjoying my surroundings, but when going along the trail I was moving as fast as I could. People would be waiting for me at the end, so I wanted to arrive at a not entirely unsociable hour, and I had plenty more kilometres to go. Aside from the soft trail, the dirt and the grass, progress was fast. It was almost entirely flat, save for a few bumps here and there.

Further along, I passed a spot where a few people were taking lunch, and resting their dog teams. They came to overtake me later, led by their guide from Muktuk Adventures, on a snowmobile. I chatted with him for a few minutes. He commented that the trail was in such bad order that he might be cancelling a month of tours, if no new snowfall came. He continued on, his clients and the dogs passing soon after. They would be setting up for the night a few kilometres further along.

The trail was in a dire state, along this final section towards the Takhini River. There was a considerable amount of dirt and grass where before there had always been an abundance of snow. I often left the trail so I could use the remaining snow off-trail. There was no clearer sign that spring was upon us.

I had supported a sled dog race here a few years ago, meaning I had travelled this section four times before, and it was pleasingly familiar. Power lines came into view to my right, a sure sign I was getting closer to town. I also saw the Takhini River, which the trail usually joins, but not this year. I passed by where the Muktuk Adventures folk had set-up their camp.

* * * * * * *

My evening break was under a whiter, cloudier sky. The road had been ploughed, but still left sufficient snow. Moving on, I soon crossed a small bridge, struggled up a hill where the mud clung at the base of the sled, and reached the spot where this year's Quest trail left the Trans-Canada Trail, the latter continuing on towards the Takhini River.

That there were trail markers here was a huge relief. The only stakes between here and Braeburn had been the crossed markers, around spots where mushers had to take extra care. Jessica had sent me directions, and Murray had confirmed the message, but there were so many snowmobile tracks I could have easily chosen the wrong route, without the remaining markers. The trail continued along a road, then took a right turn, taking me along a stretch beneath and around overhead power lines.

A few kilometres later and it was dark, and I was using my headtorch to pick up the reflective light from the markers. I could see homes beyond a line of trees to my right, and occasionally to my left. I was approaching Takhini, but did not know the way to the finish at the Hot Springs. If I had to work it out without the markers, and chose the wrong trail, I would have to continue to the Klondike Highway, and then work back along the Hot Springs road – that was the only way I knew. As it was, when the Quest trail left this straight road for a winding road through the hills and woodland, it was extremely well-marked.

The trail doubled-back on itself, and I found myself observing the constellations, noticing my direction changes relative to them. The trail became undulating in no small measure, with some fairly steep descents here and there, and a few long and winding climbs, but then everything does seem to feel harder when night has fallen, and my patience has waned.

The area had always seemed flat in the daylight, so walking the trail by night and unable to see signs of Takhini, I became disorientated and confused. I just kept moving as fast as I could, knowing people were waiting for me, and that I wanted this final section completed.

With the winding route so often doubling-back on itself, I lost all ideas of distance. This was not a simple straight line, along a residential road from the main trail to the hot springs, but a winding woodland trail across hillsides. How much longer could it be?

It was more than 12 kilometres (7.5 miles) since leaving the original Quest Trail, that I passed through an open gate by a field. I could see the lit ice tower of the Hot Springs, and I knew I was close. I broke into a run, moving faster along the cold trail, the sled sliding easily along behind me. I reached the far end of the Hot Springs car park and kept the momentum going. I moved quickly along the wooden fenced side of the Hot Springs baths, on a snowy pavement adjacent to the car park, with the main entrance ahead. Before the entrance itself was a café, the closest component of the main complex, just ahead to my left.

I came to an abrupt stop outside, just as a couple of ladies were leaving the main building for their car, giving me the sort of perplexed look that I deserved, having arrived at a hot springs a 21:40, on a late winter's eve, from a field rather than a car, and towing a sled. There was no finish banner, no applause, and no ceremony. My journey was at an end in the dark of a quiet place and at a quiet time.

Within the café, a friend, Glenn, spotted me outside; doubtless my headtorch giving me away. He was first to come out and greet me, shaking my hand and giving me a much appreciated bear hug. I deharnessed, abandoning my sled where it was, and headed inside to meet Mike, together with his wife, Jessica, and Glenn's wife, Trisha. They had finished dinner, and I joined them for a restoring beer and a contemplative chat, strategically positioning myself what I hoped would be a safe distance, accepting my last wash was some time ago.

And that was it; the end of the journey. I had succeeded but I was not overjoyed at the accomplishment, which some might consider odd. I was satisfied and pleased, but no more. As ever, the adventure was the trail herself, and, although I could not have wished for a better conclusion than a quiet drink with these wonderful, Yukon friends, I drank with Ambivalence, knowing it would take some days for the weight of it all to sink in.

For now, the emotions were a combination of light relief, happiness at being with friends, and a slight feeling of disbelief, that, after more than a month of little else, tomorrow I did not have *any* distance or trail time to think about. Melancholy patted my arm; but the memories would all come flooding back soon enough, as I reflected on this incredible journey, through this unparalleled land.

Epilogue

What is considered amongst the mushers to be the toughest sled dog race in the world came to an end in Canada's Yukon Territory for another year. The winner of this year's Yukon Quest sled dog race is Hugh Neff, from Alaska. The prize money for his win is $23,000. Second place went to Brent Sass, who led the race throughout the first half. Brent's prize for being first into Dawson City, just over halfway along the race route, was four ounces of gold. This prize acknowledges the gold rush history of Dawson City, and all the people who pitted themselves against this brutal landscape in pursuit of their dreams.

Race report by the author, MH

Once in the final quarter of my journey, in the day or so after leaving Pelly Crossing, I became fully aware that I would finish within about another week. Perhaps it will perplex some that this awareness did not fill me with joy.

Granted, there was certainly some reassurance that reaching the city meant my adventure had been a success. Still, a not insignificant part of me would have liked to about-turn, and head once more for the remoteness and solitude of the hills and deeper wilderness.

That Melancholy had gripped my sleeve at this juncture was unsurprising. I always regret nearing the end of a journey, and, by then, I felt that Takhini was pulling me in. I did not begin from Fairbanks with a

Epilogue

primary aim of arriving at the finish in a fast time; not that I wanted to be overly slow either.

My primary aims were to enjoy the journey, and to maximise my experiences along the trail. As much as I could have, I achieved that, and I felt pleased and satisfied with my time along the way. Arriving at the end signified all the best moments being over, until the next adventure. Perhaps that is why I was dreaming then, more and more, about what my next Yukon adventure might be.

The day after arriving in Whitehorse I was back out on the trail, this time in the company of Tom and his friend Rich. We sled-hauled to Coghlan Lake and back, then out to the other side of Braeburn Lake, and along the trail there. This was a useful experience for me to get back out on the trail for a recovery hike. My sled was lighter and I was carrying plenty of food. It took my total mileage above 1600 kilometres (1000 miles) of sled-hauling along the Quest trail that year. It was pleasant to have short days, and to spend a couple of nights by a fireside.

A highlight was the second night, when we camped beneath spruce trees, on thick spruce mattresses, and spent the night and the first half of the next day by a good fire. It was an opportunity for me to practice guiding and bushcraft. It had snowed overnight, but had not been overly cold, perhaps just pushing -20C (-4F), or thereabouts. Our trees had given us sufficient protection, although it was always possible to see areas for improvement in makeshift camps.

Back at Braeburn lodge, awaiting our transport back to Whitehorse, I had walked in to hushed whispers, from a table of people discussing *'That's the guy who hiked the Quest trail'*. That was a nice touch. Equally pleasant was being able to chat with Steve, both before and after the return to the trail. I have a lot of time for Steve, not least because he is an honest and genuine character; a description that I firmly believe cannot be contradicted by anyone.

Steve comes across as very comfortable in his life, and with all the friends he needs. If Steve speaks, it is because he wants to, not because he thinks he must. I have stopped by the lodge countless times and barely exchanged more than a few words with him, so this time it was good to just chat a bit.

When our transport arrived, I picked up my third cinnamon bun of the short trip, and finished it within half an hour – a feat perhaps only Yukoners will understand (a people who will drive 45 minutes from Whitehorse, each way, just to collect one of these mammoth items, which can last any normal human a matter of days).

This act surprised our driver somewhat. What seemed to surprise him even more was the fact that we had been sleeping-out without a tent, which was a reaction that lifted us all up. We had done something unusual, even in the eyes of local outdoorsy folk, and we had enjoyed success. Tom and Rich spent their last couple of days in the Yukon at the Sky High Ranch, staying in a yurt, and going out on a snowmobile journey.

I enjoyed my days in Whitehorse, frequenting my favourite spots, getting some press coverage, catching-up with old friends, and consuming mountains of food.

Epilogue

It was always going to be a real shame to leave, but necessary. One adventure must always be fully concluded before the next can begin. As much as I needed to leave the Yukon for now, it was clear to me that I had experienced the greatest adventure of my life so far, and I would be certain to return.

The Yukon is the most wonderful place, where so many people live for the outdoors. Perhaps that is why it feels to me like home, and a place I could happily live my life.

A realisation that occurred to me, during my final days on the trail, was that it was not only the physical environment that makes the Yukon so special to me, but the people who live here, and my friends most of all. After all, as much as I love spending time alone in the wilderness, I also love having the best of friends to come back to afterwards. As for the Quest Trail; I smashed it, my way.

Postscript

It was not long before the detractors began to query the legitimacy of my adventure, which is always a reassuring sign that one has done something really quite special. One individual, who thought I must have become lost, to have decided to leave Pelly Ranch for Stepping Stone, also seemed to believe I should have finished in Whitehorse rather than Takhini. I did the out-and-back to Stepping Stone because that was all part of the Quest trail, and I had no wish to cut any corners.

When the race official advised me to avoid the re-route over the Top Of The World Highway and take the shorter, easier path along the Yukon River, I did not do so, because my plan from the beginning had always been to experience that year's trail, whatever that meant, and however it might evolve during the course of the race.

I ended the route at the Quest finish point in Takhini, because that was where the Quest finished that year, once the Takhini River had opened-up, after the first mushers arrived in Whitehorse. For me to reach Whitehorse would have meant using the highway, which was absolutely not the Quest trail, nor the route the rest of the mushers took. I could not take the original Quest route to Whitehorse, because of all the open water along the river, and me not being Jesus Christ.

To claim my journey was not the full Quest route is to delegitimise the Quest results for all the mushers who finished in Takhini ahead of me that year, and every musher every other year that the Quest finished in Takhini. Hence the Quest diversion. Hence the Quest markers leading me to Takhini instead of Whitehorse. Hence me being able to finish without the need of a snorkel or scuba gear. But I digress.

I was informed that a friend and fellow foot racer, Joachim, who had also sled-hauled the Quest trail, had started out from Two Rivers instead of Fairbanks, although nobody seemed to understand the reason for this, and I had no interest in following it up, because he was certainly fit enough to do it all, and could have gone from Fairbanks to Two Rivers on a training journey beforehand, for all I knew. Besides, it is possible to complete a thing purely for the challenge of realising a goal, without the need to make claims about it being something extraordinary.

Although my journey was solo, I certainly enjoyed the hospitality offered to me along the way, meaning it was not self-sufficient or unsupported, and particularly as I was making use of an established trail.

I left the Yukon and returned to my then home in Serbia, where, for the princely sum of about £15, I had my chest x-rayed. The rib fractures were confirmed, by which time they were already well-healed. I also received news that my frostbite had resulted from the mitts not being made to design specifications, meaning the fingertip areas had been wholly deficient in down insulation. The manufacturer recalled all the mitts they could, including from someone on Everest at the time.

I had dipped my feet into the world of guiding, by taking a couple of companions out along the trail. As we sat by a campfire above Coghlan Lake, one produced his iPhone and began playing music, to drown out the silence, which had been occasionally punctuated by the distant sounds of the Braeburn wolf pack, howling into the night.

I knew in that moment that solo adventures were my best way of enjoying the world, and the chances of me realising a career in guiding were a very long way off indeed. My paradise is the peace, wonder, beauty, silence and serenity of the sublime Yukon and Alaskan trails. I long to return, and, until I do, I relive my moments of heaven in some of my happiest memories.

****

Aside from fear of re-fracturing my ribs during the days following the injury, and the fear that my frostbite would worsen dramatically (during the hours after it first occurred), I never experienced any real fear during my time on the trail. There were a handful of occasions when I felt vulnerable, such as when aware of how cold it was, or that large and potentially dangerous animals were near. I think this is only natural.

My vulnerability was part of what made it real and exciting. My sense of comfort, despite the potential dangers of the environment, fuelled my confidence. And I really did feel comfortable out there, and deeply, deeply happy and satisfied too. My time was my own. The empty land surrounding me felt like it was all there for me to experience. I was separate, individual, and disconnected from the world beyond what I could see and feel. Nothing else mattered but savouring each moment, and making progress.

Postscript

Realising this was grounding, uplifting and magnificent. I felt free; a man unchained and untethered by the trappings of the modern world. I had escaped; not only on a long leash for a short holiday, but I felt truly free of the farcical ways of the modern world; its expectations and requirements. I relished being free in the wilderness, and I revelled in it. All I had to do each day was walk, and it was beautiful, both in its act and in its simplicity.

I am aware this book is rather long. I can only assure you that I already cut thousands of pages of only partially gripping material, for the sake of brevity. The only way I can protect against such tomes in the future is to do this sort of thing with faster transport, and I really do enjoy fat-biking, for example. Still, as my dear friend Klaus once told me. "When you are on foot, each step you take is your own".

Kit List

Sled
Paris Expedition Sled
Snowsled harness
Rab kit bag
Paracord
PVC conduit

Sleeping kit
Thermarest Ridgerest Sleeping Mat
Rab Expedition 1400 sleeping bag
Rab Latok Summit tent
Rab Vapour barrier liner
Nalgene pee bottle

Footwear
Salomon XA Pro 3D GTX trail shoes
Injinji socks
Sealskinz socks
Winter hiking socks (various)
Rab Gaiters
MSR Lightning Ascent Snowshoes
NEOS overboots
Yaktrax

Clothing
Baselayer leggings (Subzero F1)
Baselayer top (Subzero F1, Alpkit, Rab)
Rab Vapour Rise Guide jacket
Rab Vapour Rise Guide trousers
Rab Batura down jacket

Rab Neutrino vest
Rab Phantom grip gloves
Expedition mitts
Balaclava (acrylic)
Buffs x 2
Neoprene face mask
Bloc eyewear goggles
Bloc eyewear Chameleon sunglasses

Stove kit
Kovea Booster +1 dual fuel stove
Kovea fuel bottle
MSR titanium cooking pot
Coleman fuel (white gas – liquid fuel)

Navigation & Tracking
Suunto Traverse GPS watch
Delorme PN-60 handheld GPS
Spot Tracker

Fire Starting Kit
Small folding saw
Cycle inner tube
Matches in waterproof container
Cigarette lighters (x3)
Magnesium striker
Tampons

First Aid Kit
Assorted plasters
Fabric tape
Elastoplast wide adhesive tape

Anti-histamine
Imodium

Food
Droewors
Biltong
Dried tropical fruit
Cup-a-soup
Homemade high energy chocolate truffles
Shortbread

Miscellaneous
Black Diamond trekking poles
Black Diamond Polar Icon headtorch
Petzl Tikki Headtorch
1 Litre Platypus soft water bottle
3L MSR Hydromedary water bladder
Diving knife
Spork
Titanium mug
Emergency whistle
Camera
Suntan lotion sachets
Hand warmer pads

Support Your Authors

It is a sad reality that my books appeal to a singularly niche market, of folks able to boast excessive intellects, coupled with adventurous spirits and sturdy, rugged good looks. As much as my readers are a blueprint for a superior evolutionary branch of the species, this elite few is scarcely able to keep me in affordable accommodation and hot dinners. Other authors, whilst not so fortunate in the quality, intelligence and beauty of their readers, suffer similarly. Indeed, simply because an author appeals more to the denser, pustule-ridden tribes, this is no reason for them to die long slow deaths, whilst cowering from the rain in a field somewhere grim.

It is for this reason that – on behalf of all of us – I wish to ask for your assistance. We writers write for our passion, and would like to write more books more often, but are typically forced into other labour camps that prove more reliable, the result of which is that all humanity suffers this lack of our art. By supporting us, we have more freedom to develop and to produce, from which humankind may once again be elevated above the level of drones and robots, at risk of being outpaced and outmanoeuvred by the exponential progress of A.I.. The best ways to support us are:

1. Write positive reviews on as many platforms as you can

2. Share your favourite lines, quotes or short excerpts online

3. Recommend others to buy our books (people buying books is what keeps us in the trade)

Books by Mark Hines

In Extremis series:
The Marathon des Sables
The Jungle Marathon
The Yukon Arctic Ultra
Hiking the Yukon Quest
Your Only Option

Human Evolution, Diet and Health
Our Natural Diet

Chapter contributions to:
Thesigers Silence: The Endurance Issue

Keep up to date with my shenanigans, courses, and new releases by taking a look at my website:
www.drmarkhines.com